THE REBEL

Albert Camus was born in Algeria in 1913 of French and Spanish parentage. He was brought up in North Africa and had many jobs there (one of them playing goal for the Algiers football team) before he came to Metropolitan France and took up journalism. He was active in the Resistance during the German occupation and became editor of the clandestine paper *Combat*. Before the war he had written a play *Caligula* (1939), and during the war the two books which brought him fame, *L'Etranger* (*The Outsider*) and *Le Mythe de Sisyphe*. Abandoning politics and journalism he devoted himself to writing and established an international reputation with such books as *La Peste* (*The Plague*) (1947), *Les Justes* (1949), and *La Chute* (*The Fall*) (1956). *The Plague, The Fall, The Outsider, A Happy Death* and *Exile and the Kingdom* have been published in Penguins along with *Selected Essays and Notebooks*, a collection of early essays, verse, parables and fairy tales in *Youthful Writings*, and his philosophical statement on the problem of suicide, *The Myth of Sisyphus*. He was awarded the Nobel Prize for Literature in 1957. In January 1960 he was killed in a road accident.

ALBERT CAMUS

THE REBEL

Translated by Anthony Bower

WITH A FOREWORD BY
SIR HERBERT READ

PENGUIN BOOKS
in association with Hamish Hamilton

Penguin Books Ltd, Harmondsworth, Middlesex, England
Penguin Books, 40 West 23rd Street, New York, New York 10010, U.S.A.
Penguin Books Australia Ltd, Ringwood, Victoria, Australia
Penguin Books Canada Ltd, 2801 John Street, Markham, Ontario, Canada L3R 1B4
Penguin Books (N.Z.) Ltd, 182–190 Wairau Road, Auckland 10, New Zealand

—

L'Homme révolté first published 1951
This translation first published by Hamish Hamilton 1953
Published in Peregrine Books 1962
Reprinted 1965, 1967, 1969
Reissued in Penguin Modern Classics 1971
Reprinted 1973, 1974, 1975, 1977, 1978, 1981, 1982, 1984

—

—

Set, printed and bound in Great Britain by
Cox & Wyman Ltd, Reading
Set in Monotype Plantin

Contents

FOREWORD by Sir Herbert Read   7

INTRODUCTION   11

1 THE REBEL   19

2 METAPHYSICAL REBELLION   29

The Sons of Cain   32
   A Man of Letters   33
   The Dandy's Rebellion   43
The Rejection of Salvation   50
Absolute Affirmation   57
Nihilism and History   72

3 HISTORICAL REBELLION   76

The Regicides   82
   The New Gospel   84
   The Execution of the King   87
   The Religion of Virtue   91
   The Terror   94
The Deicides   103
Individual Terrorism   118
   The Renunciation of Virtue   119
   Three of the Possessed   122
   The Fastidious Assassins   133
   The Path of Chigalev   142
State Terrorism and Irrational Terror   146
State Terrorism and Rational Terror   156
   The Bourgeois Prophecy   157
   The Revolutionary Prophecy   165
   The Check to the Prophecy   177
   The Kingdom of Ends   192

5

Totality and Trial   199
Rebellion and Revolution   212

4 REBELLION AND ART   219

Rebellion and the Novel   224
Rebellion and Style   233
Creation and Revolution   237

5 THOUGHT AT THE MERIDIAN   243

Rebellion and Murder   243
Nihilistic Murder   246
Historic Murder   250
Moderation and Excess   258
Thought at the Meridian   261
Beyond Nihilism   266

Foreword

WITH the publication of this book a cloud that has oppressed the European mind for more than a century begins to lift. After an age of anxiety, despair, and nihilism, it seems possible once more *to hope* – to have confidence again in man and in the future. M. Camus has not delivered us by rhetoric, or by any of the arts of persuasion, but by the clarity of his intelligence. His book is a work of logic. Just as an earlier work of his (*Le Mythè de Sisyphe*) began with a meditation on living or not living – on the implications of the act of suicide; so this work begins with a meditation on enduring or not enduring – on the implications of the act of rebellion. If we decide to live, it must be because we have decided that our personal existence has some positive value; if we decide to rebel, it must be because we have decided that a human society has some positive value. But in each case the values are not 'given' – that is the illusionist trick played by religion or by philosophy. They have to be deduced from the conditions of living, and are to be accepted along with the suffering entailed by the limits of the possible. Social values are rules of conduct implicit in a tragic fate; and they offer a hope of creation.

The Rebel, that is to say, offers us a philosophy of politics. It is a kind of book that appears only in France, devoted, in a passionate intellectual sense, to the examination of such concepts as liberty and terror. Not that it is a theoretical work – on the contrary, it is an examination of the actual situation of Europe today, informed by a precise historical knowledge of the past two centuries of its social development. It is 'an attempt to understand the times'.

Camus believes that revolt is one of the 'essential dimensions' of mankind. It is useless to deny its historical reality – rather we must seek in it a principle of existence. But the nature of revolt has changed radically in our times. It is no longer the revolt of the slave against the master, nor even the revolt of the poor against the rich; it is a metaphysical revolt, the revolt of man against the conditions of life, against creation itself. At the same time, it is an aspiration towards clarity and unity of thought – even, paradoxically, towards order. That, at least, is what it becomes under the intellectual guidance of Camus.

He reviews the history of this metaphysical revolt, beginning with the absolute negation of Sade, glancing at Baudelaire and the 'dandies', passing on to Stirner, Nietzsche, Lautréamont, and the Surrealists.* His attitude to these prophetic figures is not unsympathetic, and once more it is interesting to observe the influence of André Breton on the contemporary mind. Camus then turns to the history of revolt in the political sense, his main object being to draw a clear distinction between rebellion and revolution. Here, and not for the first time, Camus' ideas come close to anarchism, for he recognizes that revolution always implies the establishment of a new government, whereas rebellion is action without planned issue – it is spontaneous protestation. Camus reviews the history of the French Revolution, of the regicides and deicides, and shows how inevitably, from Rousseau to Stalin, the course of revolution leads to authoritarian dictatorship. Saint-Just is the precursor of Lenin. Even Bakunin, to whom Camus devotes some extremely interesting pages (pointing out, for example, that he alone of his time, with exceptional profundity, declared war against the idolatry of science) – even Bakunin, if we examine the statutes of the Fraternité Internationale (1864–7) which he drew up, is found insisting on the absolute subordination of the individual to a central committee of action.

All revolutions in modern times, Camus points out, have led to a reinforcement of the power of the State. 'The strange and terrifying growth of the modern State can be considered as the logical conclusion of inordinate technical and philosophical ambitions, foreign to the true spirit of rebellion, but which nevertheless gave birth to the revolutionary spirit of our time. The prophetic dream of Marx and the over-inspired predictions of Hegel or of Nietzsche ended by

* Unfortunately in the interests of economy certain pages relating to some of these figures have been deleted in the English edition.

conjuring up, after the City of God had been razed to the ground, either a rational or an irrational State, but one which in both cases was founded on terror.' The counter-revolutions of fascism only serve to reinforce the general argument.

Camus shows the real quality of his thought in his final pages. It would have been easy, on the facts marshalled in this book, to have retreated into despair or inaction. Camus substitutes the idea of 'limits'. 'We know at the end of this long inquiry into rebellion and nihilism that rebellion with no other limits but historical expediency signifies unlimited slavery. To escape this fate, the revolutionary mind, if it wants to remain alive, must therefore return again to the sources of rebellion and draw its inspiration from the only system of thought which is faithful to its origins; thought which recognizes limits.' To illustrate his meaning Camus refers to syndicalism, that movement in politics which is based on the organic unity of the cell, and which is the negation of abstract and bureaucratic centralism. He quotes Tolain: *'Les êtres humains ne s'émancipent qu'au sein des groupes naturels'* – human beings emancipate themselves only on the basis of natural groups. 'The masses against the State, deliberate freedom against rational tyranny, finally, altruistic individualism against the colonization of the masses, are thus the contradictions that express once again the endless opposition of moderation to excess which has animated the history of the Occident since the time of the ancient world.' This tradition of *'mesure'* belongs to the Mediterranean world, and has been destroyed by the excesses of German ideology and of Christian otherworldliness – by the denial of nature.

Restraint is not the contrary of revolt. Revolt carries with it the very idea of restraint, and 'moderation, born of rebellion, can only live by rebellion. It is a perpetual conflict, continually created and mastered by the intelligence ... Whatever we may do, excess will always keep its place in the heart of man, in the place where solitude is found. We all carry within us our places of exile, our crimes, and our ravages. But our task is not to unleash them on the world; it is to fight them in ourselves and in others. Rebellion, the secular will not to surrender of which Barrès speaks, is still, today, at the basis of the struggle. Origin of form, source of real life, it keeps us always erect in the savage formless movement of history.'

In his last pages Camus rises to heights of eloquence which are exhilarating. It is an inspiring book. It is particularly a book which should be read by all those who wish to see the inborn impulse of revolt inspired by a new spirit of action – by those who understand 'that rebellion cannot exist without a strange form of love'. Not to calculate, to give everything for the sake of life and of living men – in that way we can show that 'real generosity towards the future lies in giving all to the present'.

HERBERT READ

Introduction

THERE are crimes of passion and crimes of logic. The line that divides them is not clear. But the Penal Code distinguishes between them by the useful concept of premeditation. We are living in the era of premeditation and perfect crimes. Our criminals are no longer those helpless children who pleaded love as their excuse. On the contrary, they are adults, and they have a perfect alibi: philosophy, which can be used for anything, even for transforming murderers into judges.

Heathcliff, in *Wuthering Heights*, would kill everybody on earth in order to gain Cathie, but he would never think of saying that murder is reasonable or theoretically defensible. He would commit it; there his theory comes to a halt. This implies powerful love and it implies character. Since intense love is rare, such murders are uncommon, and they retain an air of waywardness. But as soon as a man, through lack of character, takes refuge in a doctrine, as soon as he makes his crime *reasonable*, it multiplies like Reason herself and assumes all the figures of the syllogism. It was unique like a cry; now it is universal like science. Yesterday, it was put on trial; today it is the law.

This is not the place for indignation. The purpose of this essay is once more to accept the reality of today, which is logical crime, and to examine meticulously the arguments by which it is sustained; it is an attempt to understand the time I live in. One might think that a period which, within fifty years, uproots, enslaves, or kills seventy million human beings, should only, and forthwith, be condemned. But also its guilt must be understood. In more ingenuous times, when the tyrant razed cities for his own greater glory, when the slave chained to the conqueror's chariot was dragged through the rejoicing streets, when enemies were thrown to wild animals in front of the assembled people, before such naked crimes consciousness could be steady and judgement unclouded. But slave camps under the flag of freedom, massacres justified by philanthropy or the taste for the superhuman, cripple judgement. On the day when crime puts on the apparel of innocence, through a curious reversal peculiar to our age, it is innocence that is called on to justify itself. The purpose of this essay is to accept and study that strange challenge.

It is a question of finding out whether innocence, the moment it begins to act, can avoid committing murder. We can act only in our own time, among the people who surround us. We shall be capable of nothing until we know whether we have the right to kill our fellow-men, or the right to let them be killed. Since all contemporary action leads to murder, direct or indirect, we cannot act until we know whether, and why, we have the right to kill.

What matters here is not to follow things back to their origins, but, the world being what it is, to know how to live in it. In the age of negation, it was of some avail to examine one's position concerning suicide. In the age of ideologies, we must make up our minds about murder. If murder has rational foundations, then our period and we ourselves have significance. If it has no such foundations, then we are plunged in madness and there is no way out except to find some significance or to desist. We must in any case give a clear answer to the question put to us by the blood and strife of our century. For we are being interrogated. Thirty years ago, before making the decision to kill, it was the custom to repudiate many things, to the point of repudiating oneself by suicide. God is a cheat; the whole world (including myself) is a cheat; therefore I choose to die: suicide was the question then. But Ideology, a contemporary phenomenon, limits itself to repudiating other people; they alone are the cheats. This leads to murder. Every dawn masked assassins slip into some cell; murder is the question today.

The two ideas cling together. Or rather they cling to us, and so pressingly that we ourselves are no longer able to choose our problems. They choose us, one after the other. Let us consent to being chosen. This essay proposes to follow, into the realm of murder and revolt, a mode of thinking that began with suicide and the idea of the absurd.

*

But this mode of thinking, for the moment, yields only one concept, that of the absurd. And the concept of the absurd, in its turn, only yields a contradiction where the problem of murder is concerned. The sense of the absurd, when one first undertakes to deduce a rule of action from it, makes murder seem a matter of indifference, hence, permissible. If one believes in nothing, if nothing makes sense, if we can assert no value whatsoever, everything is permissible and nothing is important. There is no pro or con; the murderer is neither right nor wrong. One is free to stoke the crematory fires, or to give one's life to the care of lepers. Wickedness and virtue are just accident or whim.

We may then decide not to act at all, which comes down to condoning other people's murder, plus a little fastidious sorrow over human imperfection. Or we may hit upon tragic dilettantism as a substitute for action; in this case, human lives become counters in a game. Finally, we may resolve to undertake some action that is not wholly arbitrary. In this case, since we have no higher value to direct our action, we shall aim at *efficiency*. Since nothing is true or false, good or bad, our principle will become that of showing ourselves to be the most effective, in other words the most powerful. And then the world will no longer be divided into the just and the unjust, but into masters and slaves. Thus, whichever way we turn in the depths of negation and nihilism, murder has its privileged position.

Hence, if we profess the absurdist position, we should be ready to kill, thus giving logic more weight than scruples we consider illusory. Certainly, some compromises will be necessary. But, on the whole, fewer than one might suppose – to judge from experience. Besides, it is always possible, as we see every day, to have the killing done for one. Thus everything would be settled in accordance with logic, if logic were really satisfied.

But logic cannot find satisfaction in an attitude which indicates first that murder is permissible and then that it is impermissible.

For the absurdist analysis, after having shown that killing is a matter of indifference, eventually, in its most important deduction, condemns killing. The final conclusion of the absurdist process is, in fact, the rejection of suicide and persistence in that hopeless encounter between human questioning and the silence of the universe. Suicide would mean the end of this encounter, and the absurdist position realizes that it could not endorse suicide without abolishing its own foundations. It would consider such an outcome running away or being rescued. But it is plain that absurdist reasoning thereby recognizes human life as the single necessary good, because it makes possible that confrontation, and because without life the absurdist wager could not go on. To say that life is absurd, one must be alive. How can one, without indulging one's desire for comfort, keep for oneself the exclusive benefits of this argument? The moment life is recognized as a necessary good, it becomes so for all men. One cannot find logical consistency in murder, if one denies it in suicide. A mind that is imbued with the idea of the absurd will doubtless accept murder that is fated; it could not accept murder that proceeds from reasoning. In view of that confrontation which they both render impossible, murder and suicide are the same thing; one must accept them both or reject them both.

Likewise, absolute nihilism, which is willing to justify suicide, advances even more easily to logical murder. If our time admits with equanimity that murder has its justification, this is because of the indifference to life which is the mark of nihilism. Certainly there have been periods in which the passion for living was so strong that it too rushed into criminal excesses. But these excesses were the outcome of a terrible enjoyment. They were not the monotonous course of events, set in motion by a compulsive logic, in whose eyes everything is equal. This logic has carried those suicidal values on which our era was nurtured to their final consequence, which is the legitimatization of murder. Likewise, it culminates in collective suicide. The most striking demonstration was furnished by the Hitlerian apocalypse of 1945. Self-destruction meant nothing to those madmen who, in their bomb-shelters, arranged their own death and apotheosis. The important thing was to not die alone, and simultaneously to destroy a whole world. In a way, the man who kills himself in solitude still recognizes a value, since, manifestly, he claims no right to the lives of other people. The proof of this is that he never uses, in order to dominate others, the terrible strength and freedom which he gains from his decision to die; every act of solitary self-destruction, when it does not proceed from passion, is in some way generous or scornful. But one is scornful on behalf of something. If the world is a matter of indifference to the suicide, this is because he has an idea of something which is not or could not be indifferent to him. One thinks that one will destroy everything or take everything along with one; but from this very death a value arises which would, perhaps, have justified existence. Absolute negation is therefore not achieved by suicide. It can be achieved only by absolute destruction, of both oneself and everybody else. Or at least it can be experienced only by striving toward that delectable end. Suicide and murder are thus two aspects of a single system, the system of an unhappy intellect which rather than suffer limitation chooses the dark victory which annihilates earth and heaven.

Equally, if one denies that there are grounds for suicide, one cannot claim them for murder. One cannot be a part-time nihilist. Absurdist reasoning cannot defend the continued existence of its spokesman and accept the sacrifice of others' lives. The moment we recognize the impossibility of absolute negation (and living is a manner of recognizing this) the very first thing that cannot be denied is the right of others to live. Thus, the self-same notion which allowed us to think that murder was a matter of indifference now undermines its justifications; we are back in the untenable position from which we tried to escape. In practice, this line of reasoning tells us at one and the same time that killing is permissible and that it is not permissible. It abandons us in contradiction, with no grounds for forbidding murder or for justifying it, menacing and exposed to menace, driven by an entire world intoxicated with nihilism, and yet lost in loneliness, with knives in our hands and a lump in our throats. Nothing remains in the absurdist attitude which can help us answer the questions of our time. The absurdist method, like that of systematic doubt, has wiped the slate clean. It leaves us in a blind alley. But, like the method of doubt, it can, by returning upon itself, disclose a new field of investigation. Reasoning follows the same reflexive course. I proclaim that I believe in nothing and that everything is absurd, but I cannot doubt the validity of my own proclamation and I am compelled to believe, at least, in my own protest. The first, and only, datum that is furnished me, within absurdist experience, is rebellion. Stripped of all knowledge, driven to commit murder or consent to it, I possess this single datum which gains greater strength from the anguish that I suffer. Rebellion arises from the spectacle of the irrational coupled with an unjust and incomprehensible condition. But its blind impetus clamours for order in the midst of chaos, and for unity in the very heart of the ephemeral. It protests, it demands, it insists that the outrage come to an end, that there be built upon rock what until now was written unceasingly upon the waters. Its aim is to transform. But to transform is to act, and to act, nowadays, is to kill while it still does not know if murder is legitimate. Hence it is absolutely necessary that rebellion derive its justifications from itself, since it has nothing else to derive them from. It must consent to study itself in order to learn how to act.

Two centuries of rebellion, metaphysical and historical, present themselves for our consideration. Only a historian could undertake to set forth in detail the doctrines and movements that followed one another during these centuries. But at least it ought to be possible to find a guiding thread. The following pages do no more than set down some historical landmarks and a provisional hypothesis. It is not the only hypothesis possible; moreover, it is far from explaining everything. But it accounts partly for the direction and, almost wholly, for the frenzy of our time. The prodigious history evoked here is the history of European pride.

In any case we cannot understand rebellion except by studying its attitudes, pretensions, and conquests. In its achievements we may perhaps discover the rule of action that the absurd could not give us; a sign at least concerning our right, or duty, to kill; hope, finally, for a new creation. Man is the only creature who refuses to be what he is. We shall try to determine whether this refusal must inevitably lead him to the destruction of others and of himself, if every rebellion must end in the defence of universal murder, or if, on the contrary, without claiming an impossible innocence, it can furnish the principle of a limited culpability.

I

THE REBEL

WHAT is a rebel? A man who says no: but whose refusal does not imply a renunciation. He is also a man who says yes as soon as he begins to think for himself. A slave who has taken orders all his life, suddenly decides that he cannot obey some new command. What does he mean by saying 'no'?

He means, for instance, that 'this has been going on too long', 'so far but no farther', 'you are going too far', or again 'There are certain limits beyond which you shall not go.' In other words, his 'no' affirms the existence of a borderline. You find the same conception in the rebel's opinion that the other person is 'exaggerating', that he is exerting his authority beyond a limit where he infringes on the rights of others. He rebels because he categorically refuses to submit to conditions that he considers intolerable and also because he is confusedly convinced that his position is justified, or rather, because in his own mind he thinks that he 'has the right to ...'. Rebellion cannot exist without the feeling that somewhere, in some way, you are justified. It is in this way that the rebel slave says yes and no at the same time. He affirms that there are limits and also that he suspects – and wishes to preserve – the existence of certain things beyond those limits. He stubbornly insists that there are certain things in him which 'are worth while ...' and which must be taken into consideration.

In every act of rebellion, the man concerned experiences not only a feeling of revulsion at the infringement of his rights but also a complete and spontaneous loyalty to certain aspects of himself. Thus he implicitly brings into play a standard of values so far from being false that he is willing to preserve them at all costs. Up to this point he has, at least, kept quiet and, in despair, has accepted a condition to which he submits even though he considers it unjust. To keep

19

quiet is to allow yourself to believe that you have no opinions, that you want nothing, and in certain cases it amounts to really wanting nothing. Despair, like Absurdism, prefers to consider everything in general and nothing in particular. Silence expresses this attitude very satisfactorily. But from the moment that the rebel finds his voice – even though he has nothing to say but no – he begins to consider things in particular. In the etymological sense, the rebel is a turn-coat. He acted under the lash of his master's whip. Suddenly he turns and faces him. He chooses what is preferable to what is not. Not every value leads to rebellion, but every rebellion tacitly invokes a value. Or is it really a question of values?

An awakening of conscience, no matter how confused it may be, develops from any act of rebellion and is represented by the sudden realization that something exists with which the rebel can identify himself – even if only for a moment. Up to now this identification was never fully realized. Previous to his insurrection, the slave accepted all the demands made upon him. He even very often took orders, without reacting against them, which were considerably more offensive to him than the one at which he balked. He was patient and though, perhaps, he protested inwardly, he was obviously more careful of his own immediate interests – in that he kept quiet – than aware of his own rights. But with loss of patience – with impatience – begins a reaction which can extend to everything that he accepted up to this moment, and which is almost always retroactive. Immediately the slave refuses to obey the humiliating orders of his master, he rejects the condition of slavery. The act of rebellion carries him beyond the point he reached by simply refusing. He exceeds the bounds that he established for his antagonist and demands that he should now be treated as an equal. What was, originally, an obstinate resistance on the part of the rebel, becomes the rebel personified. He proceeds to put self-respect above everything else and proclaims that it is preferable to life itself. It becomes, for him, the supreme blessing. Having previously been willing to compromise, the slave suddenly adopts an attitude of All or Nothing. Knowledge is born and conscience awakened.

But it is obvious that the knowledge he gains is of an 'All' that is still rather obscure and of a 'Nothing' that proclaims the possibility of sacrificing the rebel to this 'All'. The rebel himself wants to be 'All' – to identify himself completely with this blessing of which he has suddenly become aware and of which he wishes to be recognized and proclaimed as the incarnation – or 'Nothing' which means to be completely destroyed by the power that governs him. As a last resort he is willing to accept the final defeat, which is death, rather than be deprived of the last sacrament which he would call, for example, freedom. Better to die on one's feet than to live on one's knees.

Values, according to the best authorities, 'usually represent a transition from facts to rights, from what is desired to what is desirable (usually through the medium of what is generally considered desirable)'.* The transition from facts to rights is manifest, as we have seen, in the act of rebellion, as is the transition from 'this is how things should be' to 'this is how I want things to be', and still more, perhaps, the conception of the submission of the individual to the common good. The appearance of the conception of 'All or Nothing' demonstrates that rebellion, contrary to present opinion and despite the fact that it springs from everything that is most strictly individualistic in man, undermines the very conception of the individual. If an individual actually consents to die, and, when the occasion arises, accepts death as a consequence of his rebellion, he demonstrates that he is willing to sacrifice himself for the sake of a common good which he considers more important than his own destiny. If he prefers the risk of death to a denial of the rights that he defends, it is because he considers that the latter are more important than he is. He acts, therefore, in the name of certain values which are still indeterminate but which he feels are common to himself and to all men. We see that the affirmation implicit in each act of revolt is extended to something which transcends the individual in so far as it removes him from his supposed solitude and supplies him with reason to act. But it is worth noting that the conception of values as

* Lalande, *Vocabulaire philosophique.*

pre-existent to any kind of action runs counter to the purely historical schools of philosophy in which values are established (if they are ever established) by action itself. An analysis of rebellion leads us to the suspicion that, contrary to the postulates of contemporary thought, a human nature does exist, as the Greeks believed. Why rebel if th're is nothing worth preserving in oneself? The slave asserts himself for the sake of everyone in the world when he comes to the conclusion that a command has infringed on something inside him that does not belong to him alone, but which he has in common with other men – even with the man who insults and oppresses him.

Two observations will support this argument. First, we can see that an act of rebellion is not, essentially, an egoistic act. Undoubtedly it can have egoistic aims. But you can rebel equally well against a lie as against oppression. Furthermore, the rebel – at the moment of his greatest impetus and no matter what his aims – keeps nothing in reserve and commits himself completely. Undoubtedly he demands respect for himself, but only in so far as he identifies himself with humanity in general.

Then we note that revolt does not occur only amongst the oppressed but that it can also break out at the mere spectacle of oppression of which someone else is the victim. In such cases there is a feeling of identification with other individuals. And it must be made clear that it is not a question of psychological identification – a mere subterfuge by which the individual contrives to feel that it is he who has been oppressed. It can even happen that we cannot countenance other people being insulted in a manner that we ourselves have accepted without rebelling. The suicides of the Russian terrorists in Siberia, as a protest against their comrades being whipped, is a case in point. Nor is it a question of a community of interests. Injustices done to men whom we consider enemies can, actually, be profoundly repugnant to us. Our reaction is only an identification of destinies and a choice of sides. Therefore the individual is not, in himself, an embodiment of the values he wishes to defend. It needs at least all humanity to comprise them. When he rebels, a man identifies himself with other men and, from this point of view, human solidarity is metaphysical. But for the moment we are only dealing with the kind of solidarity that is born in chains.

It would be possible for us to define the positive aspect of the values implicit in every act of rebellion by comparing them to a completely negative conception like that of resentment as defined by Scheler. Actually, rebellion is more than an act of revenge, in the strongest sense of the word. Resentment is very well defined by Scheler as an auto-intoxication – the evil secretion, in a sealed vessel, of prolonged impotence. Rebellion, on the other hand, removes the seal and allows the whole being to come into play. It liberates stagnant waters and turns them into a raging torrent. Scheler himself emphasizes the passive aspect of resentment, and remarks on the prominent position it occupies in the psychology of women whose main preoccupations are desire and possession. The mainspring of revolt, on the other hand, is the principle of superabundant activity and energy. Scheler is also right in saying that resentment is always highly flavoured with envy. But we envy what we do not possess while the rebel defends what he has. He does not only claim some benefit which he does not possess or of which he was deprived. His aim is to claim recognition for something which he has and which has already been recognized by him, in almost every case, as more important than anything of which he could be envious. Rebellion is not realistic. According to Scheler, resentment always turns into either unscrupulous ambition or bitterness, depending on whether it flourishes in a weak mind or a strong one. But in both cases it is always a question of wanting to be something other than what one is. Resentment is always resentment against oneself. The rebel, on the other hand, from his very first step, refuses to allow anyone to touch what he is. He is fighting for the integrity of one part of his being. At first he does not try to conquer, but simply to impose.

Finally, it would seem that resentment takes a delight, in advance, in the pain that it would like the object of its envy to feel. Nietzsche and Scheler are right in seeing an excellent illustration of this feeling

23

in the passage where Tertullian informs his readers that one of the greatest sources of happiness in heaven will be the spectacle of the Roman emperors consumed in the fires of hell. This kind of happiness is also experienced by all the decent people who go to watch executions. The rebel, on principle, persistently refuses to be humiliated without asking that others should be. He will even accept pain provided that his integrity is respected.

It is hard to understand why Scheler absolutely identifies the spirit of revolt with resentment. His critique of resentment as a part of humanitarianism (which he considers as the non-Christian form of human love) could perhaps be applied to certain vague forms of humanitarian idealism, or to certain techniques of terror. But it is false in so far as a man's rebellion against his condition is concerned and equally false about the impulse that enlists individuals in the defence of a dignity common to all men. Scheler wants to prove that humanitarian feelings are always accompanied by misanthropy. Humanity is loved in general in order to avoid loving anybody in particular. In some cases this is correct, and it is easier to understand Scheler when we realize that for him humanitarianism is represented by Bentham and Rousseau. But man's love for man can be born of other things than an arithmetic calculation of interests or a theoretical confidence in human nature. Despite what the utilitarians say, there exists, for example, the type of logic, embodied by Dostoyevsky in Ivan Karamazov, that begins with an act of rebellion and ends in metaphysical insurrection. Scheler is aware of this and sums up the conception in the following manner: 'There is not enough love in the world to be able to squander it on anything else but the human race.' Even if this proposition were true, the profound despair that it implies would merit any other reaction but contempt. Actually, it misinterprets the tortured nature of Karamazov's rebellion. Ivan's drama, on the contrary, arises from the fact that there is too much love without an object. The existence of God being denied, love becomes redundant and then he decides to lavish it on the human race as a generous act of complicity.

Nevertheless, in the act of revolt as we have envisaged it up to now, we do not choose an abstract ideal through lack of feeling or for sterile reasons of revenge. We demand that that part of man which cannot be confined to the realm of ideas should be taken into consideration – the passionate side of his nature that serves no other purpose but to help him to live. Does that imply that no act of rebellion is motivated by resentment ? No, and we know this from the bitter experience of centuries. But we must consider the idea of revolt in its widest sense – and in its widest sense it goes far beyond resentment. When Heathcliff, in *Wuthering Heights*, says that he puts his love above God and would willingly go to Hell in order to be reunited with the woman he loves, he is prompted not only by his youth and his humiliation but by the consuming experience of a whole lifetime. The same emotion causes Eckart, in a surprising fit of heresy, to say that he prefers Hell with Jesus to Heaven without Him. This is the very essence of love. Contrary to what Scheler thinks, it would be impossible to overemphasize the passionate affirmation that underlies the act of revolt and which distinguishes it from resentment. Rebellion, though apparently negative since it creates nothing, is profoundly positive in that it reveals the part of man which must always be defended.

But finally, are not rebellion and the values that it calls into play interdependent ? Reasons for rebellion seem, in fact, to change with the times. It is obvious that a Hindu pariah, an Inca warrior, a primitive native of Central Africa, and a member of one of the first Christian communities had quite different conceptions about rebellion. We could even assert, with considerable assurance, that the idea of rebellion has no meaning in those actual cases. However, a Greek slave, a serf, a condottiere of the Renaissance, a Parisian bourgeois during the Regency, and a Russian intellectual at the beginning of the nineteenth century would undoubtedly agree that rebellion is legitimate, even if they differed about the reasons. In other words, the problem of rebellion only seems to assume a precise meaning within the confines of Western thought. It is possible to be even more explicit by saying, like Scheler, that the spirit of rebellion finds few means of expression in societies where inequalities are very great (the Hindu caste system) or, again, in those where there is absolute equality (certain primitive societies). The spirit of revolt can only exist in a society where a theoretic equality conceals great factual inequalities. The problem of revolt, therefore, has no meaning outside our Occidental society. It would be tempting to say that it was relative to the development of individualism if the preceding remarks had not put us on guard against this conclusion.

On the basis of the evidence, the only conclusion we can draw from Scheler's remark is that, thanks to the theory of political freedom, there is, in the very heart of our society, an extension of the conception of the rights of man and a corresponding dissatisfaction caused by the application of this theory of freedom. Actual freedom has not increased in proportion to man's awareness of it. We can only deduce, from this observation, that rebellion is the act of an educated man who is aware of his rights. But we cannot say that it is only a question of individual rights. Because of the sense of solidarity that we have already pointed out, it would rather seem that what is at stake is humanity's gradually increasing awareness of itself as it pursues its adventurous course. In fact, for the Inca and the pariah the problem of revolt never arises, because for them it has been solved by tradition before they had time to raise it – the answer being that tradition is sacrosanct. If, in the sacrosanct world, the problem of revolt does not arise, it is because no real problems are to be found in it – all the answers having been given simultaneously. Metaphysic is replaced by myth. But before man accepts the sacrosanct and in order for him to be able to accept it – or before he escapes from it and in order for him to be able to escape from it – there is always a period of soul-searching and revolt. The rebel is a man who is on the point of accepting or rejecting the sacrosanct and determined on creating a human situation where all the answers are human or, rather, formulated in terms of reason. From this moment every question, every word, is an act of rebellion, while in the sacrosanct world every word is an act of grace. It would be possible to demonstrate in this manner that only two possible worlds can exist for the human mind, the sacrosanct (or, to speak in Christian terms, the world of Grace)* or the rebel world. The disappearance of the one is equivalent to the appearance of the other, and this appearance can take place in disconcerting forms. Here again we find the attitude of *All or Nothing*. The pressing aspect of the problem of rebellion depends only on the fact that nowadays whole societies have wanted to re-examine their position in regard to the sacrosanct. We live in an unsacrosanct period. Insurrection is certainly not the sum total of human experience. But the controversial aspect of contemporary history compels us to say that rebellion is one of man's essential dimensions. It is our historical reality. Unless we ignore reality, we must find our values in it. Is it possible to find a rule of conduct outside the realm of religion and of absolute values? That is the question raised by revolt.

We have already noted the confused standard of values that are called into play by incipient revolt. Now we must inquire if these values are to be found in contemporary forms of rebellious thought and action and, if they do exist, we must specify their content. But, before going any farther, let us note that the basis of these values is rebellion itself. Man's solidarity is founded upon rebellion, and rebellion can only be justified by this solidarity. We then have authority to say that any type of rebellion which claims the right to deny or destroy this solidarity simultaneously loses the right to be called rebellion and actually becomes an accomplice to murder. In the same way, this solidarity, except in so far as religion is concerned, only comes to life on the level of rebellion. And so the real drama of revolutionary thought is revealed. In order to exist, man must rebel, but rebellion must respect the limits that it discovers in itself – limits where minds meet and, in meeting, begin to exist. Revolutionary thought, therefore, cannot dispense with memory: it is in a perpetual state of tension. In contemplating the results of an act of rebellion,

* There is, of course, an act of metaphysical rebellion at the beginning of Christianity, but the resurrection of Christ and the annunciation of the Kingdom of Heaven interpreted as a promise of eternal life are the answers that render it futile.

we shall have to say, each time, whether it remains faithful to its first noble promise or whether, through lassitude or folly, it forgets its purpose and plunges into a mire of tyranny or servitude.

Meanwhile, we can sum up the initial progress that the spirit of rebellion accomplishes in a process of thought that is already convinced of the absurdity and apparent sterility of the world. In absurdist experience suffering is individual. But from the moment that a movement of rebellion begins, suffering is seen as a collective experience – as the experience of everyone. Therefore the first step for a mind overwhelmed by the strangeness of things is to realize that this feeling of strangeness is shared with all men and that the entire human race suffers from the division between itself and the rest of the world. The unhappiness experienced by a single man becomes collective unhappiness. In our daily trials, rebellion plays the same role as does the '*cogito*' in the category of thought: it is the first clue. But this clue lures the individual from his solitude. Rebellion is the common ground on which every man bases his first values. I *rebel* – therefore we *exist*.

2

METAPHYSICAL REBELLION

METAPHYSICAL rebellion is the means by which a man protests against his condition and against the whole of creation. It is metaphysical because it disputes the ends of man and of creation. The slave protests against the condition of his state of slavery; the metaphysical rebel protests against the human condition in general. The rebel slave affirms that there is something in him which will not tolerate the manner in which his master treats him; the metaphysical rebel declares that he is frustrated by the universe. For both of them it is not only a problem of pure and simple negation. In fact in both cases we find an assessment of values in the name of which the rebel refuses to accept the condition in which he finds himself.

The slave who opposes his master is not concerned, let us note, with repudiating his master as a human being. He is repudiating him as master. He denies his right to deny him, as a slave, by making excessive demands. The master fails to the extent that he does not respond to a demand that he ignores. If men cannot refer to common values, which they all separately recognize, then man is incomprehensible to man. The rebel demands that these values should be clearly recognized as part of himself because he knows or suspects that, without them, crime and disorder would reign in the world. An act of rebellion seems to him like a demand for clarity and unity. The most elementary rebellion, paradoxically, expresses an aspiration to order.

This description can be applied, word for word, to the metaphysical rebel. He attacks a shattered world to make it whole. He confronts the injustice at large in the world with his own principles of justice. Thus all he originally wants is to resolve this contradiction and establish a reign of justice, if he can, or of injustice if he is driven to the end of his tether. Meanwhile he denounces the contradiction. Metaphysical rebellion is the justified claim of a desire for unity against the suffering of life and death – in that it protests against the incompleteness of human life, expressed by death, and its dispersion, expressed by evil. If a mass death sentence defines man's condition, then rebellion, in one sense, is its contemporary. When he refuses to recognize his mortality, the rebel simultaneously refuses to recognize the power that makes him live in this condition. The metaphysical rebel is, therefore, certainly not an atheist, as one might think him, but inevitably he is a blasphemer. He simply blasphemes, primarily in the name of order, by denouncing God as the origin of death and as the supreme disillusionment.

Let us return to the rebel slave to clear up this point. By protesting, he established the existence of the master against whom he rebelled. But, at the same time, he demonstrated that his master's power was dependent on his own subordination and he affirmed his own power: the power of continually questioning the superiority of his master. In this regard master and slave are in the same boat; the temporary sway of the former is as relative as the latter's submission.

At the moment of rebellion, the two forces assert themselves alternately, until the time comes for them to attempt to destroy each other and one or other temporarily disappears.

In the same way, if the metaphysical rebel ranges himself against a power whose existence he simultaneously affirms, he only admits the existence of this power at the very instant when he calls it into question. And then he draws this superior power into the same humiliating adventure as himself – the power being equally as ineffectual as our condition. He subjects it to the power of our refusal, bends it to the unbending part of human nature, forcibly integrates it into an existence which we render absurd, and finally drags it from its refuge outside time and involves it in history – very far from the eternal stability that it can only find in the unanimous consent of all men. Thus rebellion affirms that, on this level, any superior being is contradictory if nothing else.

And so the history of metaphysical revolt cannot be confused with that of atheism. From one angle, it is even identified with the contemporary history of religious sentiment. The rebel defies more than he denies. Originally, at least, he does not deny God, he simply talks to Him as an equal. But it is not a polite dialogue. It is a polemic animated by the desire to conquer. The slave starts by begging for justice and ends by wanting to wear a crown. He too wants to dominate. His insurrection against his condition is transformed into an unlimited campaign against the heavens for the purpose of capturing a king who will first be dethroned and finally condemned to death. Human rebellion ends in metaphysical revolution. It progresses from appearances to facts, from dilettantism to revolutionary commitment. When the throne of God is overthrown, the rebel realizes that it is now his own responsibility to create the justice, order, and unity that he sought in vain within his own condition and, in this way, to justify the fall of God. Then begins the desperate effort to create, at the price of sin if necessary, the dominion of man. This cannot come about without appalling consequences of which we are only, so far, aware of a few. But these consequences are in no way due to rebellion itself or, at least, they only occur to the extent that rebellion forgets its original purpose, tires of the tension caused by its positive and negative attitude, and finally abandons itself to complete negation or total submission. Metaphysical insurrection in its primary stages offers us the same positive content as the slave's rebellion. Our task is to examine what becomes of this positive content of rebellion in the actions that it entails and to point out the path where the rebel is led by his fidelity or infidelity to the origins of his revolt.

The Sons of Cain

METAPHYSICAL revolt, in the proper sense, does not appear in any coherent form in the history of ideas until the end of the eighteenth century: modern times begin with the crash of falling ramparts. But, from this moment on, its consequences develop uninterruptedly and it is no exaggeration to say that they have shaped the history of our times. Historically speaking, the first coherent offensive is Sade's: he musters, into one vast war machine, the arguments of the freethinkers up to Voltaire and Father Meslier. Naturally, his is also the most extreme negation of all. From rebellion, Sade can only deduce an absolute negative. Twenty-seven years in prison do not, in fact, produce a very conciliatory form of intelligence. Such a lengthy confinement makes a man either a weakling or a killer – or sometimes both. If the mind is strong enough to construct, in a prison cell, a a moral philosophy which is not one of submission, it will generally be one of domination. Every ethic conceived in solitude implies the exercise of power. In this respect Sade is the archetype, for in so far as society treated him atrociously he responded in an atrocious fashion. The writer, despite a few happy phrases and the unconsidered praises of contemporary critics, is secondary. He is admired today, with so much ingenuity, for reasons which have nothing to do with literature.

He is exalted as the philosopher in chains and the first theoretician of absolute rebellion. He might well have been. In prison, dreams have no limits and reality is no curb. Intelligence in chains loses in lucidity what it gains in intensity. The only logic known to Sade was the logic of his feelings. He did not create a philosophy, he pursued a monstrous dream of revenge. Only the dream turned out to be prophetic. His desperate claim to freedom led Sade into the kingdom of servitude; his inordinate thirst for a form of life he could never attain was assuaged in the successive frenzies of a dream of universal destruction. In this way, at least, Sade is our contemporary. Let us follow the steps of his successive negations.

A MAN OF LETTERS

Is Sade an atheist? He says so, we believe, before he goes to prison in his *Dialogue between a Priest and a Dying Man*; and from then on we are staggered by his passion for sacrilege. One of his cruellest characters, Saint-Fond, does not in any sense deny God. He is content to develop a gnostic theory of a wicked demi-urge and to draw the suitable conclusions from it. Saint-Fond, we remark, is not Sade. Of course not. A character is never the writer who created him. However, there are occasions when a writer is all his characters simultaneously. Now, all Sade's atheists admit the non-existence of God, on principle, for the obvious reason that His existence would imply that He was indifferent, wicked, or cruel. Sade's greatest work ends with a demonstration of the stupidity and spite of the divinity. The innocent Justine runs through the storm and Noirceul, the criminal, swears to be converted if her life is spared by the divine anger (the celestial thunderbolt). Justine is struck by lightning, Noirceul triumphs, and human sin continues to be man's answer to divine sin. And so there is a libertine wager in answer to the Pascalian wager.

The idea of God that Sade conceives for himself is, thus, of a criminal divinity who oppresses and denies mankind. That murder is a divine attribute is quite apparent from the history of religions. Why, then, should men be virtuous? Sade's first step as a prisoner is to jump to the most extreme conclusions. If God kills and repudiates mankind there is nothing to stop one repudiating and killing one's fellow-men. This angry challenge in no way resembles the tranquil negation which is still to be found in the *Dialogue* of 1782. The man who exclaims: 'I have nothing, I am nothing' and who concludes 'No, no, virtue and vice are indistinguishable in the tomb' is neither happy nor tranquil. The conception of God is the only thing,

33

according to him, 'for which man cannot be forgiven'. The word 'forgiven' sounds strange in the mouth of this expert in torture. But it is himself whom he cannot forgive for a conception that his desperate view of the world, and his condition as a prisoner, completely refute. A double rebellion – against the order of things and against himself – is the guiding principle of Sade's reasoning. As this double revolt is self-contradictory, except in the agitated mind of a victim, his reasoning is always either ambiguous or legitimate according to whether it is judged in the light of logic or in an effort to be compassionate.

He repudiates man and his morality, because God repudiates them both. But he repudiates God even though He has served as his accomplice and guarantor up to now. For what reason? Because of the strongest instinct to be found in someone who is condemned by his hatred for mankind to live behind prison walls: the sexual instinct. What is this instinct? On the one hand, it is the ultimate expression of nature and, on the other, the blind force which demands the total subjection of human beings, even at the price of their destruction.

Sade denies God in the name of nature (the ideological conceptions of his time presented it in mechanistic form) and makes nature a power bent on destruction. For him, nature is sex; his logic leads him to a lawless universe where the only master is the inordinate energy of desire. This is his impassioned kingdom, where he finds his finest means of expression: 'What are all the creatures of the earth in comparison to a single one of our desires!' The long processes of reasoning by which Sade's heroes demonstrate that nature has need of crime, that it must destroy in order to create, and that thus we help it to create from the moment that we embark on self-destruction, are only aimed at creating an absolute liberty for Sade, the prisoner, who is too unjustly repressed not to long for the explosion that will blow everything sky high. In this, he goes against his times: the freedom that he demands is one not of principles but of instincts.

Sade dreamed, no doubt, of a universal republic, whose scheme he reveals through his wise reformer, Zamé. He shows us, by this means, that one of the aims of rebellion is the liberation of the entire world – in so far as rebellion is less and less willing to recognize limits as its demands become more pressing. But everything about him contradicts this pious dream. He is no friend of humanity, he hates philanthropists. The equality of which he sometimes speaks is a mathematical concept: the equivalence of the objects that comprise the human race, the abject equality of the victims. What drives him on, what makes him want to dominate everything, his real accomplishment, is hatred. Sade's republic is not founded on liberty but on libertinism. 'Justice', this peculiar democrat writes, 'has no real existence. She is the divinity of all the passions.'

Nothing is more revealing, in this respect, than the famous lampoon, read by Dolmance in the *Philosophie du boudoir* and which has the curious title: *People of France, one more effort if you want to be republican!* Pierre Klossowski is right in attaching so much importance to it, for this lampoon demonstrates to the revolutionaries that their republic is founded on the murder of the King – who was King by divine right – and that by guillotining God on 21 January 1793, they deprived themselves, forever, of the right to proscribe crime or to censure wicked instincts. The monarchy supported the conception of a God who, in conjunction with itself, created all laws. As for the Republic, it stood alone and morality was supposed to exist without benefit of the Commandments. However, it is doubtful if Sade, as Klossowski would have it, was profoundly convinced that this was a sacrilege and that an almost religious horror led him to the conclusions that he expresses. It is much more likely that he had already come to these conclusions and that afterwards he perceived the correct arguments to justify the absolute licence of morals that he wanted to impose on the government of his time. Logic founded on passions reverses the traditional sequence of reasoning and places the conclusion before the premises. To be convinced of this we only have to appreciate the admirable sequence of sophisms by which Sade, in this passage, justifies calumny, theft, and murder and demands that they be tolerated in the New World.

35

However, it is then that his thoughts are most penetrating. He rejects, with exceptional perspicacity for his times, the presumptuous alliance of freedom with virtue. Freedom, particularly when it is a prisoner's dream, cannot endure limitations. It must embrace crime or it is no longer freedom. On this essential point, Sade never varies. This man who never preached anything but contradictions only achieves coherence – and of a most complete kind – when he talks of capital punishment. An addict of refined ways of execution, a theoretician of sexual crime, he was never able to tolerate legal crime. 'My imprisonment, with the guillotine under my very eyes, was far more horrible to me than all the Bastilles imaginable.' From this feeling of horror he drew the strength to be moderate, publicly, during the Terror, and to intervene generously on behalf of his mother-in-law, despite the fact that she had had him imprisoned. A few years later, Nodier summed up, without knowing it perhaps, the position obstinately defended by Sade: 'To kill a man in a paroxysm of passion is understandable. To have him killed by someone else after serious meditation and on the pretext of a duty honourably discharged is incomprehensible.' Here we find the germ of an idea which will be further developed by Sade: he who kills must pay in kind. Sade is more moral, we see, than our contemporaries.

But his hatred for the death penalty is at first no more than a hatred for the men who are sufficiently convinced of their own virtue to dare to inflict capital punishment, when they themselves are criminals. You cannot simultaneously choose crime for yourself and punishment for others. You must open the prison gates or give an impossible proof of your own innocence. From the moment you accept murder, even if only once, you must allow it universally. The criminal who acts according to nature cannot, without prevarication, range himself on the side of the law. 'One more effort if you want to be republicans' means: 'Accept the freedom of crime, the only reasonable step, and enter forever into a state of insurrection as you enter into a state of grace.' Thus total submission to evil leads to an appalling penitence which cannot fail to horrify the Republic of enlightenment and natural goodness. By a significant coincidence, the manuscript of *One Hundred and Twenty Days of Sodom* was burned during the first riot of the Republic which could hardly fail to denounce Sade's heretical theories of liberty and to throw so compromising a supporter into prison once more. By doing so it gave him the regrettable opportunity of developing his rebellious logic still further.

The universal republic could be a dream for Sade, but never a temptation. In politics, his real position is cynicism. In his *Society of The Friends of Crime*, he declares himself ostensibly in favour of government and its laws which he, meanwhile, has every intention of violating. It is the same impulse which drives the lowest criminals to vote for the conservative candidate. The republic of crime cannot, for the moment at least, be universal. It must pretend to obey the law. However, in a world that knows no other rule but murder, beneath a criminal heaven, and in the name of a criminal nature, Sade, in reality, obeys no other law but that of inexhaustible desire. But to desire without limit comes to accepting being desired without limit. Licence to destroy supposes that you yourself can be destroyed. Thus you must struggle and dominate. The law of this world is nothing but the law of strength; its driving force the will to power.

The advocate of crime really only respects two kinds of power: one, which he finds in his own class, founded on the accident of birth, and the other by which, through sheer villainy, an underdog raises himself to the level of the libertines of noble birth whom Sade makes his heroes. This powerful little group of initiates know that they have all the rights. Anyone who doubts, even for a second, in his formidable privileges, is immediately driven from the flock, and once more becomes a victim. Thus a sort of aristocratic morality is created where a little group of men and women entrench themselves above a caste of slaves because they withhold the secret of a strange knowledge. The only problem, for them, consists in organizing themselves for the complete exercise of their rights which have the terrifying scope of desire.

They cannot hope to dominate the entire universe until the law of crime has been accepted by the universe. Sade never even believed that his own nation could be capable of the additional effort which would make it 'republican'. But if crime and desire are not the law of the entire universe, if they do not reign at least over a specified territory, they are no longer unifying principles, but ferments of conflict. They are no longer the law and man returns to chaos and confusion. Thus it is necessary to create, from all these fragments, a world which coincides exactly with the new law. The need for unity, which Creation never satisfies, is fulfilled, at all costs, in a microcosm. The law of force never has the patience to await complete control of the world. It must fix the boundaries, without delay, of the territory where it holds sway, even if it means surrounding it with barbed wire and observation towers.

For Sade, the law of force implies barred gates, castles with seven-foot walls from which it is impossible to escape, and where a society founded on desire and crime functions unimpeded, according to an implacable system. Unbridled rebellion, insistence on complete liberty, lead to the subjection of the majority. Man's emancipation is fulfilled, for Sade, in these strongholds of debauchery where a kind of bureaucracy of vice rules over the life and death of the men and women who have entered, forever, the hell of their desires. His works abound with descriptions of these privileged places where feudal libertines, to demonstrate to their assembled victims their absolute impotence and servitude, always resume the Duc de Glangis' speech to the common people of the *One Hundred and Twenty Days of Sodom*: 'You are already dead to the world.'

Sade, likewise, occupied the tower of Freedom, but in the Bastille. Absolute rebellion took refuge with him in a sordid fortress from which none, neither persecuted nor persecutors, could ever escape. To establish his liberty, he had to create absolute necessity. Unlimited liberty of desire implies the negation of others and the suppression of pity. The heart, that 'weak spot of the intellect', must be exterminated: the locked room and the system will take its place. The system, which plays a role of capital importance in Sade's fabulous castles, sanctifies a universe of mistrust. It helps to anticipate everything so that no unexpected tenderness or pity occurs to upset the plans for complete enjoyment. It is a curious kind of pleasure, no doubt, which obeys the commandment 'We shall rise every morning at ten o'clock . . .!' But enjoyment must be prevented from degenerating into attachment, it must be put in parentheses and tempered. Objects of enjoyment must also never be allowed to appear as persons. If a man is an 'absolutely material species of plant', he can only be treated as an object and as an object for experiment. In Sade's fortress republic, there are only machines and mechanics. The system, which dictates the method of employing the machines, puts everything in its right place. His infamous convents have their rule – significantly copied from that of religious communities. Thus the libertine indulges in public confession. But the process is changed: 'If his conduct is pure, he is censured.'

Sade, as was the custom of his period, constructed ideal societies. But, contrary to the custom of his period, he codifies the natural wickedness of mankind. He meticulously constructs a citadel of force and hatred – pioneer that he is – even to the point of calculating mathematically the freedom he succeeded in destroying. He sums up his philosophy with an unemotional accounting of crimes: 'Massacred before the first of March: 10. After the first of March: 20. To come: 16. Total: 46.' A pioneer, no doubt, but a limited one, as we can see.

If that were all, Sade would not be worthy of the interest that attaches to all misunderstood pioneers. But once the drawbridge is up, life in the castle must go on. No matter how meticulous the system, it cannot foresee every eventuality. It can destroy, but it cannot create. The masters of these tortured communities do not find the satisfaction that they covet. Sade often evokes the 'charming habit of crime'. Nothing here, however, seems very charming – more like the fury of a man in chains. The point is to enjoy oneself, and the maximum of enjoyment coincides with the maximum of destruction. To possess what one is going to kill, to copulate with suffering – those are the moments of freedom towards which the entire organization of Sade's castles is oriented. But from the moment when sexual crime destroys the object of desire, it also destroys desire which exists only at the precise moment of destruction. Then another object must be brought under subjection and killed, and then another, and so on to an infinity of all possible objects. Thus occurs the depressing and dense accumulation of erotic and criminal scenes in Sade's novels, which leaves the reader with a paradoxical memory of a hideous chastity.

What part, in this universe, could pleasure play or the exquisite joy of acquiescent and accomplice bodies ? In it we find an impossible quest for escape from despair – a quest which finishes, nevertheless, in a desperate race from servitude to servitude and from prison to prison. If only nature is real and if, in nature, only desire and destruction are legitimate, then, in that all humanity does not suffice to assuage the thirst for blood, the path of destruction must lead to universal annihilation. We must become, according to Sade's formula, nature's executioner. But even that position is not achieved too easily. When the accounts are closed, when all the victims are massacred, the executioners are left face to face in the deserted castle. Something is still missing. The tortured bodies return, in their elements, to nature and will be born again. Even murder cannot be fully consummated: 'Murder only deprives the victim of his first life: a means must be found of depriving him of his second. . . .' Sade contemplates an attempt against nature: 'I abhor nature . . . I would like to upset its plans, to thwart its progress, to halt the stars in their courses, to overturn the floating spheres of space, to destroy what serves nature and to succour all that harms it; in a word, to insult it in all its works, and I cannot succeed in doing so.' It is in vain that he dreams of a technician who can pulverize the universe: he knows that, in the dust of the spheres, life will continue. The attempt against creation is doomed to failure. It is impossible to destroy everything, there is always a remainder. 'I cannot succeed in doing so. . . .' the icy and implacable universe suddenly relents at the appalling melancholy by which Sade, in the end and quite un-willingly, always moves us. 'When crimes of passion no longer measure up to our intensity, we could, perhaps, attack the sun, deprive the universe of it, or use it to set fire to the world – those would be real crimes. ....' Crimes, yes, but not the definitive crime. It is necessary to go farther; the executioners eye each other with suspicion.

They are alone, and one law alone governs them – the law of power. Since they accepted it when they were masters they cannot reject it if it turns against them. All power tends to be unique and solitary. One must kill again and again: the masters will destroy each other in their turn. Sade accepts this consequence and does not flinch. A curious kind of stoicism derived from vice sheds a little light in the dark places of his rebellious soul. He will not try to live again in the world of affection and compromise. The drawbridge will not be lowered and he will accept personal annihilation. The unbridled force of his rejection, at its extremity, achieves an unconditional consent which is not without nobility. The master consents to be the slave in his turn and even, perhaps, wishes to be. 'The scaffold would be for me the throne of voluptuousness.'

Thus the greatest degree of destruction coincides with the greatest degree of affirmation. The masters throw themselves on one another and Sade's work, dedicated to the glory of libertinism, ends by being 'strewn with corpses of libertines struck down at the height of their powers'. The most powerful, the one who will survive, is the solitary, the unique, whose glorification Sade has undertaken – in other words himself. At last he reigns supreme, master and God. But at the moment of his greatest victory, the dream vanishes. The Unique turns back towards the prisoner whose unbounded imagination gave birth to him and they become one. In fact he is alone, imprisoned in a blood-stained Bastille, entirely constructed around a still unsatisfied, and henceforth undirected, desire for pleasure. He has only triumphed in a dream and these ten volumes crammed with philosophy and atrocities recapitulate an unhappy spiritual experience, an illusory advance from the final no to the absolute yes, an acquiescence in death at last, which transfigures the assassination of everything and everyone into a collective suicide.

Sade was executed in effigy; he, too, only killed in his imagination. Prometheus ends his days as Onan. Sade is still a prisoner when he dies, but this time in a lunatic asylum, acting plays on an improvised stage with other lunatics. A derisory equivalent of the satisfaction that the order of the world failed to give him was provided for him by dreams and by creative activity. The writer, of course, has no need to refuse himself anything. For him, at least, boundaries disappear and desire can be allowed free reign. In this respect, Sade is the perfect man of letters. He created a fable in order to give himself the illusion of existing. He put 'the moral crime which is committed by writing' above everything else. His incontestable merit lies in having immediately demonstrated, with the unhappy perspicacity of accumulated rage, the extreme consequences of a rebel's logic – at least when it forgets its true origins. These consequences are a hermetic totalitarianism, universal crime, an aristocracy of cynicism, and the desire for an apocalypse. They will be found again many years after his death. But having tasted them, he was caught, it seems, on the horns of his own dilemma and he could only escape the dilemma in literature. Strangely enough, it is Sade who sets rebellion on the path of literature down which it will be led still farther by romanticism. He himself is one of those writers of whom he says 'their corruption is so dangerous, so active, that they have no other aim in printing their monstrous works but to extend beyond their own lives the sum total of their crimes; they can commit no more, but their accursed writings will lead others to do so, and this comforting thought which they carry with them to the tomb consoles them for the obligation which death imposes on them of renouncing this life'. Thus his rebellious writings bear witness to his desire for survival. Even if the immortality he longs for is the immortality of Cain, at least he longs for it, and despite himself bears witness to what is most true in metaphysical rebellion.

Moreover, even his followers compel us to do him homage. His heirs are not all writers. Of course he suffered and died to stimulate imagination in the right circles and in literary cafés. But that is not all. Sade's success in our day is explained by the dream that he had in common with contemporary thought: the demand for total freedom and dehumanization coldly planned by the intelligence. The reduction of man to an object of experiment, the rule which specifies the relation between the will to power and man as an object, the sealed laboratory which is the scene of this monstrous experiment, are lessons which the theoreticians of power will learn again when they have to organize the age of slavery.

Two centuries ahead of time and on a reduced scale, Sade extolled totalitarian societies in the name of unbridled freedom – which, in reality, rebellion does not desire. With him really begin the history and the tragedy of our times. He only believed that a society founded on the freedom of crime must coincide with freedom of morals, as though servitude had its limits. Our times have only gone as far as to blend, in a curious manner, his dream of a universal republic and his technique of degradation. At last, what he hated most, legal murder, has availed itself of the discoveries that he wanted to put to the service of impulsive murder. Crime, which he wanted to be the exotic and delicious fruit of unbridled vice, is no more, today, than the dismal habit of a police-controlled morality. Such are the surprises of literature.

THE DANDY'S REBELLION

Even after Sade's time, men of letters still continue to dominate the scene. Romanticism, with its satanic rebellion, serves only for adventures of the imagination. Like Sade, romanticism is separated from earlier forms of rebellion by its preference for evil and for the individual. By putting emphasis on its powers of defiance and refusal, rebellion, at this stage, forgets its positive content. Since God claims all that is good in man, it is necessary to deride what is good and choose what is evil. Hatred of death and of injustice will lead, therefore, if not to the exercise at least to the vindication of evil and murder.

The struggle between Satan and death in *Paradise Lost*, the favourite poem of the romantics, symbolizes this drama; all the more profoundly in that death (and, of course, sin) is the child of Satan. In order to combat evil, the rebel renounces good, because he considers himself innocent, and once again gives birth to evil. The romantic hero first of all brings about the profound and, so to speak, religious blending of good and evil.* This type of hero is 'fatal' because fate confuses good and evil without man being able to defend himself. Fate does not allow evaluations. It replaces them by the statement that 'It is so' – which excuses everything, with the exception of the Creator who alone is responsible for this scandalous state of affairs. The romantic hero is also 'fatal' because, to the extent that he increases in power and genius, the power of evil increases in him. Every manifestation of power, every excess is thus covered by this 'It is so'. That the artist, particularly the poet, should be demoniac, is a very ancient idea which is formulated, provocatively, in the work of the romantics. At this period, there is even a demoniac imperialism whose aim is to annex everything, even the orthodox genius. 'What made Milton write with constraint', Blake observes, 'when he spoke of angels and of God, and with audacity when he spoke of demons and of hell, is that he was a real poet and on the side of the demons, without knowing it.' The poet, the genius, man himself in his most exalted image, therefore cry out simultaneously with Satan: 'So farewell hope, and with hope farewell fear, farewell remorse. ... Evil, be thou my good.' It is the cry of outraged innocence.

The romantic hero, therefore, considers himself compelled to do evil by his nostalgia for impracticable good. Satan rises against his creator because the latter employed force to subjugate him. 'Whom reason hath equal'd,' says Milton's Satan, 'force hath made above his equals.' Divine violence is thus explicitly condemned. The rebel flees from this aggressive and unworthy God, 'Farthest from him is best', and reigns over all the forces hostile to the divine order. The Prince of Darkness has only chosen this path because good is a notion defined and utilized by God for unjust purposes. Even innocence irritates the Rebel in so far as it implies being duped. This 'dark

* A dominant theme in William Blake, for example.

spirit of evil who is enraged by innocence' creates a human injustice parallel to divine injustice. Since violence is at the root of all creation, deliberate violence shall be its answer. An excess of despair adds to the causes of despair and brings rebellion to that state of contemptible debility which follows the long experience of injustice and where the distinction between good and evil finally disappears. Vigny's Satan can

> ... no longer find in good or evil any pleasure
> nor of the sorrow that he causes take the measure.

This gives a definition of nihilism and authorizes murder.

Murder, in fact, is on the way to becoming attractive. It is enough to compare the Lucifer of the renaissance painters with the Satan of the romantics. An adolescent 'young, sad, charming' (Vigny) replaces the horned beast. 'Beautiful, with a beauty unknown on this earth' (Lermontov), solitary and powerful, unhappy and scornful, he is off-hand even in oppression. But his excuse is sorrow. 'Who here', says Milton's Satan, 'will envy whom the highest place ... condemns to greatest share of endless pain.' So many injustices suffered, a sorrow so unrelieved, justify every excess. The rebel can therefore allow himself certain advantages. Murder, of course, is not recommended for its own sake. But it is implicit in the value – supreme for the romantic – attached to frenzy. Frenzy is the reverse of boredom: Lorenzaccio dreams of Han of Iceland. Exquisite sensibilities evoke the elementary furies of the beast. The Byronic hero, incapable of love, or only capable of an impossible love, suffers endlessly. He is solitary, languid, his condition exhausts him. If he wants to feel alive, it must be in the terrible exaltation of a brief and destructive action. To love someone whom you will never see again is to love like a flame and to cry out for self-annihilation into the bargain. One lives only in and for the moment, in order to achieve

> the brief and vivid union
> of a tempestuous heart united to the tempest.
>
> (Lermontov)

The threat of mortality which hangs over us sterilizes everything. Only the cry of anguish can bring us to life; exaltation takes the place of truth. To this extent, the apocalypse becomes an absolute value in which everything is confounded – love and death, conscience and culpability. In a topsy-turvy universe no other life exists but that of the abyss where, according to Alfred Le Poittevin, human beings come 'trembling with rage and exulting in their crimes' to curse the Creator. The intoxication of frenzy and, ultimately, crime reveal, in a moment, the whole meaning of a life. Without exactly advocating crime, the romantics insist on paying homage to a basic system of revenge which they illustrate with the conventional images of the outlaw, the criminal with the heart of gold, and the kind brigand. Their works are bathed in blood and shrouded in mystery. The soul is delivered, at minimum expenditure, of its most hideous desires – desires which will later be assuaged in extermination camps. Of course these works are also a challenge to the society of the times. But romanticism, at the source of its inspiration, is chiefly concerned with defying moral and divine law. That is why its most original creation is not primarily the revolutionary, but logically enough, the dandy.

Logically, because this obstinate persistence in satanism can only be justified by the endless affirmation of injustice and, to a certain extent, by its consolidation. Pain, at this stage, is only acceptable on condition that it is incurable. The rebel chooses the metaphysics of 'expecting the worst', which is expressed in the literature of damnation from which we have not yet escaped. 'I was conscious of my power and I was conscious of my chains' (Petrus Borel). But these chains are valuable objects. Without them it would be necessary to prove, or to exercise, this power which, after all, one is not very sure of having. It is only too easy to end up by becoming a government employee in Algiers, and Prometheus, like the above-mentioned Borel, will devote the rest of his days to closing the cabarets and reforming colonial morals. All the same, every poet to be received into the fold must be damned. Charles Lassailly, the same one who planned a philosophic novel *Robespierre and Jesus Christ*, never went to bed without uttering several fervent blasphemies to give himself courage. Rebellion puts on mourning and exhibits itself for public admiration. Much more than the cult of the individual, romanticism inaugurates the cult of the 'character'. It is at this point that it is logical. Hoping no longer for the rule or unity of God, determined to take up arms against an antagonistic destiny, anxious to preserve everything of which the living are still capable in a world dedicated to death, romantic rebellion looked for a solution in the attitude it assumed. The attitude brought together, in aesthetic unity, all mankind who were in the hands of fate and destroyed by divine violence. The human being who is condemned to death is, at least, magnificent, before he disappears, and his magnificence is his justification. It is an established fact, the only one that can be thrown in the petrified face of the God of Hate. The impassive rebel does not flinch before the eyes of God. 'Nothing', says Milton, 'will change this determined mind, this high disdain born of an offended conscience.' Everything is drawn or rushes towards the void, but even though man is humiliated, he is obstinate and at least preserves his pride. A baroque romantic, discovered by Raymond Queneau, claims that the aim of all intellectual life is to become God. This genuine romantic is a little ahead of his time. The aim, at that time, was only to equal God and remain on His level. He is not destroyed, but by incessant effort He is never submitted to. Dandyism is a degraded form of asceticism.

The dandy creates his own unity by aesthetic means. But it is an aesthetic of singularity and of negation. 'To live and die before a mirror': that, according to Baudelaire, was the dandy's slogan ... It is a coherent slogan, at any rate. The dandy is, by occupation, always in opposition. He can only exist by defiance. Up till now, man derived his coherence from his Creator. But from the moment that he consecrates his rupture with Him, he finds himself delivered over to the fleeting moment, to the passing days, and to wasted sensibility. Therefore he must take himself in hand. The dandy rallies his forces and creates a unity for himself by the very violence of his refusal. Disoriented, like all people without a rule of life, he is coherent as a character. But a character implies a public; the dandy can only play a part by setting himself up in opposition. He can only be sure of his own existence by finding it in the expression of others' faces. Other people are his mirror. A mirror that quickly becomes obscured, it is true, since human capacity for attention is limited. It must be ceaselessly stimulated, spurred on by provocation. The dandy is, therefore, always compelled to astonish. Singularity is his vocation, excess his way to perfection. Perpetually incomplete, always on the margin of things, he compels others to create him, while denying their values. He plays at life because he is unable to live it. He plays at it until he dies, except for the moments when he is alone and without a mirror. For the dandy, to be alone is not to exist. The romantics only talked so grandly about solitude because it was their real horror, the one thing they could not bear. Their rebellion thrusts its roots deep, but from the Abbé Prévost's *Cleveland* up to the time of the Dadaists – including the frenetics of 1830 and Baudelaire and the decadents of 1880 – more than a century of rebellion was completely satiated by the audacities of 'eccentricity'. If they all were able to talk of unhappiness it is because they despaired of ever being able to conquer it, except in futile comedies, and because they instinctively felt that it remained their sole excuse and their real claim to nobility.

That is why the heritage of romanticism was not claimed by Victor Hugo, peer of the realm, but by Baudelaire and Lacenaire, poets of crime. 'Everything in this world exudes crime,' says Baudelaire, 'the newspaper, the walls, and the face of man.' Nevertheless crime, which is the law of nature, singularly fails to wear a distinguished air. Lacenaire, the first of the gentleman criminals, exploits it effectively; Baudelaire displays less tenacity but is a genius. He creates the garden of evil where crime only figures as one of the rarer species. Terror itself becomes an exquisite sensation and a collector's item 'Not only would I be happy to be a victim, but I would not even hate being an executioner in order to *feel* the revolution from both sides.' Even Baudelaire's conformity has the odour of crime. If he chose Maistre as his master, it is to the extent that this conservative goes as far as he can and centres his doctrine on death and on the executioner.

48

'The real saint', Baudelaire pretends to think, 'is someone who flogs and kills people for their own good.' His argument will be heard. A race of real saints is beginning to spread over the earth for the purpose of confirming these curious conclusions about rebellion. But Baudelaire, despite his satanic arsenal, his taste for Sade, his blasphemies, remains too much of a theologian to be a real rebel. His real drama, which made him the greatest poet of his time, was something else. Baudelaire can only be cited here to the extent that he was the most profound theoretician of dandyism and gave definite form to one of the conclusions of romantic rebellion.

Romanticism demonstrates, in fact, that rebellion is part and parcel of dandyism: one of its objectives is outward appearances. In its conventional forms, dandyism admits a nostalgia for ethics. It is only honour degraded as a point of honour. But at the same time it inaugurates an aesthetic which is still valid in our world, an aesthetic of solitary creators, who are obstinate rivals of a God they condemn. From romanticism onward, the artist's task will not only be to create a world, or to exalt beauty for its own sake, but also to define an attitude. Thus the artist becomes a model and offers himself as an example: art is his ethic. With him begins the age of the directors of conscience. When the dandies fail to commit suicide or do not go mad, they make a career and pursue prosperity. Even when, like Vigny, they exclaim that they are going to keep quiet, their silence is piercing.

But at the very heart of romanticism, the sterility of this attitude becomes apparent to a few rebels who provide a transitional type between the eccentrics and our revolutionary adventurers. Between the days of the eighteenth-century eccentric and the 'adventurers' of the twentieth century, Byron and Shelley are already fighting, however ostentatiously, for freedom.

The Rejection of Salvation

IF the romantic rebel exalts evil and the individual, he does not do so on behalf of mankind, but merely on his own behalf. Dandyism, of whatever kind, is always dandyism in relation to God. The individual, in so far as he is created being, can oppose himself only to the Creator. He has need of God with whom he carried on a kind of baleful intrigue. Armand Hoog rightly says that, despite the Nietzschean atmosphere of such works, God is not yet dead in them. The damnation, so clamorously demanded, is only a clever trick played on God. But with Dostoyevsky the account of rebellion goes a step farther. Ivan Karamazov sides with mankind and stresses human innocence. He affirms that the death sentence which hangs over them is unjust. Far from making a plea for evil, his first impulse, at least, is to plead for justice which he ranks above divinity. He does not absolutely deny the existence of God. He refutes Him in the name of a moral value. The romantic rebel's ambition was to talk to God as man to man. Here evil was the answer to evil, pride the answer to cruelty. Vigny's ideal, for example, is to answer silence with silence. Obviously, the point is to raise oneself to the level of God, and that is already blasphemy. But there is no thought of disputing the power or position of the deity. The blasphemy is reverent, since every blasphemy is, ultimately, a participation in holiness.

With Ivan, however, the tone changes. God is put on trial, in His turn. If evil is essential to divine creation, then creation is unacceptable. Ivan will no longer have recourse to this mysterious God, but to a higher principle, namely justice. He launches the essential undertaking of rebellion, which is that of replacing the reign of grace by the reign of justice. Simultaneously, he begins the attack on Christianity. The romantic rebels broke with God for being the fountainhead of hate. Ivan explicitly rejects mystery and, consequently, God as the fountainhead of love. Only love can make us consent to the injustice done to Martha, to the exploitation of workers, and, to go a step farther, to the death of innocent children.

'If the suffering of children', says Ivan, 'serves to complete the sum of suffering necessary for the acquisition of truth, I affirm from now onwards that truth is not worth such a price.' Ivan rejects the profound relationship, introduced by Christianity, between suffering and truth. Ivan's most profound utterance, the one which opens the deepest chasms beneath the rebel's feet, is his *even if*: 'I would persist in my indignation, even if I were wrong.' Which means that even if God existed, even if the mystery cloaked a truth, even if Zosime were right, Ivan would not admit that truth should be paid for by evil, suffering, and the death of innocents. Ivan incarnates the refusal of salvation. Faith leads to immortal life, but faith presumes the acceptance of the mystery and of evil and resignation to injustice. The man who is prevented by the suffering of children from accepting faith will certainly not accept eternal life. Under these conditions, even if eternal life existed, Ivan would refuse it. He rejects this bargain. He would only accept grace unconditionally and that is why he makes his own conditions. Rebellion wants all or nothing. 'All the knowledge in the world is not worth a child's tears.' Ivan does not say that there is no truth. He says that if truth does exist it can only be unacceptable. Why? Because it is unjust. The struggle between truth and justice is brought into the open for the first time – and it will never end. Ivan, by nature a solitary and therefore a moralist, will satisfy himself with a kind of metaphysical Don Quixotism. But a few decades more and a huge political conspiracy will attempt to prove that justice is truth.

In addition, Ivan is the incarnation of the refusal to be the only one saved. He throws in his lot with the damned, and for their sake rejects eternity. If he had faith, he could, in fact, be saved, but others would be damned and suffering would continue. There is no possible salvation for the man who feels real compassion. Ivan will continue to put God in the wrong by doubly rejecting faith as he would reject injustice and privilege. One step more and from *All or Nothing* we arrive at *All or No one.*

This extreme determination, and the attitude that it implies, would have sufficed for the romantics. But Ivan* even though he also gives way to dandyism, really lives his problems, torn between the negative and the affirmative. From this moment onwards, he accepts the consequences. If he rejects immortality, what remains for him? Life in its most elementary form. When the meaning of life has been suppressed, there still remains life. 'I live,' says Ivan, 'in spite of logic.' And again: 'If I no longer had any faith in life, if I doubted a woman I loved, or the universal order of things, if I were persuaded, on the contrary, that everything was only an infernal and accursed chaos – even then, I would want to live.' Ivan will live, then, and will love as well 'without knowing why'. But to live is also to act. To act in the name of what? If there is no immortality, then there is neither reward nor punishment. 'I believe that there is no virtue without immortality.' And also: 'I only know that suffering exists, that no one is guilty, that everything is connected, that everything passes and equals out.' But if there is no virtue, there is no law: 'All is permitted.'

With this 'all is permitted' the history of contemporary nihilism really begins. Romantic rebellion did not go so far. It was content with saying, in short, that everything was not permitted but that, through insolence, it allowed itself to do what was forbidden. On the other hand, with the Karamazovs the logic of indignation turned rebellion against itself and confronted it with a desperate contradiction. The essential difference is that the romantics allowed themselves to be complacent, while Ivan compelled himself to do evil so as to be coherent. He would not allow himself to be good. Nihilism is not only despair and negation, but above all the desire to despair and to negate. The very man who so violently took the part of innocence, who trembled at the suffering of a child, who wanted to see 'with his own eyes' the lamb lie down with the lion, the victim embrace his murderer, from the moment that he rejects divine coherence and tries to discover his own rule of life, recognizes the legitimacy of

* It is worth noting that Ivan is, in a certain way, Dostoyevsky, who is more at his ease in this role than in the role of Alyosha.

murder. Ivan rebels against a murderous God; but from the moment that he begins to consider the reasons for his rebellion, he deduces the law of murder. If all is permitted, he can kill his father or at least allow him to be killed. Long reflection on our condition as people sentenced to death only leads to the justification of crime. Ivan simultaneously hates the death penalty (describing an execution, he says ferociously: 'His head fell, in the name of divine grace') and condones crime, in principle. Every indulgence is allowed the murderer, none is allowed the executioner. This contradiction, which Sade swallowed with ease, chokes Ivan Karamazov.

He pretends to reason as though immortality did not, in fact exist, while he only goes so far as to say that he would refuse it if it did exist. In order to protest against evil and death, he deliberately chooses to say that virtue exists no more than does immortality and to allow his father to be killed. He consciously accepts his dilemma; to be virtuous and illogical, or logical and criminal. His double, the devil, is right when he whispers: 'You are going to commit a virtuous act and yet you do not believe in virtue, that is what angers and torments you.' The question which Ivan finally poses, the question which constitutes the real progress achieved by Dostoyevsky in the history of rebellion, is the only one we are interested in here: can one live and hold one's ground in a permanent state of rebellion?

Ivan allows us to guess his answer: one can only live in a permanent state of rebellion by pursuing it to the bitter end. What is the bitter end of metaphysical rebellion? Metaphysical revolution. The master of the world, after his legitimacy has been contested, must be over-thrown. Man must occupy his place. 'As God and immortality do not exist, the new man is permitted to become god.' But what does becoming god mean? To recognize any other law but one's own. Without it being necessary to develop the intervening arguments, we can see that to become God is to accept crime (a favourite idea of Dostoyevsky's intellectuals). Ivan's personal problem is then to know if he can be faithful to his logic and if, on the grounds of an indignant protest at innocent suffering, he can accept the murder of his father with the indifference of a man-god. We know his solution: Ivan allows his father to be killed. Too profound to be satisfied with appearances, too sensitive to perform the deed himself, he is content to allow it to be done. But he goes mad. The man who could not understand how one could love one's neighbour, cannot understand, either, how one can kill him. Caught between unjustifiable conceptions of virtue and unacceptable crime, consumed with pity and incapable of love, a solitary deprived of the benefits of cynicism, this man of supreme intelligence is killed by contradiction. 'My mind is of this world,' he said, 'what good is it to try to understand what is not?' But he only lived for what is not of this world, and his proud search for the absolute is precisely what removed him from the world of which he loved no part.

The fact that Ivan was defeated does not obviate the fact that once the problem is posed, the consequence must follow: rebellion has started on the path of action. This has already been demonstrated by Dostoyevsky, with prophetic intensity, in his legend of the Grand Inquisitor. Ivan, finally, does not separate the creator from his creation. 'It is not God whom I reject,' he says, 'it is creation.' In other words it is God the father, inseparable from what He has created. His plot to usurp the throne, therefore, remains completely moral. He does not want to reform anything in creation. But creation being what it is, he claims the right to free himself of it morally and to free all the rest of mankind with him. On the other hand, from the moment that the spirit of rebellion, having accepted the concept of 'all is permitted' and 'everyone or no one', aims at reconstructing creation in order to assert the sovereignty and divinity of man – from the moment that metaphysical rebellion extends itself from ethics to politics – a new undertaking, of incalculable import, begins, which is also born, we must note, of the same nihilism. Dostoyevsky, the prophet of the new religion, had foreseen and announced it: 'If Alyosha had come to the conclusion that neither God nor immortality existed, he would have immediately become an atheist and a socialist. For socialism is not only a question of the working classes, it is, above all, in its contemporary incarnation, a question of atheism, a question of the tower of Babel which is constructed without God's help, not to reach the heavens, but to bring the heavens down to earth.'

After that Alyosha can in fact treat Ivan with compassion as a 'real greenhorn'. The latter only made an attempt at self-domination and failed. Others will appear who are more serious-minded and who, on the basis of the same despairing nihilism, are going to demand to rule the world. These are the Grand Inquisitors who imprison Christ and come to tell Him that His is not the right method, that universal happiness cannot be achieved by the immediate freedom of choosing between good and evil, but by the domination and unification of the world. The first step is to conquer and rule. The kingdom of heaven will, in fact, appear on earth, but it will be ruled over by men – a mere handful to begin with who will be the Caesars, the ones who were the first to understand – and later, with time, by all men. The unity of all creation will be achieved by every possible means, since everything is permitted. The Grand Inquisitor is old and tired, for the knowledge he possesses is bitter. He knows that men are lazy rather than cowardly and that they prefer peace and death to the liberty of discerning between good and evil. He has pity, a cold pity, for the silent prisoner whom history endlessly deceives. He urges him to speak, to recognize his misdeeds, and, in one sense, to approve the undertaking of the Inquisitors and of the Caesars. But the prisoner does not speak. The enterprise will continue, therefore, without him: he will be killed. Legitimacy will come at the end of time when the kingdom of men is assured. 'The affair has only just begun, it is far from being terminated, and the world has many other things to suffer, but we shall achieve our aim, we shall be Caesar, and meanwhile we shall dream of universal happiness.'

Long before that, the prisoner will have been executed: the Grand Inquisitors reign alone, listening to 'the profound spirit, the spirit of destruction and death'. The Grand Inquisitors proudly refuse freedom and the bread of heaven and offer the bread of this earth without freedom. 'Come down from the cross and we shall believe in you', their police agents already cry on Golgotha. But He does not come down and, even, at the most tortured moment of His agony, he protests to God at having been abandoned. There are thus no other proofs but faith and the mystery that the rebels reject and the Grand Inquisitors scoff at. Everything is permitted and centuries of crime are prepared in that cataclysmic moment. From Paul to Stalin, the popes who have chosen Caesar have prepared the way for Caesars who quickly learn to despise popes. The unity of the world which was not achieved with God will, nevertheless, be attempted without Him.

But we have not yet reached that point. For the moment, Ivan only offers us the tortured face of the rebel plunged in the abyss, incapable of action, torn between the idea of his own innocence and his desire to kill. He hates the death penalty because it is the image of the human condition, and, at the same time, he is drawn to crime. For having taken the side of mankind, solitude is his lot. With him the rebellion of reason ends in madness.

Absolute Affirmation

WHEN man submits God to moral judgement, he kills Him in his own heart. And then what is the basis of morality? God is denied in the name of justice but can the idea of justice be understood without the idea of God? Have we not arrived at absurdity? It is absurdity that Nietzsche meets face to face. The better to avoid it, he pushes it to extremities: morality is the final aspect of God which must be destroyed before the period of reconstruction begins. Then God no longer exists and no longer guarantees our existence; man, in order to exist, must decide to act.

'We deny God, we deny the responsibility of God, it is only thus that we will deliver the world.' With Nietzsche, nihilism seems to become prophetic. But we can draw no conclusions from Nietzsche, except the base and mediocre cruelty that he hated with all his strength, unless we give first place in his work – well ahead of the prophet – to the diagnostician. The provisional, methodical, strategic character of his thought cannot be doubted for a moment. With him, nihilism becomes conscious for the first time. Diagnosticians have this in common with prophets – they think and operate in terms of the future. Nietzsche never thought except in terms of an apocalypse to come, not in order to extol it, for he guessed the sordid and calculating aspect that this apocalypse would finally assume, but in order to avoid it and to transform it into a renaissance. He recognized nihilism for what it was and examined it like a clinical fact.

He said of himself that he was the first complete nihilist of Europe. Not by choice, but by condition, and because he was too great to refuse the heritage of his time. He diagnosed in himself, and in others, the inability to believe and the disappearance of the primitive foundation of all faith – namely the belief in life. The 'Can one live as a rebel?' became with him 'Can one live, believing in nothing?' His reply is in the affirmative. Yes, if one creates a

57

system out of absence of faith, if one accepts the final consequences of nihilism, and if, on emerging into the desert and putting one's confidence in what is going to come, one feels, with the same primitive instinct, both pain and joy.

Instead of systematic doubt, he practised systematic negation, the determined destruction of everything that still hides nihilism from itself, of the idols which camouflage God's death. 'To raise a new sanctuary, a sanctuary must be destroyed, that is the law.' According to Nietzsche, he who wants to be a creator of good and of evil, must first of all destroy all values. 'Thus the supreme evil becomes part of the supreme good, but the supreme good is creative.' He wrote, in his own manner, the *Discours de la Méthode* of his period, without the freedom and exactitude of the seventeenth-century French he admired so much, but with the mad lucidity which characterizes the twentieth century which, according to him, is the century of rebellion.

Nietzsche's first step is to accept what he knows. Atheism for him goes without saying and is 'constructive and radical'. Nietzsche's superior vocation, so he says, is to provoke a kind of crisis and a final decision about the problem of atheism. The world continues on its course at random and there is nothing final about it. Thus God is useless, since He wants nothing in particular. If He wanted something, and here we recognize the traditional formulation of the problem of evil, we would have to assume Him responsible for 'a sum-total of pain and inconsistency which would debase the entire value of being born'. We know that Nietzsche was publicly envious of Stendhal's formula: 'the only excuse for God is that he does not exist'. Deprived of the divine will, the world is equally deprived of unity and finality. That is why it is impossible to pass judgement on the world. Any attempt to apply a standard of values to the world leads finally to a slander on life. Judgements are based on what is, with reference to what should be – the kingdom of heaven, eternal concepts, or moral imperatives. But what should be does not exist: and this world cannot be judged in the name of nothing. 'The advantages of our times; nothing is true, everything is permitted.'

These magnificent or ironic formulae, which are echoed by thousands of others, at any rate suffice to demonstrate that Nietzsche accepts the entire burden of nihilism and rebellion. In his somewhat puerile reflections on 'training and selection' he even formulated the extreme logic of nihilistic reasoning: 'Problem: by what means could we obtain an exact definition of nihilism in its most extreme and infectious aspect which would teach and practise, with a completely scientific awareness, voluntary death?'

But Nietzsche enlists values in the cause of nihilism which, traditionally, have been considered as restraints on nihilism – principally morality. Moral conduct, as explained by Socrates, or as recommended by Christianity, is in itself a sign of decadence. It wants to substitute the mere shadow of a man for a man of flesh and blood. It condemns the universe of passion and emotion in the name of an entirely imaginary world of harmony. If nihilism is the inability to believe, then its most serious symptom is not found in atheism, but in the inability to believe in what is, to see what is happening, and to live life as it is offered. This infirmity is at the root of all idealism. Morality has no faith in the world. For Nietzsche, real morality cannot be separated from lucidity. He is severe on the 'calumniators of the world' because he discerns in the calumny a shameful taste for evasion. Traditional morality, for him, is only a special type of immorality. 'It is virtue', he says, 'which has need of justification.' And again: 'It is for moral reasons that good will, one day, cease to be done.'

Nietzsche's philosophy, undoubtedly, revolves around the problem of rebellion. More precisely, it begins by being a rebellion. But we sense the change of position that Nietzsche makes. With him, rebellion begins at 'God is dead' which is assumed as an established fact; then rebellion hinges on everything that aims at falsely replacing the vanished deity and reflects dishonour on a world which undoubtedly has no direction but which remains the only proving-ground of the gods. Contrary to the opinion of certain of his Christian critics, Nietzsche did not form a project to kill God. He found Him dead in the soul of his contemporaries. He was the first to understand the immense importance of the event and to decide that this rebellion among men could not lead to a renaissance unless it were controlled and directed. Any other attitude towards it, whether it were regret or complacency, must lead to the apocalypse. Thus Nietzsche did not formulate a philosophy of rebellion, but constructed a philosophy on rebellion.

If he attacks Christianity in particular, it is only in so far as it represents morality. He always leaves intact the person of Jesus on the one hand, and on the other the cynical aspects of the Church. We know that he admired, from the point of view of the connoisseur, the Jesuits. 'Basically,' he writes, 'only the God of morality is rejected.' Christ, for Nietzsche as for Tolstoy, is not a rebel. The essence of His doctrine is summed up in total consent and in non-resistance to evil. Thou shalt not kill, even to prevent killing. The world must be accepted as it is, nothing must be added to its unhappiness, but you must consent to suffer personally from the evil it contains. The kingdom of heaven is within our immediate reach. Not faith but deeds – that, according to Nietzsche, is Christ's message. From then on, the history of Christianity is nothing but a long betrayal of this message. The New Testament is already corrupt, and from the time of Paul until the Councils subservience to faith has led to the obliteration of deeds.

What is the profoundly corrupt addition made by Christianity to the message of its Master? The idea of judgement, completely foreign to the teachings of Christ, and the correlative notions of punishment and reward. From this moment, human nature becomes the subject of history, and significant history expressed by the idea of human totality is born. From the Annunciation until the Last Judgement, humanity has no other task but to conform to the strictly moral ends of a narrative that has already been written. The only difference is that the characters, in the epilogue, separate themselves into the good and the bad. While Christ's sole judgement consists in saying that the sins of nature are unimportant, historical Christianity makes nature the sole source of sin. 'What does Christ deny? Everything that, at the moment, bears the name Christian.' Christianity believes that it is fighting against nihilism because it gives the world a sense of direction, while it is nihilist itself in so far as it prevents, in imposing an imaginary meaning on life, the discovery of its real meaning: 'Every Church is a stone rolled on to the tomb of the man-god; it tried to prevent the resurrection, by force.' Nietzsche's paradoxical but significant conclusion is that God had been killed by Christianity, in that Christianity has secularized the sacred. Here we must understand historical Christianity and 'its profound and contemptible duplicity'.

The same process of reasoning leads to Nietzsche's attitude towards socialism and all forms of humanitarianism. Socialism is only a degenerate form of Christianity. In reality, he preserves a belief in the finality of history which betrays life and nature, which substitutes ideal ends for real ends, and contributes to enervating both the will and the imagination. Socialism is nihilistic, in the henceforth precise sense which Nietzsche confers on the word. A nihilist is not someone who believes in nothing, but someone who does not believe in what he sees. In this sense, all forms of socialism are manifestations, degraded once again, of Christian decadence. For Christianity, reward and punishment imply the truth of history. But, by inescapable logic, all history ends by implying punishment and reward; and from this day on collective Messianism is born. Similarly, the equality of souls before God leads, now that God is dead, to equality pure and simple. There again, Nietzsche wages war against socialist doctrines in so far as they are moral doctrines. Nihilism, whether manifested in religion or in socialist preachings, is the logical conclusion of our so-called superior values. The free mind will destroy these values and denounce the illusions on which they are built, the bargaining that they imply, and the crime they commit in preventing the lucid intelligence from accomplishing its mission: of transforming passive nihilism into active nihilism.

In this world rid of God and of moral idols, man is now alone and without a master. No one has been less inclined than Nietzsche (and in this way he distinguishes himself from the romantics) to allow himself to believe that such freedom would be easy. This unbridled freedom put him among the ranks of those of whom he himself said that they suffered a new form of anguish and a new form of happiness. But, at the beginning, it is only anguish which makes him cry out: 'Alas, grant me madness. . . . By being above the law, I am the most outcast of all outcasts.' He who cannot stand his ground above the law, must find another law or take refuge in madness. From the moment that man believes neither in God nor in immortal life, he becomes 'responsible for everything alive, for everything that, born of suffering, is condemned to suffer from life'. It is to himself, and to himself alone, that he returns in order to find law and order. Then the time of exile begins, the endless search for justification, the nostalgia without an aim, 'the most painful, the most heart-breaking question, that of the heart which asks itself: where can I feel at home?'

Because his mind was free, Nietzsche knew that freedom of the mind is not a comfort, but an achievement that one aspires to and obtains, at long last, after an exhausting struggle. He knew that there is a great risk in wanting to consider oneself above the law, of finding oneself beneath that law. That is why he understood that the mind only found its real emancipation in the acceptance of new obligations. If nothing is true, if the world is without order, then nothing is forbidden; to prohibit an action, there must, in fact, be a standard of values and an aim. But, at the same time, nothing is authorized; there must also be values and aims in order to choose another course of action. Absolute domination by the law does not represent liberty, but nor does absolute freedom of choice. Chaos is also a form of servitude. Freedom only exists in a world where what is possible is defined at the same time as what is not possible. Without law there is no freedom. If fate is not guided by superior values, if chance is king then there is nothing but the step in the dark and the appalling freedom of the blind. At the conclusion of the most complete liberation, Nietzsche therefore chooses the most complete subordination. 'If we do not make of God's death a great renunciation and a perpetual victory over ourselves, we shall have to pay for that omission.' In other words, with Nietzsche, rebellion ends in asceticism. A profounder logic replaces the 'if nothing is true, everything is permitted' of Karamazov by 'if nothing is true, nothing is permitted'. To deny that one single thing is forbidden in this world amounts to renouncing everything that is permitted. At the point where it is no longer possible to say what is black and what is white, the light is extinguished and freedom becomes a voluntary prison.

It can be said that Nietzsche rushes, with a kind of frightful joy, towards the impasse into which he methodically drives his nihilism. His avowed aim is to render the situation untenable to his contemporaries. His only hope seems to be to arrive at the extremity of contradiction. Then if man does not wish to perish in the coils that strangle him, he will have to cut them at a single blow, and create his own values. The death of God accomplishes nothing and can only be lived through in terms of preparing a resurrection. 'If we fail to find grandeur in God,' says Nietzsche, 'we find it nowhere; it must be denied or created.' To deny was the task of the world around him which he saw rushing towards suicide. To create was the superhuman task for which he was willing to die. He knew in fact that creation is only possible in the extremity of solitude and that man would only commit himself to this staggering task if, in the most extreme distress of mind, he must undertake it or perish. Nietzsche cries out to man that his only truth is the world – to which he must be faithful and on which he must live and find his salvation. But, at the same time, he teaches him that to live in a lawless world is impossible because to live implies, explicitly, the law. How can one live freely and without law? To this enigma, man must find an answer, on pain of death.

Nietzsche, at least, does not flinch. He answers and his answer is bold: Damocles never danced better than beneath the sword. One must accept the unacceptable and contend the untenable. From the moment that it is admitted that the world pursues no end, Nietzsche proposes to concede its innocence, to affirm that it accepts no judgement since it cannot be judged on any intention, and consequently to replace all judgements based on values by absolute assent, a complete and exalted allegiance to this world. Thus, from absolute despair will spring infinite joy, from blind servitude freedom without obligation. To be free is, precisely, to abolish ends. The innocence of the ceaseless change of things, as soon as one consents to it, represents the maximum liberty. The free mind willingly accepts what is necessary. Nietzsche's most intimate concept is that the necessity of phenomena, if it is absolute, does not imply any kind of restraint. Total acceptance of total necessity is his paradoxical definition of freedom. The question 'Free of what?' is thus replaced by 'Free for what?' Liberty coincides with heroism. It is the asceticism of the great man: 'the bow bent to the breaking-point'.

This magnificent consent, born of affluence and fullness of spirit, is the unreserved affirmation of human imperfection and suffering, of evil and murder, of all that is problematic and strange in our existence. It is born of an arrested wish to be what one is in a world which is what it is. 'To consider oneself a fatality, not to wish to be other than one is . . .' The Nietzschean experiment, which is part of the recognition of fatality, ends in a deification of fate. The more implacable destiny is, the more it becomes worthy of adoration. A moral God, pity, and love are enemies of fate to the extent that they try to make amends for it. Nietzsche wants no redemption. The joy of self-realization is the joy of annihilation. But only the individual is annihilated. The movement of rebellion, in which man claimed his own self, disappears in the individual's absolute submission to self-realization. *Amor fati* replaces what was an *odium fati*. 'Every individual collaborates with the entire cosmos, whether we know it or not, whether we want it or not.' The individual is lost in the destiny of the species and the eternal movement of the spheres. 'Everyone who has existed is eternal, the sea throws him back upon the shore.'

Nietzsche then returns to the origins of thought – to the pre-Socratics. The latter suppressed ultimate causes so as to leave intact the eternal values of the principles they upheld. Only power without purpose, only Heraclitus's 'strife', is eternal. Nietzsche's whole effort is directed towards demonstrating the existence of laws which govern future events and that there is an element of chance in the inevitable: 'A child is innocence and forgetfulness, a new beginning, a gamble, a wheel which spins automatically, a first step, the divine gift of consent.' The world is divine because the world is illogical. That is why art alone, by being equally illogical, is capable of grasping it. It is impossible to give a clear account of the world, but art can teach us to reproduce it – just as the world reproduces itself in the course of its eternal gyrations. The primordial sea indefatigably repeats the same words and casts up the same astonished beings on the same sea-shore. But at least he who consents to his own return and to the return of all things, who becomes an echo and an exalted echo, participates in the divinity of the world.

By this subterfuge, the divinity of man is finally introduced. The rebel, who at first denies God, finally aspires to replace him. But Nietzsche's message is that the rebel can only become God by entirely renouncing rebellion, even the type of rebellion that produces gods to chastise humanity. 'If there is a God, how can one tolerate not being God oneself?' There is, in fact, a god ... namely the world. To participate in his divinity, all that is necessary is to consent. 'No longer to pray, but to give one's blessing', and the earth will abound in men-gods. To say yes to the world, to reproduce it, is simultaneously to recreate the world and oneself, to become the great artist, the creator. Nietzsche's message is summed up in the word 'creation', with the ambiguous meaning it has assumed. Nietzsche's sole admiration was for the egotism and austerity proper to all creators. The transmutation of values consists only in replacing critical values by creative values; by respect and admiration for what exists. Divinity without immortality defines the extent of the creator's freedom. Dionysos, the earth-god, shrieks eternally as he is torn limb from limb. But at the same time he represents the agonized beauty which is the result of suffering. Nietzsche thought that to accept this earth and Dionysos was to accept his own sufferings. And to accept everything, both suffering and the supreme contradiction simultaneously, was to be king. Nietzsche agreed to pay the price for his kingdom. Only the 'sad and suffering' world is true – the world is the only divinity. Like Empedocles who threw himself down Etna to find truth in the only place where it exists, namely in the bowels of the earth, Nietzsche proposed that man should allow himself to be engulfed in the cosmos in order to rediscover his eternal divinity and to become Dionysos himself. The *Will to Power* ends, like Pascal's *Pensées* of which it so often reminds us, with a wager. Man does not yet obtain assurance but only the wish for assurance which is not at all the same thing. Nietzsche, too, hesitated on this brink: 'That is what is unforgivable in you. You have the authority and you refuse to sign.' Yet, finally, he had to sign. But the name of Dionysos only immortalized the notes to Ariadne which he wrote when he was mad.

In a certain sense, rebellion, with Nietzsche, ends again in the exaltation of evil. The difference is that evil is no longer a revenge. It is accepted as one of the possible aspects of good and, with rather more conviction, as part of destiny. Thus he considers it as something to be avoided and also as a sort of remedy. In Nietzsche's mind, the only problem was to see that the human spirit bowed proudly to the inevitable. We know, however, his posterity and the kind of politics that were to be authorized by the man who claimed to be the last anti-political German. He dreamed of tyrants who were artists, but tyranny comes more naturally than art to mediocre men. 'Rather Cesare Borgia than Parsifal,' he exclaimed. He begat both Caesar and Borgia, but devoid of the distinction of feeling which he attributed to the great men of the Renaissance. As a result of his insistence that the individual should bow before the eternity of the species and should submerge himself in the great cycle of time, race had been turned into a special aspect of the species and the individual has been made to bow before this sordid god. The life of which he spoke with such fear and trembling has been degraded to a sort of biology for domestic use. Finally a race of vulgar overlords, with a blundering desire for power, adopted, in his name, the 'anti-semitic deformity' on which he never ceased to pour scorn.

He believed in courage combined with intelligence, and that was what he called strength. Courage has been turned against intelligence in his name; and the virtues that were really his have thus been transformed into their opposite . . . blind violence. He confused freedom and solitude, as do all proud spirits. His 'profound solitude at midday and at midnight' was nevertheless lost in the mechanized hordes which finally inundated Europe. Advocate of classic taste, of irony, of frugal defiance, aristocrat who had the courage to say that aristocracy consisted in practising virtue without asking for a reason and that a man who had to have reasons for being honest was not to be trusted, addict of integrity ('integrity that had become an instinct, a passion'), stubborn supporter of the 'supreme equity of the supreme intelligence which is the mortal enemy of fanaticism', he was set up, thirty-three years after his death, by his own countrymen as the master of lies and violence and his ideas and attributes, made admirable by his sacrifice, have been rendered detestable. In the history of intelligence, with the exception of Marx, Nietzsche's adventure had no equivalent: we shall never finish making reparation for the injustice done to him. Of course history records other philosophies that have been misconstrued and betrayed. But up to the time of Nietzsche and national socialism, it was quite without parallel that a process of thought – brilliantly illuminated by the nobility and by the sufferings of an exceptional mind – should have been demonstrated to the eyes of the world by a parade of lies and by the hideous accumulation of corpses from concentration camps. The doctrine of the superman led to the methodical creation of sub-men – a fact that doubtless should be denounced but which also demands interpretation. If the final result of the great movement of rebellion in the nineteenth and twentieth centuries was to be this ruthless bondage, then surely rebellion should be rejected and Nietzsche's desperate cry to his contemporaries taken up: 'My conscience and yours are no longer the same conscience.'

We must first of all realize that we can never confuse Nietzsche with Rosenberg. We must be the advocates for the defence of Nietzsche. He himself has said so, denouncing in advance his bastard progeny, 'he who had liberated his mind still has to purify himself'. But the question is to find out if the liberation of the mind, as he conceived it, does not preclude purification. The idea that comes to a head with Nietzsche, and that supports him, has its laws and its logic which, perhaps, explain the bloody travesty of his philosophy. Is there nothing in his work which can be used in support of definitive murder? Cannot the killers, provided that they deny the spirit for the letter (and even what still remains of the spirit in the letter), find their pretext in Nietzsche? The answer must be yes. From the moment that the methodical aspect of Nietzschean thought is neglected (and it is not certain that he himself always observed it) his rebellious logic recognizes no limits.

We also remark that it is not in the Nietzschean refusal to worship idols that murder finds its justification, but in the passionate cohesion which crowns Nietzsche's work. To say yes to everything supposes that one says yes to murder. Moreover, it expresses two ways of consenting to murder. If the slave says yes to everything, he consents to the existence of a master and to his own sufferings; Jesus teaches non-resistance. If the master says yes to everything, he consents to slavery and to the suffering of others; and the result is the tyrant and the glorification of murder. 'Is it not laughable that we believe in a sacred, infrangible law, thou shalt not lie, thou shalt not kill, in an existence characterized by perpetual lying and perpetual murder?' Actually metaphysical rebellion, in its initial stages, was only a protest against the lie and the crime of existence. The Nietzschean affirmative, forgetful of the original negative, disavows rebellion at the same time that it disavows the ethic which refuses to accept the world as it is. Nietzsche prayed for a Roman Caesar with the soul of Christ. To his mind, this was to say yes to both slave and master. But, in the last analysis, to say yes to both was to give one's blessing to the stronger of the two, namely the master. Caesar must inevitably renounce the domination of the mind in order to rule in the realm of fact. 'How can one make the best of crime?' asks Nietzsche, a good professor faithful to his system. Caesar must answer: by multiplying it. 'When the ends are great,' Nietzsche wrote to his own detriment, 'humanity employs other standards and no longer judges crime as such even if it resorts to the most frightful means.' He died in 1900, at the beginning of the century in which that statement was to become fatal. It was in vain that he exclaimed in his hour of lucidity, 'It is easy to talk about all sorts of immoral acts; but would one have the courage to carry them through? For example, I could not bear to break my word or to kill; I should languish, and eventually I should die as a result – that would be my fate.' From the moment that assent was given to the totality of human experience, the way was open to others who, far from languishing, would gather strength from lies and murder. Nietzsche's responsibility lies in having legitimized, for worthy reasons of method – and even if only for an instant – the right to dishonour of which Dostoyevsky had already said that if one offered it to people one could always be sure of seeing them rushing at it. But his involuntary responsibility goes still further.

Nietzsche is exactly what he recognized himself as being: the most acute manifestation of nihilism's conscience. The decisive step that he compelled rebellion to take consists in making it jump from the negation of the ideal to the secularization of the ideal. Since the salvation of man is not achieved in God, it must be achieved on earth. Since the world has no direction, man, from the moment that he accepts this, must give it one which will lead eventually to a superior type of humanity. Nietzsche laid claim to the direction of the future of the human race. 'The task of governing the world is going to fall to our lot.' And elsewhere: 'The time is approaching when we shall have to struggle for the domination of the world, and this struggle will be fought in the name of philosophical principles.' In these words he predicted the twentieth century. But if he was able to predict it, it was because he was warned by the interior logic of nihilism and knew that one of its aims was ascendancy; and thus he prepared the way for this ascendancy.

There is freedom for man without God, as Nietzsche imagined him, in other words for the solitary man. There is freedom at mid-day when the wheel of the world stops spinning and man accepts things as they are. But *what is* becomes *what will be* and the ceaseless change of things must be accepted. The light finally grows dim, the axis of the day declines. Then history begins again and freedom must be sought in history; history must be accepted. Nietzschism – the theory of individual will to power – was condemned to support the universal will to power. Nietzschism was nothing without world domination. Nietzsche undoubtedly hated free-thinkers and humanitarians. He took the words 'freedom of thought' in their most extreme sense: the divinity of the individual mind. But he could not stop the free-thinkers partaking of the same historical fact as himself – the death of God – nor could he prevent the consequences being the same. Nietzsche saw clearly that humanitarianism was only a form of Christianity deprived of superior justification which preserved final causes while rejecting the first cause. But he failed to perceive that the doctrines of social emancipation must, by an inevitable logic of nihilism, lead to what he himself had dreamed of superhumanity.

Philosophy secularizes the ideal. But tyrants appear who soon secularize the philosophies which give them their rights. Nietzsche had already predicted this development in discussing Hegel whose originality, according to him, consisted in inventing a pantheism in which evil, error, and suffering could no longer serve as arguments against the divinity. 'But the State, and the powers that be, immediately made use of this grandiose initiative.' However, he himself had conceived of a system in which crime could no longer serve as an argument against anything and in which the only value resided in the divinity of man. This grandiose initiative also had to be put to use. National socialism in this respect was only a transitory heir, only the speculative and rabid outcome of nihilism. In all other respects those who, in correcting Nietzsche with the help of Marx, will choose to assent only to history and no longer to all of creation will be perfectly logical. The rebel whom Nietzsche set on his knees before the cosmos will, from now on, kneel before history. What is surprising about that? Nietzsche, at least in his theory of superhumanity, and Marx, before him, with his classless society, both replace the Beyond by the Later On. In that way, Nietzsche betrayed the Greeks and the teachings of Jesus who, according to him, replaced the Beyond by the Immediate. Marx like Nietzsche thought in strategic terms and like Nietzsche hated formal virtue. Their two rebellions, both of which finish similarly in adhesion to a certain aspect of reality, end by merging into Marxism-Leninism and being incarnated in that caste, already mentioned by Nietzsche, which would 'replace the priest, the teacher, the doctor'. The fundamental difference is that Nietzsche, in awaiting the superman, proposed to assent to what exists and Marx to what is to come. For Marx nature is to be subjugated in order to obey history, for Nietzsche nature is to be obeyed in order to subjugate history. It is the difference between the Christian and the Greek. Nietzsche at least foresaw what was going to happen: 'Modern socialism tends to create a form of secular Jesuitism, to make instruments of all men,' and again: 'What we desire is well-being . . . As a result we march towards a spiritual slavery such as has never been seen . . . Intellectual Caesarism hovers over every activity of the business man and of the philosophers.' Placed in the crucible of Nietzschean philosophy, rebellion, in the folly of freedom, ends in biological or historical Caesarism. The absolute negative had driven Stirner to defy crime simultaneously with the individual. But the absolute affirmative leads to universalizing murder and mankind simultaneously. Marxism-Leninism has really accepted the burden of Nietzsche's free-will by means of ignoring several Nietzschean virtues. The great rebel thus creates with his own hands, and for his own imprisonment, the implacable reign of necessity. Once he had escaped from God's prison, his first care was to construct the prison of history and of reason, thus putting the finishing touch to the camouflage and consecration of that nihilism whose conquest he claimed.

Nihilism and History

ONE hundred and fifty years of metaphysical revolt and of nihilism have witnessed the persistent reappearance, under different guises, of the same ravaged countenance: the face of human protest. All of them, decrying the human condition and its creator, have affirmed the solitude of man and the non-existence of any kind of morality. But at the same time they have all tried to construct a purely terrestrial kingdom where their chosen principles will hold sway. As rivals of the Creator, they have inescapably been led to the point of reconstructing creation according to their own concepts. Those who rejected, for the world they had just created, all other principles but desire and power, have been driven to suicide or madness and have predicted the apocalypse. As for the rest, who wanted to create their own principles, they have chosen pomp and ceremony, the world of appearances, murder and destruction. But Sade and the romantics, Karamazov or Nietzsche only entered the world of death because they wanted to discover the true life. So that by a process of inversion, it is the desperate appeal for order that rings through this insane universe. Their conclusions have only proved disastrous or destructive to freedom from the moment that they laid aside the burden of rebellion, fled the tension that it implies, and chose the comfort of tyranny or of servitude.

Human insurrection, in its exalted and tragic forms, is only, and can only be, a prolonged protest against death, a violent accusation against the universal death penalty. In every case that we have come across, the protest is always directed at everything in creation which is dissonant, opaque, or promises the solution of continuity. Essentially, then, we are dealing with a perpetual demand for unity. The rejection of death, the desire for immortality and for clarity, are the main springs of all these extravagances, whether sublime or puerile. Is it only a cowardly and personal refusal to die? No, since many of these rebels have paid the ultimate price in order to live up to their own demands. The rebel does not ask for life, but for reasons for living. He rejects the consequences implied by death. If nothing lasts, then nothing is justified: anything that dies has no meaning. To fight against death amounts to claiming that life has a meaning, to fighting for order and for unity.

The protest against evil which is at the very core of metaphysical revolt is significant in this regard. It is not the suffering of a child which is repugnant in itself, but the fact that the suffering is not justified. After all, pain, exile, confinement are sometimes accepted when dictated by good sense or by the doctor. In the eyes of the rebel, what is missing from the misery of the world, as well as from its moments of happiness, is some principle by which they can be explained. The insurrection against evil is, above all, a demand for unity. The rebel obstinately confronts a world condemned to death and the fatal obscurity of the human condition with his demand for life and absolute clarity. He is seeking, without knowing it, a moral philosophy or a religion. Rebellion is a form of asceticism, though it is blind. Therefore, if the rebel blasphemes it is in the hope of finding a new god. He staggers under the shock of the first and most profound of all religious experiences, but it is a disenchanted religious experience. It is not rebellion itself which is noble, but its aims, even though its achievements are at times ignoble. At least we must know how to recognize the ignoble ends it achieves. Each time that it defies the total rejection, the absolute negation of what exists, it destroys. Each time that it blindly accepts what exists and gives voice to absolute assent, it destroys again. Hatred of the creator can turn to hatred of creation or to exclusive and defiant love of what exists. But in both cases it ends in murder and loses the right to be called rebellion. One can be a nihilist in two ways, in both cases by having an intemperate recourse to absolutes. Apparently there are rebels who want to die and those who want to cause death. But they are identical, consumed with desire for the true life, frustrated by their desire, and therefore preferring generalized injustice to mutilated justice. At this point of indignation, reason becomes madness. If it is true that the instinctive rebellion of the human heart advances gradually through the centuries towards its most complete realization, it has also grown, as we have seen, in blind audacity to the inordinate extent of deciding to answer universal murder by metaphysical assassination.

The *even if*, which we have already recognized as marking the most important moment of metaphysical revolt, is in any case fulfilled only in absolute destruction. It is not the nobility of rebellion which illuminates the world today, but nihilism. And it is the consequences of nihilism which we must retrace, without losing sight of the truth innate in its origins. Even if God existed, Ivan would never surrender to Him in the face of the injustice done to man. But a longer contemplation of this injustice, a more bitter approach, transformed the 'even if you exist' into 'you do not deserve to exist', therefore 'you do not exist'. The victims have found in their own innocence the justification for the final crime. Convinced of their condemnation and without hope of immortality they decided to murder God. If it is false to say that, from that day, began the tragedy of contemporary man, it is not true, either, to say that it ended there. On the contrary, this attempt indicates the highest point in a drama that began with the end of the ancient world and of which the last words have not yet been spoken. From this moment, man decides to exclude himself from grace and to live by his own means. Progress, from the time of Sade up to the present, has consisted of gradually enlarging the enclosure where, according to his own rules, man without God brutally wields power. In defiance of the divinity, the frontiers of this stronghold have been extended, to the point of making the entire universe into a fortress erected against the fallen and exiled deity. Man, at the culmination of his rebellion, incarcerated himself; from Sade's lurid castle to the concentration camps, man's greatest liberty consisted only of building the prison of his crimes. But the state of siege gradually spreads, the claim for freedom must embrace all mankind. Then the only kingdom which is opposed to the kingdom of grace must be founded, namely the kingdom of justice, and the human community must be reunited on the debris of the fallen City of God. To kill God and to build a Church is the constant and contradictory purpose of rebellion. Absolute liberty finally becomes a prison of absolute duties, a collective asceticism, a story to be brought to an end. The nineteenth century, which is the century of rebellion, thus merges into the twentieth, the century of justice and ethics, the century of violent self-recrimination. Chamfort, the moralist of rebellion, has already provided the formula: 'One must be just before being generous, as one must have bread before having cake.' Thus, the ethic of luxury will be renounced in favour of the bitter morality of the empire builder.

We must now embark on the subject of this convulsive effort to control the world and to introduce a universal rule. We have arrived at the moment when rebellion, rejecting every aspect of servitude, attempts to annex all creation. At each of its setbacks, we have already seen formulated the political solution, the solution of conquest. Henceforth, with the introduction of moral nihilism, it will retain, of all its other acquisitions, only the will to power. In principle, the rebel only wanted to conquer his own self and to maintain it in the face of God. But he forgets his beginnings and, by the law of spiritual imperialism, he sets out in search of world conquest by way of an infinitely multiplied series of murders. He drove God from His heaven, but with the spirit of metaphysical rebellion openly joining forces with revolutionary movements, the irrational claim for freedom is paradoxically going to adopt reason as a weapon, as the only means of conquest which appears to it entirely human. With the death of God, mankind remains: and by this we mean the history which we must understand and shape. Nihilism, which smothers the creative force in the very core of rebellion, only adds that one can shape it with all the means at one's disposal. Man, on an earth which he knows is henceforth solitary, is going to add, to irrational crimes, the crimes of reason that are bent on the domination of man. To the 'I rebel, therefore we exist', he adds, with prodigious plans in mind which even include the death of rebellion: 'And we are alone.'

3

HISTORICAL REBELLION

FREEDOM, 'that terrible word inscribed on the chariot of the storm', is the motivating principle of all revolutions. Without it, justice seems inconceivable to the rebel's mind. There comes a time, however, when justice demands the suspension of freedom. Then terror, on a grand or small scale, makes its appearance to consummate the revolution. Every act of rebellion expresses a nostalgia for innocence and an appeal to the essence of being. But, one day, nostalgia takes up arms and assumes the responsibility of total guilt; in other words, adopts murder and violence. The servile rebellions, the regicide revolutions, and the twentieth-century revolutions had thus, consciously, accepted a burden of guilt which increased in proportion to the degree of liberation they proposed to introduce. This contradiction, which has become only too obvious, prevents our contemporary revolutionaries from displaying that aspect of happiness and optimism which shone forth from the faces and the speeches of the members of the Constituent Assembly in 1789. Is this contradiction inevitable? Does it characterize or betray the value of rebellion? These questions are bound to arise about revolution as they are bound to arise about metaphysical rebellion. Actually, revolution is only the logical consequence of metaphysical rebellion, and we shall discover, in our analysis of the revolutionary movement, the same desperate and bloody effort to affirm the dignity of man in defiance of the things that deny its existence. The revolutionary spirit thus undertakes the defence of that part of man which refuses to submit. In other words, it tries to assure him his crown in the realm of time, and, rejecting God, it chooses history with an apparently inevitable logic.

In theory, the word revolution retains the meaning that it has in astronomy. It is a movement which describes a complete circle,

76

which leads from one form of government to another after a total transition. A change of regulations concerning property without a corresponding change of government is not a revolution, but a reform. There is no kind of economic revolution, whether its methods are violent or pacific, which is not, at the same time, manifestly political. Revolution can already be distinguished, in this way, from rebellion. The warning given to Louis XVI: 'no, sire, this is not a rebellion, it is a revolution' accents the essential difference. It means precisely that 'it is the absolute certainty of a new form of government'. Rebellion is, by nature, limited in scope. It is no more than incoherent pronouncement. Revolution, on the contrary, originates in the realm of ideas. Specifically, it is the injection of ideas into historic experience while rebellion is only the movement which leads from individual experience into the realm of ideas. While even the collective history of a movement of rebellion is always that of a fruitless struggle with facts, of an obscure protest which involves neither methods nor reasons, a revolution is an attempt to shape actions to ideas, to fit the world into a theoretic frame. That is why rebellion kills men while revolution destroys both men and principles. But, for the same reasons, it can be said that there has not yet been a revolution in the course of history. There could only be one and that would be the definitive revolution. The movement which seems to complete the circle already begins to describe another, at the precise moment when the new government is formed. The anarchists, with Varlet as their leader, were made well aware of the fact that government and revolution are incompatible in the direct sense. 'It implies a contradiction', says Proudhon, 'that a government could ever be called revolutionary, for the very simple reason that it is the government.' Now that the experiment has been made, let us qualify that statement by adding that a government can only be revolutionary in opposition to other governments. Revolutionary governments are, most of the time, obliged to be war governments. The more extensive the revolution the more considerable the chances of the war that it implies. The society born of the revolution of 1789 wanted to fight for Europe. The society born of the 1917 revolution is fighting for universal dominion. Total revolution ends by demanding – we shall see why – the control of the world.

While waiting for this to happen, if happen it must, the history of man, in one sense, is the sum total of his successive rebellions. In other words, the movement of transition which can be clearly expressed in terms of space is only an approximation in terms of time. What was devoutly called, in the nineteenth century, the progressive emancipation of the human race appears, from the outside, like an uninterrupted series of rebellions which overreach themselves and try to find their formulation in ideas, but which have not yet reached the point of definitive revolution where everything on heaven and earth would be stabilized. A superficial examination seems to infer, rather than any real emancipation, an affirmation of mankind by man, an affirmation increasingly broad in scope but which is always unrealized. In fact, if there had ever been one real revolution, there would be no more history. Unity would have been achieved and death would have been satiated. That is why all revolutionaries finally aspire to world unity and act as though they believed that history were dead. The originality of twentieth-century revolution lies in the fact that, for the first time, it openly claims to realize the ancient dream of unity of the human race and, at the same time, the definitive consummation of history. Just as rebel movements led to the point of 'All or Nothing' and just as metaphysical rebellion demanded the unity of the world, the twentieth-century revolutionary movement, when it arrived at the most obvious conclusions of its logic, insisted with threats of force on arrogating to itself the whole of history. Rebellion is therefore compelled, on pain of appearing futile or being out of date, to become revolutionary. It no longer suffices for the rebel to declare himself God or to look to his own salvation by adopting a certain attitude of mind. The species must be deified, as Nietzsche attempted to do, and his ideal of the superman must be adopted so as to assure salvation for all – as Ivan Karamazov wanted. For the first time, the Possessed appear on the scene and proceed to give the answer to one of the secrets of the times: the identity of reason and of the will to power. Now that God is dead, the world must be changed and organized by the forces at man's disposal. The force of imprecation alone is not enough and weapons are needed for the conquest of totality. Revolution, even, and above all, revolution which claims to be materialist, is only a limitless metaphysical crusade. But can totality claim to be unity? That is the question which this book must answer. So far we can only say that the purpose of this analysis is not to give, for the hundredth time, a description of the revolutionary phenomenon, nor once more to examine the historic or economic causes of great revolutions. Its purpose is to discover in certain revolutionary data the logical sequence, the explanations, and the invariable themes of metaphysical rebellion.

The majority of revolutions are shaped by, and derive their originality from, murder. All, or almost all, have been homicidal. But some, in addition, have practised regicide and deicide. Just as the history of metaphysical rebellion began with Sade, so our real inquiry only begins with his contemporaries, the regicides, who attack the incarnation of divinity without yet daring to kill the principle of eternity.

When a slave rebels against his master the situation presented is of one man pitted against another, under a cruel sky, far from the exalted realms of principles. The final result is merely the murder of a man. The servile rebellions, peasant risings, beggar tumults, rustic outbreaks, all advance the concept of a principle of equality, life for life, which despite every kind of mystification and audacity will always be found in the purest manifestations of the revolutionary spirit: Russian terrorism in 1905, for example.

Spartacus's rebellion which took place as the ancient world was coming to an end, a few decades before the Christian era, is an excellent illustration of this point. First we note that this is a rebellion of gladiators, that is to say of slaves consecrated to single combat and condemned, for the delectation of their masters, to kill or be killed. Beginning with seventy men, this rebellion ended with an army of seventy thousand insurgents which crushed the best Roman legions and advanced through Italy to march on the Eternal City itself.

However, as André Prudhommeaux remarks, this rebellion introduced no new principle to Roman life. The proclamation issued by Spartacus goes no farther than to offer 'equal rights' to the slaves. The transition from fact to right which we analysed in the first stage of rebellion is, in fact, the only logical acquisition which one can find on this level of rebellion. The insurgent rejects slavery and affirms his equality with his master. He wants to be master in his turn.

Spartacus's rebellion is a constant illustration of this principle of positive claims. The slave army liberates the slaves and immediately hands over their former masters to them in bondage. According to one tradition, of doubtful veracity it is true, gladiatorial combats were even organized between several hundred Roman citizens while the slaves sat in the grandstands delirious with joy and excitement. But to kill men only leads to killing more men. To allow a principle to triumph, another principle must be overthrown. The city of light of which Spartacus dreamed could only have been built on the ruins of eternal Rome, of its institutions, and of its gods. Spartacus's army marches to lay siege to a Rome paralysed with fear at the prospect of having to pay for its crimes. However, at the decisive moment, within sight of the sacred walls, the army halts and wavers, as if it were retreating before the principles, the institutions, the city of the gods. When these had been destroyed, what could he put in their place, except the brutal desire for justice, the wounded and exacerbated love which, until this moment, had kept these wretches on their feet.* In any case, the army retreated without having fought, and then made the curious move of deciding to return to the place where the slave rebellion originated, to retrace the long road of its victories and to return to Sicily. It was as though these outcasts, forever alone and helpless before the great tasks which awaited them and too daunted to assail the heavens, returned to what was purest and most

* Spartacus's rebellion recapitulates the programme of the servile rebellions which preceded it. But this programme is limited to the distribution of land and the abolition of slavery. It is not directly concerned with the gods of the city.

heartening in their history, to the land of their first awakening where it was easy and right to die.

Then began their defeat and martyrdom. Before the last battle, Spartacus crucified a Roman citizen to show his men the fate that was in store for them. During the battle, Spartacus himself tried with frenzied determination, the symbolism of which is obvious, to reach Crassus who was commanding the Roman legions. He wanted to perish but in single combat with the man who symbolized, at that moment, every Roman master; it was his dearest wish to die, but in absolute equality. He did not reach Crassus: principles wage war at a distance and the Roman general kept himself apart. Spartacus died as he wished, but at the hands of mercenaries, slaves like himself, who killed their own freedom with his. In revenge for the one crucified citizen, Crassus crucified thousands of slaves. The six thousand crosses which, after such a just rebellion, staked out the road from Capua to Rome, demonstrated to the servile crowd that there is no equality in the world of power and that the masters calculate, at a usurious rate, the price of their own blood.

The Cross is also Christ's punishment. One can imagine that He only chose a slave's punishment, a few years later, so as to reduce the enormous distance which henceforth would separate humiliated humanity from the implacable face of the Master. He intercedes. He submits to the most extreme injustice so that rebellion shall not divide the world in two, so that suffering will also light the way to heaven and preserve it from the curses of mankind. What is astonishing in the fact that the revolutionary spirit, when it wanted to affirm the separation of heaven and earth, should begin by disembodying the divinity by killing His representatives on earth? In certain aspects, the period of rebellions comes to an end in 1793 and revolutionary times begin – on a scaffold.*

* In that this book is not concerned with the spirit of rebellion inside Christianity, the Reformation has no place here, nor the numerous rebellions against ecclesiastical authority which preceded it. But we can say, at least, that the Reformation prepares the way for Jacobinism and in one sense initiates the reforms that 1789 carries out.

The Regicides

KINGS were put to death long before 21 January 1793, and before the regicides of the nineteenth century. But regicides of earlier times and their followers were interested in attacking the person, not the principle, of the king. They wanted another king and that was all. It never occurred to them that the throne could remain empty for ever. Seventeen eighty-nine is the starting-point of modern times, because the men of that period wished, among other things, to overthrow the principle of divine right and to introduce to the historical scene the forces of negation and rebellion which had become the essence of intellectual discussion in the previous centuries. Thus they added to traditional tyrannicide the concept of calculated deicide. The so-called free-thinkers, the philosophers and jurists, served as levers for this revolutionary concept.* In order for such an undertaking to enter into the realms of possibility and to be considered justified, it was first necessary for the Church, whose infinite responsibility it is, to place itself on the side of the masters by compromising with the executioner – a step which developed into the Inquisition and which was perpetuated by complicity with the temporal powers. Michelet is quite correct in only wanting to recognize two outstanding characters in the revolutionary saga: Christianity and the French Revolution. In fact, for him, 1789 is explained by the struggle between divine grace and justice. Although Michelet shared the taste for all-embracing abstractions with his intemperate period, he saw that this taste was one of the profound causes of the revolutionary crisis.

Even if the monarchy of the *ancien régime* was not always arbitrary in its manner of governing it was undoubtedly arbitrary in principle. It was founded on divine right, which means that its legitimacy could

* The kings themselves collaborated in this by allowing political power gradually to encroach on religious power, thus threatening the very principle of their legitimacy.

never be questioned. However, its legitimacy often was questioned, in particular by various Parliaments. But those who exercised it considered and presented it as an axiom. Louis XIV, as is well known, rigidly adhered to the principle of divine right.* Bossuet gave him considerable help in this direction by saying to the kings of France: 'You are gods.' The king, in one of his aspects, is the divine emissary in charge of human affairs and therefore of the administration of justice. Like God himself, he is the last recourse of the victims of misery and injustice. In principle, the people can appeal to the king for help against their oppressors. 'If the king only knew, if the Czar only knew . . .' was the frequently expressed sentiment of the French and Russian people during periods of great distress. It is true in France, at least, that, when it did know, the monarchy often tried to defend the lower classes against the oppressions of the aristocracy and the bourgeoisie. But was this, essentially, justice? From the absolute point of view, which was the point of view of the writers of the period, it was not. Even though it is possible to appeal to the king, it is impossible to appeal against him in so far as he is the embodiment of a principle. He dispenses his protection and his assistance if and when he wants to. One of the attributes of grace is that it is discretionary. Monarchy in its theocratic form is a type of government which wants to put grace before justice. Rousseau in his Savoyard Curate's declaration, on the other hand, is only original in so far as he submits God to justice and in this way inaugurates, with the rather naïve solemnity of the period, contemporary history.

From the moment that the free-thinkers began to question the existence of God, the problem of justice became of primary importance. The justice of the period was, quite simply, confused with equality. The throne of God totters and justice, to confirm its support of equality, must give it the final push by making a direct attack on His representative on earth. Divine right to all intents and purposes was already destroyed by being opposed and forced to compromise with natural right for three years, from 1789 to 1792. In the last

* Charles I clung so tenaciously to the principle of divine right that he considered it unnecessary to be just and loyal to those who denied it.

resort, grace is incapable of compromise. It can give in on certain points, but never on the final point. But that is not going far enough. According to Michelet, Louis XVI still wanted to be king in prison. In a France entirely governed by new principles, the principle that had been defeated still survived behind prison walls through the mere power of faith and through the existence of one human being. Justice has this in common with grace and this alone, that it wants to be total and to rule absolutely. From the moment that they conflict, they fight to the death. 'We do not want to condemn the king,' said Danton, 'who has not even got the good manners of a jurist, we want to kill him.' In fact, if God is denied, the king must die. Saint-Just, it seems, was responsible for Louis XVI's death; but when he exclaims: 'To determine the principle in virtue of which the accused is perhaps to die, is to determine the principle by which the society which judges him lives,' he demonstrates that it is the philosophers who are going to kill the king: the king must die in the name of the social contract.* But this demands an explanation.

THE NEW GOSPEL

The Social Contract is, primarily, an inquiry into the legitimacy of power. But it is a book about rights not about facts and at no time is it a collection of sociological observations. It is concerned with principles and for this very reason is bound to be controversial. It presumes that traditional legitimacy, which is supposedly of divine origin, is not acquired. Thus it proclaims another sort of legitimacy and other principles. *The Social Contract* is also a catechism of which it has both the tone and the dogmatic language. Just as 1789 completes the conquests of the English and American revolutions, so

---

* Rousseau would not, of course, have wanted this. It must be remembered before proceeding with this analysis and in order to set its limits, that Rousseau firmly declared: 'Nothing here below is worth buying at the price of human blood.'

Rousseau pushes to its limits the theory of the social contract to be found in Hobbes. *The Social Contract* amplifies and dogmatically explains the new religion whose god is reason, confused with Nature, and whose representative on earth, in place of the king, is the people considered as an expression of the general will.

The attack against the traditional order is so evident that, from the very first chapter, Rousseau is determined to demonstrate the precedence of the citizens' pact, which accorded the people their place, to the pact between the people and the king, which established royalty. Until Rousseau's time, God created kings who, in their turn, created peoples. After *The Social Contract*, peoples create themselves, before creating kings. As for God, there is nothing more to be said for the time being. Here we have, in the political field, the equivalent of Newton's revolution. Power, therefore, is no longer arbitrary, but derives its existence from general consent. In other words, power is no longer what is but what should be. Fortunately, according to Rousseau, what is cannot be separated from what should be. The people are sovereign 'only because they are always everything that they should be'. Confronted with this statement of principle, it is perfectly justifiable to say that reason, which was always obstinately invoked at that period, is not particularly well treated in the context. It is evident that, with *The Social Contract*, we are assisting at the birth of a new mystique – the will of the people being substituted for God Himself. 'Each of us', says Rousseau, 'places his person and his entire capabilities under the supreme guidance of the will of the people and we receive each individual member into our bodies as an indivisible part of the whole.'

This political entity, proclaimed sovereign, is also defined as a divine entity. Moreover, it has all the attributes of a divine entity. It is, in fact, infallible in that, in its role of sovereign, it cannot even wish to commit abuses. 'Under the law of reason, nothing is done without cause.' It is totally free, if it is true that absolute freedom is freedom in regard to oneself. Thus Rousseau declares that it is against the nature of the body politic for the sovereign power to impose a law upon itself that cannot be enforced. It is also inalienable, indivisible, and, finally, it even aims at solving the great theological problem, the contradiction between absolute power and divine innocence. The will of the people is, in fact, coercive; its power has no limits. But the punishment it inflicts on those who refuse to obey it is nothing more than a means of 'compelling them to be free'. The deification is completed when Rousseau, separating the sovereign from his very origins, reaches the point of distinguishing between the general will and the will of all. This can be logically deduced from Rousseau's premises. If man is naturally good, if Nature as expressed in him is identified with reason,* he will express the pre-eminence of reason, on the one condition that he expresses himself freely and naturally. He can no longer, therefore, go back on his decision, which henceforth overshadows him. The will of the people is, primarily, the expression of universal reason, which is categorical. The new God is born.

That is why the words that are to be found most often in *The Social Contract* are the words 'absolute', 'sacred', 'inviolable'. The body politic thus defined, whose laws are sacred commandments, is only a by-product of the mystic body of temporal Christianity. *The Social Contract*, moreover, terminates with a description of a civil religion and makes of Rousseau a harbinger of contemporary forms of society which exclude not only opposition but even neutrality. Rousseau is, in fact, the first man in modern times to institute the profession of civil faith. He is also the first to justify the death penalty in a civil society and the absolute submission of the subject to the authority of the sovereign. 'It is in order not to become victim of an assassin that we consent to die if we become assassins.' A strange justification, but one which firmly establishes the fact that you must know how to die if the sovereign commands and must, if necessary, concede that he is right and you are wrong. This mystic idea explains Saint-Just's silence from the time of his arrest until he goes to the scaffold. Suitably developed, it equally well explains the enthusiasm of the defendants in the Moscow trials.

We are witnessing the dawn of a new religion with its martyrs, its ascetics, and its saints. To be able to estimate the influence achieved

* Every ideology is contrary to human psychology.

by this gospel, one must have some idea of the inspired tones of the proclamations of 1789. A revolutionary, confronted with the skeletons discovered in the Bastille, exclaims: 'The day of revelation is upon us. . . . The very bones have risen at the sound of the voice of French freedom; they bear witness against the centuries of oppression and death, and prophesy the regeneration of human nature and of the life of nations.' Then he predicts: 'We have reached the heart of time. The tyrants are ready to fall.' It is the moment of astonished and generous faith when a remarkably enlightened mob overthrows the scaffold and the wheel at Versailles.* Scaffolds seemed to be the very altars of religion and injustice. The new faith could not tolerate them. But a moment comes when faith, if it becomes dogmatic, erects its own altars and demands unconditional adoration. Then scaffolds reappear and despite the altars, the oaths, the feasts, and the freedom of reason, the masses of the new faith must now be celebrated with blood. In any case, in order that 1789 shall mark the beginning of the reign of 'holy humanity'† and of 'Our Lord the human race',‡ the fallen sovereign must first of all disappear. The murder of the king-priest will sanction the new age – which endures to this day.

THE EXECUTION OF THE KING

Saint-Just introduced Rousseau's ideas into the pages of history. At the king's trial, the essential part of his arguments consisted of saying that the king is not inviolable and should be judged by the assembly and not by a special tribunal. His method of proof he owed to Rousseau. A tribunal cannot be the judge between the king and the sovereign people. The general will cannot be tried by ordinary judges. It is above everything. The inviolability and the transcendence of the general will are thus proclaimed. We know that the predominant

* The same idyll takes place in Russia, in 1905, where the soviet of St Petersburg parades through the streets carrying placards demanding the abolition of the death penalty, and again in 1917.

† Vergniaud.   ‡ Anarchasis Cloots.

theme of the trial was the inviolability of the royal person. The struggle between grace and justice finds its most provocative illustration in 1793 when two different conceptions of transcendence meet in mortal combat. Moreover, Saint-Just is perfectly aware of how very much is at stake: 'The spirit in which the king is judged will be the same as the spirit in which the Republic is established.'

Saint-Just's famous speech has, therefore, all the earmarks of a theological treatise. 'Louis, the stranger in our midst,' is the thesis of this youthful prosecutor. If a contract, either civil or natural, could still bind the king and his people, there would be a mutual obligation; the will of the people could not set itself up as absolute judge to pronounce absolute judgement. Therefore it is necessary to prove that no agreement binds the people and the king. In order to prove that the people are themselves the embodiment of eternal truth it is necessary to demonstrate that royalty is the embodiment of eternal crime. Saint-Just, therefore, postulates that every king is a rebel or a usurper. He is a rebel against the people whose absolute sovereignty he usurps. Monarchy is not a king, 'it is crime'. Not *a* crime, but crime itself, says Saint-Just; in other words, absolute desecration. That is the precise, and at the same time, ultimate meaning of Saint-Just's remark the import of which has been stretched too far*: 'No one can rule innocently.' Every king is guilty, because any man who wants to be king is automatically on the side of death. Saint-Just says exactly the same thing when he proceeds to demonstrate that the sovereignty of the people is a 'sacred matter'. Citizens are inviolable and sacred and can only be constrained by the law which is an expression of their common will. Louis himself does not benefit by this particular inviolability or by the assistance of the law, for he is placed outside the contract. He is not part of the general will; on the contrary, by his very existence he is a blasphemer against this all-powerful will. He is not a 'citizen' which is the only way of participating in the new divine dispensation. 'What is a king in comparison

---

* Or at least the significance of which has been anticipated. When Saint-Just made this remark he did not know that he was already speaking for himself.

to a Frenchman ?' Therefore, he should be judged and no more than that.

But who will interpret the will of the people and pronounce judgement ? The Assembly, which by its origin has retained the right to administer this will, and which participates as an inspired council in the new divinity. Should the people be asked to ratify the judgement ? We know that the efforts of the monarchists in the Assembly were finally concentrated on this point. In this way the life of the king could be rescued from the logic of the bourgeois-jurists and at least entrusted to the spontaneous emotions and compassion of the people. But here again Saint-Just pushes his logic to its extremities and makes use of the conflict, invented by Rousseau, between the general will and the will of all. Even though the will of all would be willing to pardon, the general will cannot do so. Even the people cannot efface the crime of tyranny. Cannot the victims, according to law, withdraw their complaint ? We are not dealing with law, we are dealing with theology. The crime of the king is, at the same time, a sin against the ultimate nature of things. A crime is committed, then it is pardoned, punished, or forgotten. But the crime of royalty is permanent, it is inextricably bound to the person of the king, to his very existence. Christ Himself, though He can forgive sinners, cannot absolve false gods. They must disappear or conquer. If the people forgive today, they will find the crime intact tomorrow, even though the criminal sleeps peacefully in prison. Therefore there is only one issue: 'To avenge the murder of the people by the death of the king'.

The only purpose of Saint-Just's speech is, once and for all, to block every egress for the king, except the one leading to the scaffold. If, in fact, the premises of *The Social Contract* are accepted, this is inevitable. At last, after Saint-Just, 'kings will flee to the desert and Nature will resume her rights'. It was quite pointless of the Convention to vote a reservation and say that it did not intend to create a precedent if it passed judgement on Louis XVI and if it pronounced a security measure. In doing so it fled before its own principles and tried to camouflage, with shocking hypocrisy, its real purpose, which was to found a new form of absolutism. Jacques Roux, at least, was speaking the truth of the times when he called the king Louis the Last, thus indicating that the real revolution, which had already been accomplished on the economic level, was then taking place on the philosophic plane and that it implied a twilight of the gods. Theocracy was attacked in principle in 1789 and killed in person in 1793. Brissot was right in saying: 'The most solid monument to our revolution is philosophy.'

On 21 January, with the murder of the king-priest, was consummated what has significantly been called the passion of Louis XVI. Undoubtedly, it is a crying scandal that the public assassination of a weak but good-hearted man has been presented as a great moment in French history. That scaffold marked no climax: far from it. But the fact remains that, by its results and consequences, the condemnation of the king is at the crux of our contemporary history. It symbolizes the secularization of our history and the dematerialization of the Christian God. Up to now God played a part in history through the medium of the kings. But His representative in history has been killed, for there is no longer a king. Therefore there is nothing but a semblance of God, relegated to the heaven of principles.*

The revolutionaries may well refer to the Gospel, but in fact, they dealt a terrible blow to Christianity from which it has not yet recovered. It really seems as if the execution of the king, followed, as we know, by hysterical scenes of suicide and madness, took place entirely in the conscience of the victim. Louis XVI seems, sometimes, to have doubted his divine right, although he systematically rejected any projected legislation which threatened this concept. But from the moment that he suspected or knew his fate, he seemed to identify himself, as his language betrayed, with his divine mission, so that there would be no possible doubt that the attempt on his person was aimed at the King-Christ, the incarnation of the divinity, and not at the craven flesh of a mere man. His bedside book, in the Temple, was the *Imitation*. The calmness and perfection that this man of rather average sensibility displayed during his last moments, his indifference

* This will later become the god of Kant, Jacobi, and Fichte.

to everything of this world and, finally, his brief display of weakness on the solitary scaffold so far removed from the people whose ears he had wanted to reach, while the terrible rolling of the drum drowned his voice, give us the right to imagine that it was not Capet who died, but Louis appointed by divine right, and that with him, in a certain manner, died temporal Christianity. To emphasize this sacred bond, his confessor sustained him, in his moment of weakness, by reminding him of his 'resemblance' to the God of Sorrows. And Louis XVI recovers himself and speaks in the language of this God: 'I shall drink', he says, 'the cup to the last dregs.' Then he commits himself, trembling, into the hands of the executioner.

THE RELIGION OF VIRTUE

A religion which executes its obsolete sovereign must now establish the power of its new sovereign; it closes the churches and this leads to an endeavour to build a temple. The blood of the gods, which for a second bespatters the confessor of Louis XVI, announces a new baptism. Joseph de Maistre qualified the Revolution as satanic. We can see why and in what sense. Michelet, however, was closer to the truth when he called it a purgatory. An era blindly embarks on an attempt to discover a new illumination, a new happiness, and the face of the real God. But what will this new god be? Let us ask Saint-Just once more.

Seventeen eighty-nine does not yet affirm the divinity of man, but the divinity of the people, to the degree in which the will of the people coincides with the will of Nature and of reason. If the general will is freely expressed, it can only be the universal expression of reason. If the people are free, they are infallible. Once the king is dead, and the chains of the old despotism thrown off, the people are going to express what, at all times and in all places, is, had been, and will be the truth. They are the oracle that must be consulted to know what the eternal order of the world demands. *Vox populi, vox naturae.* Eternal principles govern our conduct: Truth, Justice, finally, Reason. There we have the new God. The Supreme Being, whom cohorts of young girls come to adore at the Feast of Reason, is only the ancient god disembodied, peremptorily deprived of any connexion with the earth, and launched like a balloon into a heaven empty of all transcendent principles. Deprived of all his representatives, of any intercessor, the god of the lawyers and philosophers only has the value of logic. He is very feeble indeed and we can see why Rousseau, who preached tolerance, thought that atheists should be condemned to death. To insure the adoration of a theorem for any length of time, faith is not enough, a police force is needed as well. But that will only come later. In 1793 the new faith is still enough, and it will suffice, to take Saint-Just's word, to govern according to the dictates of reason. The art of ruling, according to him, has only produced monsters because, before his time, no one wished to govern according to Nature. The period of monsters has come to an end with the termination of the period of violence. 'The human heart advances from Nature to violence, from violence to morality.' Morality is, therefore, only Nature finally restored after centuries of alienation. Man only has to be given law 'in accord with Nature and with his heart', and he will cease to be unhappy and corrupt. Universal suffrage, the foundation of the new laws, must inevitably lead to a universal morality. 'Our aim is to create an order of things which establishes a universal tendency towards good.'

The religion of reason quite naturally establishes the Republic of law and order. The general will is expressed in laws codified by its representatives. 'The people make the revolution, the legislator makes the Republic.' 'Immortal, impassive' institutions, 'sheltered from the temerity of man', will govern in their turn the lives of all men by universal accord and without possibility of contradiction since by obeying the laws everyone will only be obeying themselves. 'Outside the law', says Saint-Just, 'everything is sterile and dead.' It is the formal and legalistic Republic of the Romans. We know the passion of Saint-Just and his contemporaries for ancient Rome. The decadent young man who, in Rheims, spent hours in a room painted black and decorated with white tear-drops, with the shutters closed, dreamed of the Spartan Republic. The author of *Organt*, a long and licentious poem, was absolutely convinced of the necessity for frugality and virtue. In his institutions, Saint-Just refused to allow children to eat meat until the age of sixteen and dreamed of a nation which was both vegetarian and revolutionary. 'The world has been empty since the Romans,' he exclaimed. But heroic times were near at hand. Cato, Brutus, Scaevola, had become possible once more. The rhetoric of the Latin moralists flourished again. 'Vice, virtue, corruption', were terms which constantly recurred in the oratory of the times, and, even more, in the speeches of Saint-Just of which they were the perpetual burden. The reason for this is simple. This perfect structure, as Montesquieu had already seen, could not exist without virtue. The French Revolution, by claiming to build history on the principle of absolute purity, simultaneously introduces modern times and the era of formal morality.

What, in fact, is virtue? For the bourgeois philosopher of the period it is conformity with Nature and, in politics, conformity with the law which expresses the general will. 'Morality', says Saint-Just, 'is stronger than tyrants.' In effect, it amounts to killing Louis XVI. Every form of disobedience to law therefore comes, not from an imperfection in the law, which is presumed to be impossible, but from a lack of virtue in the refractory citizen. That is why the Republic is not only an assembly, as Saint-Just forcibly says, it is also virtue. Every form of moral corruption is at the same time political corruption, and vice versa. A principle of infinite repression, derived from this very doctrine, is then established. Undoubtedly Saint-Just was sincere in his desire for a universal idyll. He really dreamed of a Republic of ascetics, of humanity reconciled and dedicated to the chaste pursuits of the age of innocence, under the watchful eye of those wise old men whom he decked out in advance with a tricolour scarf and a white plume. We also know that, at the beginning of the Revolution, Saint-Just pronounced himself, together with Robespierre, against the death penalty. He only insisted that murderers should be dressed in black for the rest of their lives. He wanted to establish a form of justice which did not attempt 'to find the culprit guilty but to find him weak' – an admirable ambition. He also dreamed of a Republic of forgiveness which would recognize that though the fruits of crime are bitter its roots are nevertheless tender. One of his outbursts, at least came from the heart and is not easily forgotten: 'it is a frightful thing to torment the people'. Yes, indeed, it is a frightful thing. But a man can realize this and yet submit to principles which imply, in the final analysis, the torment of the people.

Morality, when it is formal, devours. To paraphrase Saint-Just, nothing is virtuous innocently. From the moment that laws fail to make harmony reign, or when the unity which should be created by adherence to principles is destroyed, who is to blame? Factions. Who comprises the factions? Those who deny by their very actions the necessity of unity. Factions divide the sovereign; therefore they are blasphemous and criminal. They, and they alone, must be combated. But what if there are many factions? All shall be fought to the death. Saint-Just exclaims: 'Either the virtues or the Terror.' Freedom must be guaranteed and the draft constitution presented to the Convention already mentions the death penalty. Absolute virtue is impossible and the republic of forgiveness leads, with implacable logic, to the republic of the guillotine. Montesquieu had already denounced this logic as one of the causes of the decadence of societies, saying that the abuse of power is greatest when laws do not anticipate it. The pure law of Saint-Just did not take into account the truth, which is as old as history itself, that law, in its essence, is bound to be transgressed.

THE TERROR

Saint-Just, the contemporary of Sade, finally arrives at the justification of crime, although he starts from very different principles.

Saint-Just is, of course, the anti-Sade. If Sade's formula were 'open the prisons and prove your virtue', then Saint-Just's would be: 'Prove your virtue or go to prison.' However, both justify terrorism – the libertine justifies individual terrorism, the high priest of virtue, State terrorism. Absolute good or absolute evil, if the necessary logic is applied, both demand the same degree of ecstasy. Of course, there is a certain ambiguity in the case of Saint-Just. The letter which he wrote to Vilain D'Aubigny in 1792 has something really insane about it. It is a profession of faith by a persecuted persecutor which ends with a hysterical avowal: 'If Brutus does not kill others, he will kill himself.' A personality so obstinately serious, so voluntarily cold, logical, and imperturbable, leads one to imagine every kind of aberration and disorder. Saint-Just invented the kind of seriousness which makes the history of the last two centuries so tedious and depressing. 'He who makes jokes as the head of a government,' he said, 'has a tendency to tyranny.' An astonishing maxim, above all if one thinks of the penalty for the mere accusation of tyranny, and one which, in any case, prepared the way for the pedant Caesars. Saint-Just sets the example; even his tone is definitive. That cascade of peremptory affirmatives, that axiomatic and sententious style, portrays him better than the most faithful painting. His sentences drone on; his definitions follow one another with the coldness and precision of commandments. 'Principles should be moderate, laws implacable.' It is the style of the guillotine.

Such pertinacity in logic, however, implies a profound passion. Here, as elsewhere, we again find the passion for unity. Every rebellion implies some kind of unity. The rebellion of 1789 demands the unity of the whole country. Saint-Just dreams of an ideal city where manners and customs, in final agreement with the law, will proclaim the innocence of man and the identity of his nature with reason. And if factions arise to interrupt this dream, passion will exaggerate its logic. No one will dare to imagine that, since factions exist, the principles are conceivably wrong. Factions will be condemned as criminal because principles remain inviolable. 'It is time that everyone returned to morality and the aristocracy to the Terror.' But the aristocratic factions are not the only ones to be reckoned with, there are the republicans, too, and anyone else who criticizes the actions of the Legislature and of the Convention. They, too, are guilty since they threaten unity. Saint-Just, then, proclaims the major principle of twentieth-century tyrannies. 'A patriot is he who supports the republic in general; whoever opposes it in detail is a traitor.' Whoever criticizes it is a traitor, whoever fails to give open support is a suspect. When neither reason, nor the free expression of individual opinion, succeeds in systematically establishing unity, it must be decided to suppress all alien elements. Thus the guillotine becomes a logician whose function is refutation. 'A rogue who has been condemned to death by the tribunal says he wants to resist oppression simply because he wants to resist the scaffold!' Saint-Just's indignation is hard to understand in that, until his time, the scaffold was precisely nothing else but one of the most obvious symbols of oppression. But at the heart of this logical delirium, at the logical conclusion of this morality of virtue, the scaffold represents freedom. It assures rational unity and that harmony will reign in the ideal city. It purifies (the word is apt) the republic, and eliminates malpractices which arise to contradict the general will and universal reason. 'They question my right to the title of philanthropist,' Marat exclaims; in quite a different style, 'Ah! What injustice!' 'Who cannot see that I want to cut off a few heads to save a great number?' A few – a faction? Naturally – and all historic actions are performed at this price. But Marat, making his final calculations, claimed two hundred and sixty-three thousand heads. But he compromised the therapeutic aspect of the operation by screaming during the massacre: 'Brand them with hot irons, cut off their thumbs, tear out their tongues.' This philanthropist wrote day and night, in the most monotonous vocabulary imaginable, of the necessity of killing in order to create. He wrote again, by candlelight deep down in his cellar, during the September nights while his henchmen were installing spectators' benches in prison courtyards – men on the right, women on the left – to display as a gracious example of philanthropy, the spectacle of the aristocracy having their heads cut off.

Do not let us confuse, even for a moment, the imposing figure of Saint-Just with the sad spectacle of Marat – Rousseau's monkey as Michelet rightly calls him. But the drama of Saint-Just lies in having at moments joined forces, for superior and much deeper reasons, with Marat. Factions join with factions and minorities with minorities, and in the end he is not even sure that the scaffold functions in the service of the will of all. But at least Saint-Just will affirm, to the bitter end, that it functions in the service of the general will, since it functions in the service of virtue. 'A revolution such as ours is not a trail, but a clap of thunder for the wicked.' God strikes like a thunderbolt, innocence is a flash of lightning – a flash of lightning which brings justice. Even the pleasure-seekers, in fact they above all, are counter-revolutionaries. Saint-Just, who said that the idea of happiness was new to Europe (actually it was mainly new for Saint-Just for whom history stopped at Brutus), remarks that some people have an 'appalling idea of what happiness is and confuse it with pleasure'. They, too, must be taught a lesson. Finally, it is no longer a question of majority or minority. Paradise, lost and always coveted by universal innocence, disappears into the distance; on the unhappy earth, racked with the cries of civil and national wars. Saint-Just decrees, against his nature and against his principles, that when the whole country suffers then all are guilty. The series of reports on the factions abroad, the law of the 22 Prairial, the speech of 15 April 1794, on the necessity of the police, mark the stages of this conversation. The man who with such nobility held that it was infamous to lay down one's arms while there remained, somewhere in the world, one master and one slave, is the same man who had to agree to suspend the Constitution of 1793 and to adopt arbitrary rule. In the speech that he made to defend Robespierre, he rejects fame and posterity and only refers himself to an abstract providence. At the same time, he recognized that virtue, of which he made a religion, has no other reward but history and the present, and that it must, at all costs, lay the foundations of its own reign. He did not like power which he called 'cruel and wicked' and which, he said, 'advanced towards repression, without any guiding principle'. But the guiding principle was virtue and was derived from the people. When the people failed, the guiding principle became obscured and oppression increased. Therefore, it was the people who were guilty and not power which must remain, in principle, innocent. Such an extreme and outrageous contradiction could only be resolved by an even more extreme logic and by the final acceptance of principles in silence and in death. Saint-Just at least remained equal to this demand, and in this way was at last to find his greatness and that independent life in time and space of which he spoke with such emotion.

For a long time he had, in fact, had a presentiment that the demands he made implied a total and unreserved sacrifice on his part and had said himself that those who make revolutions in this world – 'Those who do good' – can only sleep in the tomb. Convinced that his principles, in order to triumph, must culminate in the virtue and happiness of his people, aware, perhaps, that he was asking the impossible, he cut off his own retreat in advance by declaring that he would stab himself in public on the day when he despaired of the people. Nevertheless, he despairs, since he has doubts about the Terror. 'The revolution is frozen, every principle has been attenuated; all that remains are red caps worn by intriguers. The exercise of terror has blunted crime as strong drink blunts the palate.' Even virtue 'unites with crime in times of anarchy'. He said that all crime sprang from tyranny which was the greatest crime of all, and yet, confronted with the unflagging obstinacy of crime, the Revolution itself resorted to tyranny and became criminal. Thus crime cannot be obliterated, nor can factions, nor the despicable desire for enjoyment; the people must be despaired of and subjugated. But nor is it possible to govern innocently. Thus, evil must either be suffered or served, principles must be declared capable of error or the people and mankind must be recognized as guilty. Then Saint-Just averts his mysterious and handsome face: 'It would be leaving very little to leave a life in which one must either be the accomplice or the silent witness of evil.' Brutus, who must kill himself if he does not kill others, begins by killing others. But the others are too many; they cannot all be killed.

In that case he must die and demonstrate, yet again, that rebellion, when it gets out of hand, swings from the annihilation of others to the destruction of the self. This task, at any rate, is easy; it suffices to follow logic, once more, to the bitter end. In his speech in defence of Robespierre, shortly before his death, Saint-Just reaffirms the guiding principle of his actions which is the very same principle that leads to his condemnation: 'I belong to no faction, I shall fight against them all.' He accepted then, and in advance, the decision of the general will – in other words, of the Assembly. He agreed to go to his death for love of principle and despite all the realities of the situation, since the opinion of the Assembly could only really be swayed by the eloquence and fanaticism of a faction. But that is beside the point! When principles fail, men have only one way to save them and to preserve their faith, which is to die for them. In the stifling heat of Paris in July, Saint-Just, ostensibly rejecting reality and the world, confesses that he stakes his life on the decision of principles. When this had been said, he seems to have a fleeting perception of another truth, and ends with a restrained denunciation of his colleagues, Billaud-Varennes and Collot d'Herbois. 'I want them to justify themselves and I want us to become wiser.' The style and the guillotine are here suspended for a moment. But virtue, in that it has too much pride, is not wisdom. The guillotine is going to fall again on that head as cold and beautiful as morality itself. From the moment that the Assembly condemns him, until the moment when he stretches his neck to the knife, Saint-Just keeps silent. This long silence is more important than his death. He complained that silence reigned around thrones and that is why he wanted to speak so much and so well. But in the end, contemptuous of the tyranny and the enigma of a people who do not conform to pure reason, he resorts to silence himself. His principles cannot accept the condition of things; and things not being what they should be his principles are therefore fixed, silent, and alone. To abandon oneself to principles is really to die – and to die for an impossible love which is the contrary of love. Saint-Just dies, and with him all hope of a new religion.

'All the stones are cut to build the structure of freedom,' said

Saint-Just; 'you can build a palace or a tomb of the same stones.' The very principles of *The Social Contract* presided at the elevation of the tomb which Napoleon Bonaparte came to seal. Rousseau, who was not wanting in common sense, understood very well that the society envisioned by *The Social Contract* was only suitable for gods. His successors took him at his word and tried to establish the divinity of man. The red flag – a symbol of martial law and therefore of the executive under the *ancien régime* – became the revolutionary symbol on 10 August 1792. A significant transfer about which Jaurès comments as follows: 'It is we the people who are the law. . . . We are not rebels. The rebels are in the Tuileries.' But it is not so easy as that to become God. Even the gods of the ancients did not die at the first blow and the revolutions of the nineteenth century were intended to achieve the final liquidation of the principle of divinity. Paris rose to place the king once more under the rule of the people and to prevent him from restoring an authority of principle. The corpse which the rebels of 1830 dragged through the rooms of the Tuileries and installed on the throne in order to pay it derisory homage has no other significance. The king could still be, at that period, a respected minister, but his authority is now derived from the people and his guiding principle is the Charter. He is no longer Majesty. Now that the *ancien régime* had definitely disappeared in France, the new régime must again, after 1848, reaffirm itself and the history of the nineteenth century up to 1914 is the history of the restoration of popular sovereignties against *ancien régime* monarchies; in other words, the history of the principle of nations. This principle finally triumphs in 1919 which witnesses the disappearance of all Absolutist monarchies in Europe.* Everywhere, the sovereignty of the nation is substituted, in law and in fact, for the sovereign king. Only then can the consequences of the principles of 1789 be seen. We survivors are the first to be able to judge them clearly.

* With the exception of the Spanish monarchy. But the German Empire collapsed, of which Wilhelm II said that it was 'the proof that we Hohenzollerns derive our crown from heaven alone and that it is to heaven alone that we must give an accounting'.

The Jacobins reinforced the eternal moral principles to the extent to which they supressed the things which, up to then, had supported these principles. As preachers of a gospel, they wanted to base fraternity on the abstract law of the Romans. They substituted the law for divine commandments on the supposition that it must be recognized by all because it was the expression of the general will. The law found its justification in natural virtue and then proceeded to justify natural virtue. But immediately a single faction manifests itself, this reasoning collapses and we perceive that virtue has need of justification in order not to be abstract. In the same way, the bourgeois jurists of the eighteenth century, by burying under the weight of their principles the just and vital conquests of their people, prepared the way for the two contemporary forms of nihilism: individual nihilism and State nihilism.

Law can reign, in fact, in so far as it is the law of universal reason.* But it never is and it loses its justification if man is not naturally good. A day comes when ideology conflicts with psychology. Then there is no more legitimate power. Thus the law evolves to the point of becoming confused with the legislator and with a new form of absolutism. Where to turn then? The law has gone completely off its course; and, losing its precision, it becomes more and more inaccurate to the point of making everything a crime. The law always reigns supreme, but it no longer has any fixed limits. Saint-Just had foreseen that this form of tyranny might be exercised in the name of a silent people. 'Ingenious crime will be exalted into a kind of religion and criminals will be in the sacred hierarchy.' But this is inevitable. If major principles have no foundation, if the law expresses nothing but a provisional inclination, it is only made in order to be broken or to be imposed. Sade or dictatorship, individual terrorism or State terrorism, both justified by the same absence of justification, are, from the moment that rebellion cuts itself off from its roots and abstains from any concrete morality, one of the alternatives of the twentieth century.

* Hegel saw clearly that the philosophy of enlightenment wanted to deliver man from the irrational. Reason reunites mankind while the irrational destroys unity.

The revolutionary movement which was born in 1789 could not, however, stop there. God, for the Jacobins, is not completely dead, any more than He was dead for the romantics. They still preserve the Supreme Being. Reason, in a certain way, is still a mediator. It implies a pre-existent order. But God is at least dematerialized and reduced to the theoretical existence of a moral principle. The bourgeoisie succeeded in reigning only during the entire nineteenth century by referring itself to abstract principles. Less worthy than Saint-Just, it simply made use of this frame of reference as an alibi, while employing on all occasions the opposite values. By its essential corruption and disheartening hypocrisy, it helped finally to discredit the principles it proclaimed. Its culpability, in this regard, is infinite. From the moment that eternal principles are put in doubt simultaneously with formal virtue and when every value is discredited, reason will start to act without reference to anything but its own successes. It would like to rule, denying everything that exists and affirming what is to come. One day it will conquer. Russian Communism, by its violent criticism of every kind of formal virtue, puts the finishing touches to the revolutionary work of the nineteenth century by denying any superior principle. The regicides of the nineteenth century are succeeded by the deicides of the twentieth century, who want to make the earth a kingdom where man is God. The reign of history begins and, identifying himself only with his history, man, unfaithful to his real rebellion, will henceforth devote himself to the nihilistic revolution of the twentieth century which denies all forms of morality and desperately attempts to achieve the unity of the human race through an exhausting series of crimes and wars. The Jacobin Revolution which tried to institute the religion of virtue in order to achieve unity by doing so, will be followed by the cynical revolutions, which can be either of the right or of the left, which will try to achieve the unity of the world so as to found, at last, the religion of man. All that was God's will henceforth be rendered to Caesar.

The Deicides

JUSTICE, reason, truth still shone in the Jacobin heaven; performing the function of fixed stars which could, at least, serve as guides. German nineteenth-century thinkers, particularly Hegel, wanted to continue the work of the French Revolution while suppressing the causes of its failure. Hegel thought that he discerned the seeds of the Terror contained in the abstract principles of the Jacobins. According to him, absolute and abstract freedom must inevitably lead to terrorism; the rule of abstract law is identical to the rule of oppression. For example, Hegel remarks that the period between the time of Augustus and Alexander Serverus (A.D. 235) is the period of the greatest legal proficiency but also the period of the most ruthless tyranny. To avoid this contradiction, it was therefore necessary to wish to construct a concrete society, invigorated by a principle that was not formal, in which freedom could be reconciled with necessity. German philosophy therefore finished by substituting, for the universal but abstract reason of Saint-Just and Rousseau, a less artificial but more ambiguous idea: concrete universal reason. Up to this point, reason had soared above the phenomena which were related to it. Now reason is, henceforth, incorporated in the stream of historic events, which it explains while they give it substance.

It can certainly be said that Hegel rationalized to the point of being irrational. But, at the same time, he gave reason an unreasonable shock by endowing it with a lack of moderation, the results of which are now before our eyes. Into the fixed ideas of its period, German thought suddenly introduced an irresistible urge to movement. Truth, reason, and justice were brusquely incarnated in the future of the world. But by committing them to perpetual acceleration, German ideology confused their existence with their movements and fixed the conclusion of their existence at the conclusion of the historic future – if there was to be one. These values have ceased to be guides in order to become goals. As for the means of attaining these goals, in other words life and history, no pre-existent value can point the way. On the contrary, a large part of Hegelian demonstration is devoted to proving that moral conscience by being so banal as to obey justice and truth, as though these values existed independently of the world, jeopardizes, precisely for this reason, the advent of these values. The rule of action has thus become action itself – which must be performed in darkness while awaiting the final illumination. Reason, annexed by this form of romanticism, is nothing more than an inflexible passion.

The ends have remained the same, only ambition has increased; thought has become dynamic, reason has embraced the future and aspired to conquest. Action is no more than a calculation based on results, not on principles. From this moment dates the idea (hostile to every concept of ancient thought which, nevertheless, reappeared to a certain extent in the spirit of revolutionary France) that man has not been endowed with a definitive human nature, that he is not a finished creation but an experiment of which he can be partly the creator. With Napoleon and the Napoleonic philosopher Hegel, the period of efficaciousness begins. Before Napoleon, men had discovered space and the universe, with Napoleon they discovered time and the future in terms of this world: and by this discovery the spirit of rebellion is going to be profoundly transformed.

In any case, it is strange to find Hegel's philosophy at this new stage in the development of the spirit of rebellion. Actually, in one sense, his work exudes an absolute horror of dissidence: he wanted to be the very essence of reconciliation. But this is only one aspect of a system which, by its very method, is the most ambiguous in all philosophic literature. To the extent that, for him, what is real is rational, he justifies every ideological encroachment upon reality. What has been called Hegel's panlogic is a justification of the condition of fact. But his philosophy also exalts destruction for its own sake. Everything is reconciled, of course, in the dialectic, and one extreme cannot be stated without the other arising; there exists in Hegel, as in all great thinkers, the material for contradicting Hegel.

But philosophers are rarely read with the head alone, but often with the heart and all its passions which can accept no kind of reconciliation.

Nevertheless, the revolutionaries of the nineteenth century have borrowed from Hegel the weapons with which they definitively destroyed the formal principles of virtue. All that they have preserved is the vision of a history without any kind of transcendence dedicated to perpetual strife and to the struggle of wills bent on seizing power. In its critical aspect, the revolutionary movement of our times is, primarily, a violent denunciation of the formal hypocrisy which presides over bourgeois society. The partially justified pretension of modern Communism, like the more frivolous claim of Fascism, is to denounce the mystification which undermines the principles and virtues of the bourgeois type of democracy. Divine transcendence, up to 1789, served to justify the arbitrary actions of the king. After the French Revolution, the transcendence of the formal principles of reason or justice serve to justify a rule which is neither just nor reasonable. This transcendence is therefore a mask that must be torn off. God is dead, but as Stirner predicted, the morality of principles in which the memory of God is still preserved must also be killed. The hatred of formal virtue – degraded witness to divinity and false witness in the service of injustice – has remained one of the principal themes of history today. Nothing is pure: that is the cry which rends the air of our times. Impurity, the equivalent of history, is going to become the rule, and the abandoned earth will be delivered to naked force which will decide whether or not man is divine. Thus lies and violence are adopted in the same spirit in which a religion is adopted and on the same heartrending impulse.

But the first fundamental criticism of the good conscience – the denunciation of the beautiful soul and of ineffective attitudes – we owe to Hegel for whom the ideology of the good, the true, and the beautiful is the religion of those possessed of none of them. While the mere existence of factions surprises Saint-Just and contravenes the ideal order that he affirms, Hegel not only is not surprised, but even affirms that faction is the prelude to thought. For the Jacobin, everyone is virtuous. The movement which starts with Hegel and which is triumphant today, presumes, on the contrary, that no one is virtuous but that everyone will be. At the beginning, everything, according to Saint-Just, is an idyll, while, according to Hegel, it is a tragedy. But in the end that amounts to the same thing. Those who destroy the idyll must be destroyed or destruction must be embarked on in order to create the idyll. Violence, in both cases, is the victor. The avoidance of the Terror, undertaken by Hegel, only leads to an extension of the Terror.

That is not all. Apparently the world today can no longer be anything other than a world of masters and slaves because contemporary ideologies, those that are changing the face of the earth, have learned from Hegel to conceive of history as the product of and mastery of slavery. If, on the first morning of the world, under the empty sky, there is only a master and a slave; even if there is only the bond of master and slave between a transcendent god and mankind, then there can be no other law in this world but the law of force. Only a god, or a principle above the master and the slave, could intervene and make men's history more than a simple chronicle of victories and defeats. First Hegel and then the Hegelians have tried, on the contrary, to destroy, more and more thoroughly, all idea of transcendence and any nostalgia for transcendence. Although there was infinitely more in Hegel than in the left-wing Hegelians who, finally, triumphed over him, he nevertheless furnished, on the level of the dialectic of master and slave, the decisive justification of the spirit of power in the twentieth century. The conqueror is always right; that is one of the lessons that can be learned from the most important German philosophical system of the nineteenth century. Of course, there is to be found in the prodigious Hegelian structure a means of partially contradicting these ideas. But twentieth-century ideology is not connected with what is improperly called the idealism of the master of Jena. Hegel's face, which reappears in Russian Communism, has been successively remodelled by David Strauss, Bruno Bauer, Feuerbach, Marx, and the entire Hegelian left-wing. We are only interested in him here, in that he alone has any real bearing on the history of our time. If Nietzsche and Hegel serve as alibis to the masters of Dachau and Karaganda that does not condemn their entire philosophy. But it does lead to the suspicion that one aspect of their thought, or of their logic, can lead to these appalling conclusions.

Nietzschean nihilism is methodical. *The Phenomenology of the Mind* also has a didactic aspect. At the meeting-point of two centuries, it depicts, in its successive stages, the education of the mind as it pursues its way towards absolute truth. It can be compared on the metaphysical level with Rousseau's *Émile*. Each stage is an error and is, moreover, accompanied by historic sanctions which are almost always fatal, either to the mind or to the civilization in which it is reflected. Hegel proposes to demonstrate the necessity of these painful stages. *The Phenomenology* is, in one aspect, a meditation on despair and death. The mission of despair is, simply, to be methodical in that it must be transfigured, at the end of history, into absolute satisfaction and absolute wisdom. The book has the defect, however, of only imagining highly intelligent pupils and it has been taken literally, while literally, it only wanted to proclaim the spirit. It is the same with the celebrated analysis of mastery and slavery.

Animals, according to Hegel, have an immediate knowledge of the exterior world, a perception of the self, but not the knowledge of self which distinguishes man. The latter is only really born at the moment when he becomes aware of himself as a rational being. Therefore his essential characteristic is self-consciousness. Consciousness of self, to be affirmed, must distinguish itself from what it is not. Man is a creature who, to affirm his existence and his difference, denies. What distinguishes consciousness of self from the world of nature is not the simple act of contemplation by which it identifies itself with the exterior world and finds oblivion, but the desire it can feel with regard to the world. This desire re-establishes its identity, when it demonstrates that the exterior world is something apart. In its desire, the exterior world consists of what it does not possess, but which nevertheless exists, and of what it would like to exist but which no longer does. Consciousness of self is therefore, of necessity, desire. But in order to exist it must be satisfied, and it can only be satisfied by the gratification of its desire. It therefore acts in order to gratify itself and, in so doing, it denies and suppresses its means of gratification. It is the epitome of negation. To act is to destroy in order to give birth to the spiritual reality of consciousness. But to destroy an object unconsciously, as meat is destroyed, for example, in the act of eating, is a purely animal activity. To consume is not yet to be conscious. Desire for consciousness must be directed towards something other than unconscious nature. The only thing in the world that is distinct from nature is, precisely, self-consciousness. Therefore desire must be centred upon another form of desire, self-consciousness must be gratified by another form of self-consciousness. In simple words, man is not recognized – and does not recognize himself – as a man as long as he limits himself to subsisting like an animal. He must be acknowledged by other men. All consciousness is, basically, the desire to be recognized and proclaimed as such by other consciousnesses. It is others who beget us. Only in association do we receive a human value, as distinct from an animal value.

In that the supreme value, for the animal, is the preservation of life, consciousness should raise itself above the level of that instinct in order to achieve human value. It should be capable of risking its life. To be recognized by another consciousness, man should be ready to risk his life and to accept the chance of death. Fundamental human relations are thus relations of pure prestige, a perpetual struggle, to the death, for recognition of one human being by another.

At the first stage of his dialectic, Hegel affirms that in so far as death is the common ground of man and animal, it is by accepting death and even by inviting it that the former differentiates himself from the latter. At the heart of this primordial struggle for recognition, man is thus identified with violent death. The mystic slogan 'Die and become what you are' is taken up once more by Hegel. But 'become what you are' gives place to 'become what you so far are not'. This primitive and passionate desire for recognition, which is confused with the will to exist, can only be satisfied by a recognition gradually extended until it embraces everyone. In that everyone wants equally much to be recognized by everyone, the fight for life will only cease with the recognition of all by all which will mark the termination of history. The existence which Hegelian consciousness seeks to obtain is born in the hard-won glory of collective approval. It is not beside the point to note that, in the thought inspired by our revolutions, the supreme good does not, in reality, coincide with existence but with an arbitrary facsimile. The entire history of mankind is, in any case, nothing but a prolonged fight to the death for the conquest of universal prestige and absolute power. It is, in its essence, imperialist. We are far from the gentle savage of the eighteenth century and from the *Social Contract*. In the sound and fury of the passing centuries, each separate consciousness, to ensure its own existence, must henceforth desire the death of others. In its excesses, this relentless tragedy is absurd, since, in the event of one consciousness being destroyed, the victorious conscience is not recognized as such in that it cannot be victorious in the eyes of something that no longer exists. In fact, it is here that the philosophy of appearances reaches its limits.

No human reality would therefore have been engendered if, through a natural characteristic which can be considered fortunate for Hegel's system, there had not existed, from the beginning of time, two kinds of consciousness, one of which has not the courage to renounce life and which is therefore willing to recognize the other kind of consciousness without being recognized itself in return. It consents, in short, to being considered as an object. This type of consciousness which, to preserve its animal existence, renounces independent life, is the consciousness of a slave. The type of consciousness which by being recognized achieves independence is that of the master. They are distinguished one from the other at the moment when they clash and when one submits to the other. The dilemma at this stage is not to be free or to die, but to kill or conquer. This dilemma will resound throughout the course of history.

Undoubtedly the master enjoys total freedom first as regards the slave, since the latter recognizes him totally, and then as regards the natural world, since by his work the slave transforms it into objects of enjoyment which the master consumes in a perpetual affirmation of his own identity. However, this autonomy is not absolute. The master, to his detriment, is recognized in his autonomy by a consciousness which he himself does not recognize as autonomous. Therefore he cannot be satisfied and his autonomy is only negative. Mastery is a blind alley. Since, moreover, he cannot renounce mastery and become a slave again, the eternal destiny of masters is to live unsatisfied or to be killed. The master serves no other purpose in history but to arouse servile consciousness, the only form of consciousness that really makes history. The slave, in fact, is not bound to his condition, but wants to change it. Thus, unlike his master, he can improve himself, and what is called history is nothing but the effects of his long efforts to obtain real freedom. Already, by work, by his transformation of the natural world into a technical world, he manages to escape from the nature which was the basis of his slavery in that he did not know how to raise himself above it by accepting death.* The very agony of death experienced in the humiliation of the entire being lifts the slave to the level of human totality. He knows, henceforth, that this totality exists; now it only remains for him to realize it through a long series of struggles against nature and against the masters. History identifies itself, therefore, with the history of endeavour and rebellion. It is hardly astonishing that Marxism-Leninism derived, from this dialectic, the contemporary ideal of the soldier-worker.

We shall leave aside the description of the various attitudes of the servile consciousness (stoicism, scepticism, guilty conscience) which then follows in *The Phenomenology*. But thanks to its consequences another aspect of this dialectic cannot be neglected, namely, the assimilation of the master-slave relationship between man and god. One of Hegel's commentators† remarks that if the master really existed, he would be God. In his description of guilty conscience, he

---

* Actually, the ambiguity is profound, for the nature in question is not the same. Does the advent of the technical world suppress death or the fear of death in the natural world? That is the real question which Hegel leaves in suspense.

† Jean Hyppolite.

shows how the Christian slave, wishing to deny the existence of his oppressor, takes refuge in the world beyond and by doing so gives himself a new master in the person of God. Elsewhere Hegel identifies the supreme master with absolute death. And so the struggle begins again, on a higher level, between man in chains and the cruel god of Abraham. The resolution of this new conflict between the universal god and the human entity will be furnished by Christ who reconciles in Himself the universal and the unique. But, in one sense, Christ is a part of the palpable world. He is visible, He lived, and He died. He is therefore only a stop on the road to the universal: He too must be denied dialectically. It is only necessary to recognize Him as the man-God to obtain a higher synthesis. Skipping the intermediary stages, it suffices to say that this synthesis, after being incarnated in the Church and in reason, culminates in the absolute State, founded by the soldier-workers, where the spirit of the world will be finally self-reflected in the mutual recognition of each by all and in the universal reconciliation of everything that has ever existed under the sun. At this moment, 'when the eyes of the spirit coincide with the eyes of the body', each individual consciousness will be nothing more than a mirror reflecting another mirror, itself reflected to infinity in infinitely recurring images. The City of God will coincide with the City of Humanity; and universal history, sitting in judgement on the world, will pass its sentence by which good and evil will be justified, the State will play the part of Destiny and will proclaim its approval of every aspect of reality on 'the sacred day of the Presence'.

This sums up the essential ideas which in spite, or because, of the extreme ambiguity of their interpretation, have literally driven the revolutionary mind in apparently contradictory directions and which we are now learning to recognize in the ideology of our times. Amorality, scientific materialism, and atheism have definitely replaced the anti-theism of the rebels of former times and have made common cause, under Hegel's paradoxical influence, with a revolutionary movement which, until his time, was never really separated from its moral, evangelical, and idealistic origins. These tendencies, if they are sometimes very far from really originating with Hegel, found their source in the ambiguity of his thought and in his critique of the doctrine of transcendence. Hegel's undeniable originality lies in his definitive destruction of all vertical transcendence – particularly the transcendence of principles. There is no doubt that he restores the immanence of the spirit to the evolution of the world. But this immanence is not precisely defined and has nothing in common with the pantheism of the ancients. The spirit is and is not part of the world; it creates itself and will finally prevail. Thus the emphasis is placed on the end of history. Until then there is no suitable criterion on which to base a judgement of value. One must act and live in terms of the future. All morality becomes provisional. The nineteenth and twentieth centuries, in their most profound manifestations, are centuries which have tried to live without transcendence.

One of Hegel's commentators,* of left-wing tendencies it is true, but orthodox in his opinion on this particular point, notes Hegel's hostility to the moralists and remarks that his only axiom is to live according to the manners and customs of one's nation. A maxim of social conformity of which Hegel, in fact, gave the most cynical proofs. Kojève adds, however, that this conformity is only legitimate to the extent that the customs of the nation correspond to the spirit of the times, in other words to the extent that they are solidly established and can resist revolutionary criticism and attacks. But who will determine their solidity and who will judge their validity? For a hundred years, the capitalist régimes of the West have withstood violent assaults. Should they for that reason be considered legitimate? Inversely, should those who were faithful to the Weimar Republic have abandoned it and pledged themselves to Hitler, in 1933, because the former collapsed when attacked by the latter? Should the Spanish Republic have been betrayed at the exact moment when General Franco's forces triumphed? These are conclusions which traditional reactionary thought would have justified within its own perspectives. The novelty, of which the consequences are incalculable, lies in the

* Alexandre Kojève.

fact that revolutionary thought has assimilated them. The suppression of every moral value and of all principles and their replacement by fact, as provisional but actual king, could only lead, as we have plainly seen, to political cynicism, whether it be fact as envisioned by the individual, or more serious still, fact as envisioned by the State. The political movements, or ideologies, inspired by Hegel, are all united in the ostensible abandonment of virtue.

Hegel could not, in fact, prevent those who had read him, with feelings of anguish which were far from methodical and when Europe was already the victim of great injustice, from finding themselves precipitated into a world without innocence and without principles – into the very world of which Hegel says that it is in itself a sin, since it is separated from the spirit. Hegel, of course, permits the forgiveness of sins at the end of history. However, until then, every human activity is sinful. 'Therefore only the absence of activity is innocent, the existence of a stone and not even the existence of a child.' Thus even the innocence of stones is unknown to us. Without innocence there is no panel of reference and no reason. Without reason, there is nothing but naked force, the master and slave waiting for reason one day to prevail. Between master and slave, even suffering is solitary, joy is without foundation, and both are undeserved. Then how can one live, how endure life when friendship is reserved for the end of time? The only escape is to create order with the use of weapons. 'Kill or enslave!' ... those who read Hegel with this single and terrible purpose only really considered the first part of the dilemma. From it they have derived a philosophy of scorn and despair and have deemed themselves slaves and nothing but slaves, bound by death to the absolute Master and by the whip to their terrestrial masters. This philosophy of the guilty conscience has merely taught them that every slave is enslaved only by his own consent, and can only be liberated by an act of protest which coincides with death. Answering the challenge, the most courageous have completely identified themselves with this act of protest and have dedicated themselves to death. After all, to say that negation is in itself a positive act justified in advance every kind of negation and predicted the cry of Bakunin and Nechayev: 'Our mission is to destroy, not to construct.' A nihilist for Hegel was only a sceptic who had no other escape but contradiction or philosophic suicide. But he himself gave birth to another type of nihilist who, making boredom into a principle of action, identified suicide with philosophic murder.* It was at this point that the terrorists were born who decided that it was necessary to kill and die in order to exist, because mankind and history could only be created by sacrifice and murder. The magnificent idea that all idealism is chimerical, if it is not paid for by risking one's life, was to be developed to the fullest possible extent by young men who were not engaged in expounding the concept from the safe distance of a university chair before dying in their beds, but among the tumult of falling bombs and even on the gallows. By doing this and even by their errors they corrected their masters and demonstrated, contrary to his teaching, that one kind of aristocracy, at least, is superior to the hideous aristocracy of success exalted by Hegel: the aristocracy of sacrifice.

Another sort of follower, who read Hegel more seriously, chose the second term of the dilemma and made the pronouncement that the slave could only free himself by enslaving in his turn. Post-Hegelian doctrines, unmindful of the mystic aspect of certain of the master's tendencies, have led his followers to absolute atheism and to scientific materialism. But this evolution is inconceivable without the absolute disappearance of every transcendent principle of explanation, and without the complete destruction of the Jacobin ideal. Immanence, of course, is not atheism. But immanence in the process of development is, if one can say so, provisional atheism.† The indefinite face of God which, with Hegel, is still reflected in the mind of the world will not be difficult to efface. Hegel's successors will draw decisive con-

---

* This form of nihilism, despite appearances, is still nihilism in the Nietzschean sense, to the extent that it is a calumny of the present life to the advantage of a historic future in which one tries to believe.

† In any event, the criticism of Kierkegaard is valid. To base divinity on history is, paradoxically, to base an absolute value on approximate knowledge Something 'eternally historic' is a contradiction in terms.

clusions from his ambiguous formula: 'God without man is no more than man without God.' David Strauss in his *Life of Jesus* isolates the theory of Christ considered as the God-man. Bruno Bauer (*The Critique of Evangelist History*) institutes a materialist Christianity by insisting on the humanity of Jesus. Finally Feuerbach (whom Marx considered as a great mind and of whom he acknowledges himself the critical disciple), in his *Essence of Christianity*, replaces all theology by a religion of man and the species, which has converted a large part of contemporary thought. His task is to demonstrate that the distinction between human and divine is illusory, that it is nothing but the distinction between the essence of humanity – in other words, human nature – and the individual. 'The mystery of God is only the mystery of the love of man for himself.' The accents of a strange new prophecy ring out: 'Individuality has replaced faith, reason the Bible, politics, religion, and the State, the earth heaven, work prayer, poverty, hell, and man has replaced Christ.' Thus there is only one hell and it is on this earth: and it is against this that the struggle must be waged. Politics is religion, and transcendent Christianity – that of the hereafter – establishes the masters of the earth by means of the slave's renunciation and creates one master more beneath the heavens. That is why atheism and the revolutionary spirit are only two aspects of the same movement of liberation. That is the answer to the question which is always being asked: why has the revolutionary movement identified itself with materialism rather than with idealism? Because to conquer God, to make Him a slave, amounts to abolishing the transcendence which kept the former masters in power and to preparing, with the ascension of the new tyrants, the advent of the man-king. When poverty is abolished, when historic contradictions are resolved, 'the real god, the human god, will be the State'. Then *homo homini lupus* becomes *homo homini deus*. This concept is at the root of the contemporary world. With Feuerbach, we assist at the birth of a terrible form of optimism which we can still observe at work today and which seems to be the very antithesis of nihilist despair. But that is only in appearance. We must know Feuerbach's final conclusions in the *Theogony* to perceive the profoundly nihilist derivation of his inflamed imagination. In effect, Feuerbach affirms, in the face of Hegel, that man is only what he eats, and recapitulates his ideas and predicts the future in the following phrase: 'The true philosophy is the negation of philosophy. No religion is my religion. No philosophy is my philosophy.'

Cynicism, the deification of history and of matter, individual terror and State crime, these are the inordinate consequences which will now spring, armed to the teeth, from the equivocal conception of a world which entrusts to history alone the task of producing both values and truth. If nothing can be clearly understood before truth has been brought to light, at the end of time, then every action is arbitrary and force will finally rule supreme. 'If reality is inconceivable,' Hegel exclaims, 'then we must contrive inconceivable concepts.' A concept that cannot be conceived must, perforce, like error, be contrived. But to be accepted it cannot rely on the persuasion innate in order and truth, but must finally be imposed. Hegel's attitude consists of saying: 'this is truth which however appears to us to be error, but which is true, precisely because it happens to be error. As for proof, it is not I, but history, at its conclusions, which will furnish it.' Such pretensions can only entail two attitudes: either the suspension of all affirmation until the production of proof, or the affirmation of everything, in history, which seems dedicated to success – force in particular – which, in either case, is a form of nihilism. Moreover, it is impossible to understand twentieth-century revolutionary thought if we overlook the fact that unfortunately it derived a large part of its inspiration from a philosophy of conformity and opportunism. True rebellion is not jeopardized on account of the distortion of these particular ideas.

Nevertheless, the source which authorized Hegel's claims is what renders them intellectually and forever suspect. He believed that history in 1807, with the advent of Napoleon and of himself, had come to an end and that affirmation was possible and nihilism conquered. *The Phenomenology*, the Bible which was to have prophesied only the past, put a limit on time. In 1807 all sins were forgiven, and time had stopped. But history has continued. Other sins, since then, have been hurled in the face of the world and have revived the scandal of the former crime which German philosophy had already forgiven forever. The deification of Hegel by himself, after the deification of Napoleon who could henceforth be innocent since he had succeeded in stabilizing history, only lasted seven years. Instead of total affirmation, nihilism once more covered the face of the earth. Philosophy, even servile philosophy, has its Waterloos.

But nothing can discourage the appetite for divinity in the heart of man. Others have come and are still to come who, forgetting Waterloo, still claim to terminate history. The divinity of man is still on the march, and will only be worthy of adoration at the end of time. This apocalypse must be promoted and despite the fact that there is no God, at least a Church must be built. After all, history, which has not yet come to an end, allows us a glimpse of a perspective that might even be that of the Hegelian system. When cholera carries off the philosopher of the battle of Jena at the height of his glory, everything is, in fact, prepared for what is to follow. The sky is empty, the earth delivered into the hands of power without principles. Those who have chosen to kill and those who have chosen slavery will sucessively occupy the front of the stage, in the name of a form of rebellion which has been diverted from the path of truth.

Individual Terrorism

PISAREV, the theoretician of Russian nihilism, declares that the greatest fanatics are children and adolescents. That is also true of nations. Russia, at this period, is an adolescent nation, which had been delivered with forceps, barely a century ago, by a Czar who was still ingenuous enough to cut off the heads of rebels himself. It is not astonishing that she should have pushed German ideology to extremes of sacrifice and destruction of which German professors had only been capable in their minds. Stendhal noticed an essential difference between Germans and other people in the fact that they are excited by meditation rather than soothed. That is true, but it is even more true of Russia. In that immature country, completely without philosophic tradition,* the youth enthusiastically embraced the concepts of German thought and incarnated the consequences in blood. A 'proletariat of undergraduates'† then took the lead in the great movement of human emancipation and in doing so gave it its most violent aspect. Until the end of the nineteenth century these undergraduates never numbered more than a few thousand. However, entirely on their own, and in defiance of the most compact absolutism of the time, they claimed and actually did contribute to the liberation of forty million mujiks. Almost all of them paid for this liberation by suicide, execution, prison, or madness. The entire history of Russian terrorism can be summed up in the struggle of a handful of intellectuals to abolish tyranny, against a background of a silent populace. Their attenuated victory was finally betrayed. But by their sacrifice and even by their most extreme negations they gave substance to a new standard of values or a new virtue which, even today, has not ceased to oppose tyranny and to give aid to the cause of true liberation.

The germanization of nineteenth-century Russia is not an

* Pisarev remarks that civilization, in its ideological aspects, has always been imported into Russia.

† Dostoyevsky.

isolated phenomenon. The influence of German ideology at that moment was preponderant, and we are well aware, for example that the nineteenth century in France, with Michelet and Quinet, is the century of German thought. But, in Russia, this ideology did not encounter an already established system, while in France it had to contend and compromise with libertarian socialism. In Russia, it was on conquered territory. The first Russian university, the University of Moscow, founded in 1750, is German. The slow colonization of Russia by German teachers, bureaucrats, and soldiers, which began under Peter the Great, was transformed at the instance of Nicholas I into systematic germanization. The intelligentsia developed a passion for Schelling simultaneously with their passion for French writers in the eighteen-thirties, for Hegel in the eighteen-forties, and, in the second half of the century, for German socialism derived from Hegel.* Russian youth then proceeds to pour into these abstract thoughts the inordinate violence of its passions and authentically experiences these already moribund ideas. The religion of man already formulated by its German pastors was still missing its apostles and martyrs. Russian Christians, led astray from their original vocation, played this role. For this reason they had to accept life without transcendence and without virtue.

THE RENUNCIATION OF VIRTUE

In the eighteen-twenties, among the first Russian revolutionaries, the Decembrists, virtue still existed. Jacobin idealism had not yet been uprooted from the hearts of these gentlemen. They even practised conscious virtue: 'Our fathers were sybarites, we are Catos,' said one of them, Peter Viasemsky. To this he only adds the opinion, which will still be found in Bakunin and the revolutionary socialists of 1905, that suffering regenerates. The Decembrists remind us of the French nobles who allied themselves with the third estate and renounced

* *Das Kapital* was translated in 1872.

their privileges. Patrician idealists deliberately chose to sacrifice themselves for the liberation of the people. Despite the fact that their leader, Pestel, was a political and social theorist, their abortive conspiracy had no fixed programme; it is not even sure that they ever believed in the possibility of success. 'Yes, we shall die,' one of them said on the eve of the insurrection, 'but it will be a fine death.' It was, in fact, a fine death. In December 1825 the rebels, arranged in formation, were mown down by cannon fire in the square in front of the Senate at St Petersburg. The survivors were deported, but not before five had been hanged, and so clumsily that it had to be done twice. It was easy to understand why these ostensibly inefficacious victims have been venerated, with feelings of exaltation and horror, by all of revolutionary Russia. They were exemplary, if not efficacious. They indicated, at the beginning of this chapter of revolutionary history, the ambitions and the greatness of what Hegel ironically called the beautiful soul in relation to which Russian revolutionary ideas were, nevertheless, to be defined.

In this atmosphere of exaltation, German thought came to combat French influence and impose its prestige on minds torn between their desire for vengeance and justice and the realization of their impotent isolation. It was first received, extolled, and commented upon as though it were revelation itself. The best minds were inflamed with a passion for philosophy. They even went so far as to put Hegel's *Logic* into verse. For the most part, Russian intellectuals at first inferred the justification of a form of social quietism. To be aware of the rationality of the world sufficed, the Spirit would realize itself, in any case, at the end of time. That is the first reaction of Stankevitch, Bakunin, and Bielinsky, for example. Then the Russian mind recoiled at this factual, if not intentional, complicity with absolutism and, immediately, jumped to the opposite extreme.

Nothing is more revealing, in this respect, than the evolution of Bielinsky, one of the most remarkable and most influential minds of the eighteen-thirties and forties. Beginning with a background of rather vague libertarian idealism, Bielinsky suddenly discovers Hegel. In his room, at midnight, under the shock of revelation, he bursts into tears like Pascal, and casts the latter off without further ado: 'Neither chance nor the absolute exist, I have made my adieux to the French.' At the same time he is still a conservative and a partisan of social quietism. He writes to that effect without a single hesitation and defends his position, as he perceives it, courageously. But this essentially kind-hearted man then sees himself allied with what is most detestable in this world – injustice. If everything is logical, then everything is justified. One must consent to the whip, to serfdom, to Siberia. To accept the world and its sufferings seemed to him, at one moment, the noble thing to do because he imagined that he would only have to bear his own sufferings and his own contradictions. But if it also implied consent to the sufferings of others, he suddenly discovered that he has not the heart to continue. He sets out again in the opposite direction. If one cannot accept the suffering of others, then something in the world cannot be justified and history, at one point at least, no longer coincides with reason. But reason must be altogether reasonable or it is not reason at all. Man's solitary protest, quieted for a moment by the idea that everything can be justified, bursts forth again in vehement terms. Bielinsky addresses Hegel himself: 'With all the esteem due to your philistine philosophy, I have the honour to inform you that even if I had the opportunity of climbing to the very top of the ladder of evolution, I should still ask you to account for all the victims of life and history. I do not want happiness, even gratuitous happiness, if my mind is not at rest concerning all my blood brothers.'

Bielinsky understood that what he wanted was not the absolute of reason but the fullness of life. He did not allow himself to identify it. He wants the immortality of the entire man, clothed in his living body, not the abstract immortality of the species become Spirit. He argues with equal passion against new adversaries, and draws, from this fierce inferior debate, conclusions which he owes to Hegel, but which he turns against him.

These are the conclusions of individualism in revolt. The individual cannot accept history as it is. He must destroy reality, not collaborate with it, in order to affirm his own existence. 'Negation is my god, as reality formerly was. My heroes are the destroyers of the past: Luther, Voltaire, the Encyclopedists, the Terrorists, Byron in *Cain*.' Thus we rediscover here, simultaneously, all the themes of metaphysical rebellion. Certainly, the French tradition of individualistic socialism always remained alive in Russia. Saint-Simon and Fourier who were read in the eighteen-thirties and Proudhon, who was imported in the forties, inspired the great concepts of Herzen, and, very much later, those of Pierre Lavrov. But this system which remained attached to ethical values finally succumbed, provisionally at any rate, during its great debate with cynical thought. On the other hand, Bielinsky rediscovers both with and against Hegel the same tendencies to social individualism, but under the aspect of negation, in the rejection of transcendental values. When he dies, in 1848, his thought will, moreover, be very close to that of Herzen. But, when he confronts Hegel, he defines, with precision, an attitude which will be adopted by the nihilists, and at least in part by the terrorists. Thus he furnishes a type of transition between the idealist aristocrats of 1825 and the 'nothing-ist' students of 1860.

THREE OF THE POSSESSED

When Herzen, in making his apology for the nihilist movement – only to the extent, it is true, that he sees in it a still greater emancipation from ready-made ideas – writes: 'The annihilation of the past is the procreation of the future', he is using the language of Bielinsky. Kotiarevsky, speaking of the so-called radicals of the period, defined them as apostles 'who thought that the past must be completely renounced and the human personality must be constructed to quite another plan'. The next step was the total rejection of history and the determination to construct the future, no longer with regard to the historic spirit, but so as to coincide with the man-king. But the man-king cannot raise himself to power unaided. He has need of others and therefore enters into a nihilist contradiction which Pisarev, Bakunin, and Nechayev will try to resolve while each slightly extends the area of destruction and negation, to the point where terrorism finally kills the contradiction itself, in a simultaneous act of sacrifice and murder.

The nihilism of the eighteen-sixties began, apparently, by the most radical negation imaginable: the rejection of any action which was not purely egotistic. We know that the very term nihilism was invented by Turgenev in his novel *Fathers and Sons*, whose hero, Bazarov, was an exact portrayal of this type of man. Pisarev, when he wrote a review of this book, proclaimed that the nihilists recognized Bazarov as their model ... 'we have nothing', said Bazarov, 'to boast about but the sterile knowledge of understanding, up to a certain point, the sterility of what exists.' – Is that, he was asked, what is called nihilism? 'Yes, that is what is called nihilism.' Pisarev praises Bazarov's attitude, which for the sake of clarity he defines thus: 'I am a stranger to the order of existing things, I have nothing to do with it.' Thus the only value resides in rational egoism.

In denying everything that is not satisfaction of the self, Pisarev declares war on philosophy, on art which he considers absurd, on erroneous ethics, on religion, and even on customs and on good manners. He constructs a theory of intellectual terrorism which makes one think of the present-day surrealists. Provocation is made into a doctrine, but on a level of which Raskolnikov provides the perfect example. At the height of this fine transport, Pisarev asks himself, without even laughing, whether he is justified in killing his own mother and answers: 'And why not, if I want to do so, and if I find it useful?'

From that point on, it is surprising not to find the nihilists engaged in making a fortune or acquiring a title or in cynically taking advantage of every opportunity that offers itself. It is true that there were nihilists to be found in advantageous positions on all levels of good society. But they did not construct a theory from their cynicism and preferred on all occasions to pay visible and quite inconsequential homage to virtue. As for those we are discussing, they contradicted themselves by the defiance they hurled in the face of society which, in itself, was the affirmation of a value. They called themselves materialists; their bedside book was Buchner's *Force and Matter*. But one of them confessed: 'Every one of us was ready to go to the scaffold and to give his head for Moleschott and Darwin', thus putting doctrine well ahead of matter. Doctrine, taken seriously to this degree, has an air of religion and fanaticism. For Pisarev, Lamarck was a traitor because Darwin was right. Whoever in this intellectual sphere began talking about the immortality of the soul was immediately excommunicated. Vladimir Veidle is therefore right when he defined nihilism as rationalist obscurantism. Reason among the nihilists, strangely enough, annexed the prejudices of faith; the least of the contradictions made by these individualists was not choosing for the prototype of reason the most common form of science-worship. They denied everything by the most debatable of values, the values of Flaubert's Monsieur Homais.

However, it was by choosing to make reason, in its most limited aspect, into an act of faith that the nihilists provided their successors with a model. They believed in nothing but reason and self-interest. But instead of scepticism, they chose the apostolate and became socialists. Therein lies their basic contradiction. Like all adolescent minds they simultaneously experienced doubt and the need to believe. Their personal solution consists of endowing their negation with the intransigence and passion of faith. What after all is astonishing about that? Veidle quotes the scornful phrase used by Soloviev, the philosopher, in denouncing this contradiction: 'Man is descended from monkeys, therefore let us love one another.' However, Pisarev's truth is to be found in this dilemma. If man is the image of God then it does not matter that he is deprived of human love; the day will come when he will be satiated with it. But if he is a blind creature, wandering in the darkness of a cruel and circumscribed condition, he has need of his equals and of their ephemeral love. Where can charity take refuge, after all, if not in the world without god? In the other, grace provides for all, even for the rich. Those who deny everything at least understand that negation is a calamity. They can then open their hearts to the misery of others and finally deny themselves. Pisarev did not shrink from the idea of murdering his mother, and yet he managed to find the exact words to describe injustice. He wanted to enjoy life egoistically, but he suffered imprisonment and finally went mad. Such an ostentatious display of cynicism finally led him to an understanding of love, to be exiled from it, and to suffer from it to the point of suicide, thus revealing, in place of the man-god he wanted to create, the unhappy, suffering old man whose greatness illuminates the pages of contemporary history.

Bakunin embodies, but in a manner spectacular in a different way, the very same contradictions. He died on the eve of the terrorist epic.* Moreover, he rejected, in advance, individual outrages and denounced 'the Brutuses of the period'. However, he had a certain respect for them since he reproached Herzen for having openly criticized Karakosov for his abortive attempt to assassinate Alexander II in 1866. This feeling of respect had its reasons. Bakunin influenced the course of events in the same manner as Bielinsky and the nihilists, and directed them into the channel of individual revolt. But he contributed something more: a germ of political cynicism which will congeal, with Nechayev, into a doctrine and will drive the revolutionary movement to extremes.

Bakunin had hardly emerged from adolescence when he was overwhelmed and uprooted by Hegelian philosophy, as if by a gigantic earthquake. He buries himself in it day and night 'to the point of madness', he says, and adds, 'I saw absolutely nothing but Hegel's categories.' When he emerges from this initiation, it is with the exaltation of a neophyte. 'My personal self is dead forever, my life is the true life. It is in some way identified with the absolute life.' He required very little time to see the dangers of that comfortable position. He who has understood reality does not rebel against it, but rejoices in it; in other words, he becomes a conformist. Nothing in Bakunin's character predestined him to that watchdog philosophy. It is possible, also, that his travels in Germany, and the unfortunate opinion he formed of the Germans, may have ill-prepared him to agree with the aged Hegel, that the Prussian state was the privileged depositary of the final fruits of the mind. More Russian than the Czar himself, despite his dreams of universality, he could in no event

* 1876.

subscribe to the apology of Prussia when it was founded on a logic brash enough to assert that: 'The will of other peoples has no rights for it is the people who represent the will (of the Spirit) who dominate the world.' In the eighteen-forties, moreover, Bakunin discovered French socialism and anarchism from which he appropriated a few tendencies. Bakunin rejects, with a magnificent gesture, any part of German ideology. He approached the absolute in the same way as he approached total destruction, with the same passionate emotion, and with the blind enthusiasm for the 'All or Nothing' which we find in him, again in its purest form.

After having extolled absolute Unity, Bakunin enthusiastically embraces the most elementary form of Manichaeism. What he wants, of course, is once and for all 'the universal and authentically democratic Church of freedom'. That is his religion; it is the religion of his times. He is not sure, however, that his faith on this point has been perfect. In his *Confession* to Czar Nicholas I, he seems to be sincere when he says that he has never been able to believe in the final revolution 'except with a supernatural and painful effort to stifle forcibly the interior voice which whispered to me that my hopes were absurd'. His theory of obligatory immorality is, on the other hand, much more firmly based and he is often to be seen plunging about in it with the ease and pleasure of a mettlesome horse. History is only governed by two principles, the State and social revolution, revolution and counter-revolution, which can never be reconciled, and which are engaged in a death struggle. The State is the incarnation of crime. 'The smallest and most inoffensive State is still criminal in its dreams.' Therefore revolution is the incarnation of good. This struggle, which surpasses politics, is also the struggle of satanic principles against the divine principle. Bakunin explicitly reintroduces one of the themes of romantic rebellion into rebellious action. Proudhon had already decreed that God is Evil and exclaimed: 'Come, Satan, victim of the calumnies of kings and of the petty-minded!' Bakunin also gives a glimpse of the broader implications of an apparently political rebellion: 'Evil is the satanic rebellion against divine authority, a rebellion in which we, nevertheless, see the fruitful seed of every form of human emancipation.' Like the Fraticellis of fourteenth-century Bohemia, revolutionary socialists today use this phrase as a password: 'In the name of him to whom a great wrong has been done.'

The struggle against creation will therefore be without mercy and without ethics, the only salvation lies in extermination. 'The passion for destruction is a creative passion.' Bakunin's burning words on the subject of the revolution of 1848 vehemently proclaim this pleasure in destruction. 'A feast without beginning and without end', he says. In fact, for him as for all who are oppressed, the revolution is a feast, in the religious sense of the word. Here we are reminded of the French anarchist Coeurderoy who, in his book *Hurrah, or the Cossack Revolution*, summoned the hordes of the North to lay waste to the whole world. He also wanted to 'apply the torch to my father's house' and proclaimed that the only hope lay in the deluge and human chaos. Pure rebellion is grasped, in these manifestations, in its biological truth. That is why Bakunin with exceptional perspicacity was the only one of his period to declare war on the concept of government by scientists. Against the claims of every abstract idea, he pleaded the cause of the complete man, completely identified with his rebellion. If he glorifies the brigand leader of the peasant rising, if he chooses to model himself on Stenka Razin and Pugachev, it is because these men fought, without either doctrine or principle, for the ideal of pure freedom. Bakunin introduces, into the midst of revolution, the naked principle of rebellion. .... 'The tempest and life, that is what we need. A new world, without laws, and consequently free.'

But is a world without laws a free world? That is the question posed by any rebellion. If the question were to be asked of Bakunin, the answer would not be in doubt. Despite the fact that he was opposed in all circumstances, and with the most extreme lucidity, to authoritarian socialism, yet from the moment when he himself begins to define the society of the future, he does so – without being at all concerned about the contradiction – in terms of a dictatorship. The statutes of the *International Fraternity* (1864–7), which he edited himself, already establish the absolute subordination of the individual to the central committee, during the period of action. It is the same for the period which will follow the revolution. He hopes to see in liberated Russia 'a strong dictatorial power . . . a power supported by partisans, enlightened by their advice, fortified by their free collaboration, but which would be limited by nothing and by no one'. Bakunin contributed as much as his enemy Marx to Leninist doctrine. The dream of the revolutionary Slav empire, moreover, as Bakunin conjures it up before the Czar, is exactly the same, down to the last detail of its frontiers, as that realized by Stalin. Coming from a man who was wise enough to say that the essential driving-force of Czarist Russia was fear and who rejected the Marxist theory of part dictatorship, these conceptions may seem contradictory. But this contradiction demonstrates that the origins of authoritarian doctrines are partially nihilistic. Pisarev justifies Bakunin. Certainly, the latter wanted total freedom: but he hoped to realize it through total destruction. To destroy everything is to pledge oneself to building without foundations, and then to supporting the walls with one's arms. He who rejects the entire past, without keeping any part of it which could serve to breathe life into the revolution, condemns himself to finding justification only in the future and, in the meantime, to entrusting the police with the task of justifying the provisional state of affairs. Bakunin proclaims dictatorship, not despite his desire for destruction, but in accordance with it. Nothing, in fact, could turn him from this path since his ethical values had already been dissolved in the crucible of total negation. In his openly obsequious *Confession* to the Czar, which he wrote in order to gain his freedom, he spectacularly introduces the double game into revolutionary politics. With his *Catechism of a Revolutionary*, which he probably drafted in Switzerland, with the help of Nechayev, he voices, even though he denies it later, the political cynicism which will never cease to weigh on the revolutionary movement and which Nechayev himself has so provocatively illustrated.

A less well-known figure than Bakunin, still more mysterious, but more significant for our purpose, Nechayev pushed nihilism to the farthest coherent point. His thought presents practically no contradiction. He appeared, about 1860, in revolutionary intellectual circles, and died, obscurely, in January 1882. In this short space of time he never ceased to suborn the students around him, Bakunin himself, the revolutionary refugees, and finally the guards in his prison whom he succeeded in persuading to take part in a crazy conspiracy. When he first appears, he is already quite sure of what he thinks. If Bakunin was fascinated by him to the point of consenting to entrust him with imaginary authority, it is because he recognized in that implacable figure the type of human being that he recommended and what he himself, in a certain manner, would have been if he had been able to silence his heart. Nechayev was not content with saying that one must unite with 'the savage world of bandits, the true and unique revolutionary environment of Russia', nor to write once more, like Bakunin, that henceforth politics would be religion and religion politics. He made himself the cruel high-priest of a desperate revolution; his most recurrent dream was to found a homicidal order which would permit him to propagate and finally enthrone the sinister divinity that he had decided to serve.

He did not only give dissertations on universal destruction, his originality lay in coldly claiming, for those who dedicate themselves to the revolution, an 'All is permitted' and in permitting himself everything in fact. 'The revolutionary is a man condemned in advance. He must have neither romantic relationships nor object to engage his feelings. He should even cast off his own name. Every part of him should be concentrated in one single passion: the revolution.' If history is, in fact, independent of all principles and comprised only of a struggle between revolution and counter-revolution, there is no other way out but to espouse wholeheartedly one of the two, and either die or be resurrected. Nechayev pursues this logic to the bitter end. For the first time, with him, revolution is going to be explicitly separated from love and friendship.

The consequences of arbitrary psychology transposed by Hegel's method can be seen for the first time in Nechayev. Hegel had allowed that the mutual recognition of minds could be accomplished in love.

However, he would not give a place in the foreground of his analysis to this 'phenomenon' which, according to him, he found 'had not the strength, the patience, nor the application of the negative'. He had chosen to demonstrate consciousness in blind combat, dimly groping on the sands, like crabs which finally come to grips in a fight to the death, and voluntarily abandoned the equally legitimate image of beams of light painfully searching for each other in the night and finally focusing together in a blaze of illumination. Those who love, friends or lovers, know that love is not only a blinding flash, but also a long and painful struggle in the darkness for the realization of definitive recognition and reconciliation. After all, if history is endowed with virtue to the extent that it gives proof of patience, real love is as patient as hatred. Moreover, the demand for justice is not the only justification throughout the centuries for revolutionary enthusiasms which are also supported by a painful insistence on universal friendship, even – and above all – in defiance of an inimical heaven. Those who die for justice, throughout history, have always been called 'brothers'. Violence, for every one of them, is directed only against the enemy, in the service of the community of the oppressed. But if the revolution is the only positive value, it has a right to claim everything – even the denunciation and therefore the sacrifice of the friend. Henceforth, violence will be directed against one and all, in the service of an abstract idea. The accession to power of the possessed had to take place so that it could be said, once and for all, that the revolution, in itself, was more important than the people it wanted to save and that friendship, which until then had transformed defeats into the semblance of victories, must be sacrificed and postponed until the still invisible day of victory.

Nechayev's originality thus lies in justifying the violence done to one's brothers. He decided, with Bakunin, on the terms of the *Catechism*. But once the latter, in a fit of mental aberration, had given him the mission of representing in Russia a European Revolutionary Union which existed only in his imagination, Nechayev in effect took over Russia, founded his *Society of the Axe* and himself defined its regulations. There we find again the secret central committee, necessary no doubt to any military or political action, to whom everyone must swear absolute allegiance. But Nechayev does more than militarize the revolution from the moment when he admits that the leaders, in order to govern their subordinates, have the right to employ violence and lies. Nechayev lies, to begin with, when he claims to be a delegate of a central committee which is still non-existent and when, to enlist certain sceptics in the action that he proposed to undertake, he describes the committee as disposing of unlimited resources. He goes still farther by distinguishing between categories of revolutionaries, with those of the first category (by which he means the leaders) reserving the right to consider the rest as 'expendable capital'. All the leaders in history may have thought in these terms but they never said so. Until Nechayev, at any rate, no revolutionary leader had dared to make this the guiding principle of his conduct. Up to his time no revolution had put at the head of its table of laws the concept that man could be a chattel. Traditionally, recruiting relied on its appeal to courage and to the spirit of self-sacrifice. Nechayev decided that the sceptics could be terrorized or blackmailed and the believers deceived. Even pseudo revolutionaries could still be used, if they were urged on systematically to perform the most dangerous deeds. As for the oppressed, since they were going to be saved once and for all, they could be oppressed still more. What they would lose, the oppressed of the future would gain. Nechayev states, in principle, that governments must be driven to take repressive measures, that the official representatives most hated by the population must never be touched and that finally the secret society must employ all its resources to increase the suffering and misery of the masses.

Although these beautiful thoughts have realized their full meaning today, Nechayev did not live to see the triumph of his principles. He tried to apply them, at all events, at the time of the student Ivanov's murder, which so struck the popular imagination of the time that Dostoyevsky made it one of the themes of *The Possessed*. Ivanov, whose only fault seems to have been that he had doubts about the central committee of which Nechayev claimed to be a delegate, was considered an enemy of the revolution because he was opposed to the man who was identified with the revolution. Therefore he must die. 'What right have we to take a man's life?' asks Ouspensky, one of Nechayev's comrades – 'It is not a question of right, but of our duty to eliminate everything that may harm our cause.' When revolution is the sole value, there are, in fact, no more rights, there are only duties. But by an immediate inversion, every right is assumed in the name of duty. For the sake of the cause, Nechayev, who has never made an attempt on the life of any tyrant, ambushes and kills Ivanov. Then he leaves Russia and returns to Bakunin who turns his back on him and condemns his 'repugnant tactics'. 'One has gradually come', writes Bakunin, 'to the conclusion that to found an indestructible society it must be based on the politics of Machiavelli and the methods of the Jesuits: for the body, only violence; for the soul, deception.' That is well said. But in the name of what value is it possible to decide that this 'tactic is repugnant' if the revolution, as Bakunin believed, is the only good? Nechayev is really in the service of the revolution; it is not his own ends that he serves, but the cause. Extradited, he yields not an inch to his judges. Condemned to twenty-five years in gaol, he still reigns over the prisons, organizes the gaolers into a secret society, plans the assassination of the Czar, and is again brought up for trial. Death in the dungeon of a fortress, after twelve years' confinement, brings an end to the life of this rebel who is the first of the contemptuous aristocrats of the revolution.

At this period, in the bosom of the revolution, everything is really permitted and murder can be elevated into a principle. It was thought, however, with the renewal of populism in 1870, that this revolutionary movement, sprung from the ethical and religious tendencies to be found in the Decembrists, and in the socialism of Lavrov and Herzen, would put a check on the evolution towards political cynicism that Nechayev had illustrated. This movement appealed to 'living souls', prompted them to turn to the people and educate them so that they would march forward to their own liberation. 'Repentant noblemen' left their families, dressed like the poor, and went into the villages to preach to the peasants. But the peasants were suspicious and held their peace. When they did not hold their peace, they denounced the apostle to the police. This check to the beautiful souls had the result of throwing back the movement on the cynicism of a Nechayev or, at any rate, on violence. In so far as the intelligentsia was unable to reclaim the allegiance of the people, it felt itself once more face to face alone with autocracy; once more the world appeared to it in the aspect of master and slave. The group known as *The Will of the People* therefore elevates individual terrorism into a principle and inaugurates the series of murders which continued until 1905 with the revolutionary socialist party. This is the point at which the terrorists are born, disillusioned with love, united against the crimes of their masters, but alone in their despair, and face to face with their contradictions which they can only resolve in the double sacrifice of their innocence and their life.

THE FASTIDIOUS ASSASSINS

In the year 1878, Russian terrorism was born. A very young girl, Vera Zassulich, on the day following the trial of one hundred and eighty-three Populists, the twenty-fourth of January, shot down General Trepov, the governor of St Petersburg. At her trial she was acquitted and then succeeded in escaping the police of the Czar. This revolver shot launched a whole series of repressive actions and attempted assassinations, which kept pace with one another and which, it was already apparent, could only be terminated by mutual exhaustion.

The same year a member of *The Will of the People*, Kravychinsky stated the principles of terror in his pamphlet *Death for Death*. Consequences always follow principles. In Europe, the Emperor of Germany, the King of Italy, the King of Spain, were victims of assassins. Again in 1878, Alexander II created, in the shape of the Okhrana, the most efficient weapon of State terrorism the world has ever seen. From then on, the nineteenth century abounds in murders, both in Russia and in the West. In 1879 another King of Spain is assassinated and there is an abortive attempt on the life of the Czar. In 1881 the Czar is murdered by terrorist members of *The Will of the People*. Sofia Perovskaya, Jeliabov, and their friends are hanged. In 1883 takes place the assassination of the Emperor of Germany, whose murderer is beheaded with an axe. In 1887 there are the executions of the Chicago martyrs and the congress of Spanish anarchists at Valencia where they issue the terrorist proclamation: 'If society does not capitulate, vice and evil must perish, even if we must all perish with them.' In France, the eighteen-nineties mark the culminating point of what is called propaganda by action. The exploits of Ravachol, Vaillant, and Henry are the prelude to Carnot's assassination. In the year 1892 alone there were more than a thousand dynamite outrages in Europe, and in America almost five hundred. In 1898 the Empress Elisabeth of Austria was murdered. In 1901 the President of the United States, Mackinley, was assassinated. In Russia, where the series of attempts against the lives of minor representatives of the régime had not ceased, the *Organization for Combat* of the Revolutionary Socialist party came into being in 1903 and brought together the most outstanding personalities of Russian terrorism. The murders of Plehve by Sazanov and of the Grand Duke Sergei by Kaliayev, in 1905, mark the culminating point of the thirty years' apostolate of blood and terminate, for revolutionary religion, the age of martyrs.

Nihilism, intimately involved with a frustrated religious movement, thus culminates in terrorism. In the universe of total negation, these young disciples try, with bombs, revolvers, and also with the courage with which they walk to the gallows, to escape from the contradiction and to create the values they lack. Until their time, men died for what they knew, or for what they thought they knew. From their time on, it became the rather more difficult habit to sacrifice oneself for something about which one knew nothing, except that it was necessary to die for whatever it was. Until then, those who had to die put themselves in the hand of God in defiance of the justice of man. But on reading the declarations of the condemned victims of that period, we are amazed to see that all, without exception, entrusted themselves, in defiance of their judges, to the justice of other men who were not yet born. These men of the future remained, in the absence of supreme values, their last recourse. The future is the only transcendental value for men without God. The terrorists undoubtedly want first of all to destroy – to make absolutism totter under the shock of exploding bombs. But by their death, at any rate, they aim at recreating a community founded on love and justice, and thus to resume a mission which the Church has betrayed. The terrorists' real mission is to create a Church from whence will one day spring the new God. But is that all? If their voluntary assumption of guilt and death gave rise to nothing but the promise of a value still to come, the history of the world today would justify us in saying, for the moment at any rate, that they have died in vain and that they never have ceased to be nihilists. A value to come is, moreover, a contradiction in terms, since it can neither explain an action nor furnish a principle of choice as long as it has not been formulated. But the men of 1905, tortured by contradictions, really did give birth, by their very negation and death, to a value which will henceforth be imperative and which they brought to light in the belief that they were only announcing its advent. They ostensibly placed, above themselves and their executioners, that supreme and painful good which we have already found at the origins of rebellion. Let us stop and consider this value, at the moment when the spirit of rebellion encounters, for the last time in our history, the spirit of compassion.

'How can we speak of terrorist activity without taking part in it?' exclaims the student Kaliayev. His companions, united ever since 1903, in the *Organization for Combat* of the Revolutionary Socialist party, under the direction of Azef and later of Boris Savinkov, all live up to the standard of this admirable statement. They are men of the highest principles: the last, in the history of rebellion, to refuse no part of their condition or their drama. If their lives were dedicated to the terror, 'if they had faith in it,' as Pokotilov says, they never ceased to be torn asunder by it. History offers few examples of fanatics who have suffered from scruples, even in action. But the men of 1905 were always prey to doubts. The greatest homage we can pay them is to say that we would not be able, in 1950, to ask them one question which they themselves had not already asked and which, in their life, or by their death, they had not partially answered.

However, they quickly passed into the realms of history. When Kaliayev, for example, in 1903, decided to take part with Savinkov in terrorist activity, he was twenty-six years old. Two years later the 'Poet', as he was called, was hanged. It was a short career. But to anyone who examines, with a little feeling, the history of that period, Kaliayev, in his breathtaking career, displays the most significant aspect of terrorism. Sazonov, Schweitzer, Pokotilov, Voinarovsky, and most of the other anarchists likewise burst upon the scene of Russian history and poised there for a moment, dedicated to destruction, as the swift and unforgettable witnesses to a more and more agonized protest.

Almost all are atheists. 'I remember', wrote Boris Voinarovsky, who died in throwing a bomb at Admiral Dubassov, 'that, before even going to high-school, I preached atheism to one of my childhood friends. Only one question embarrasses me. Where did my ideas come from? For I had not the least conception of eternity.' Kaliayev, himself, believed in God. A few moments before an attempted assassination which failed, Savinkov saw him in the street, standing in front of an ikon, holding the bomb in one hand and making the sign of the cross with the other. But he repudiated religion. In his cell, before his execution, he refused its consolations.

Secrecy compelled them to live in solitude. They did not know, except perhaps in the abstract, the profound joy experienced by the man of action in contact with a large section of humanity. But the bond that unites them replaces every other attachment in their minds. 'Chivalry', writes Sazonov, 'our chivalry was permeated with such a degree of feeling that the word "brother" in no way conveyed, with sufficient clarity, the essence of our relations with one another.' From prison, Sazonov writes to his friends: 'For my part, the indispensable condition of happiness is to keep forever the knowledge of my perfect solidarity with you.' As for Voinarovsky, he confesses that he said, to a woman whom he loved and who wished to detain him, the following phrase which he recognizes as 'slightly comic' but which, according to him, proves his state of mind: 'I should hate you if I arrived late for my comrades.'

This little group of men and women, lost among the Russian masses, bound only to one another, chose the role of executioner to which they were in no way destined. They lived in the same paradox, combining in themselves respect for human life in general and contempt for their own lives – to the point of nostalgia for the supreme sacrifice. For Dora Brilliant, the anarchist programme was of no importance – terrorist action was primarily embellished by the sacrifice it demanded from the terrorist. 'But', says Savinkov, 'terror weighed on her like a cross.' Kaliayev himself is ready to sacrifice his life at any moment. 'Even better than that, he passionately desired to make this sacrifice.' During the preparations for the attempt on Plehve, he stated his intention of throwing himself under the horses' hooves and perishing with the minister. With Voinarovsky also the desire for sacrifice coincides with the attraction of death. After his arrest, he writes to his parents: 'How many times during my adolescence the idea came to me to kill myself. . . .'

At the same time, these executioners who risked their own lives so completely, only made attempts on the lives of others after the most scrupulous examination of conscience. The first attempt on the Grand Duke Sergei failed because Kaliayev, with the full approval of his comrades, refused to kill the children who were riding in the Grand Duke's carriage. About Rachel Louriée, another terrorist, Savinkov writes: 'She had faith in Terrorist action, she considered it as honour and a duty to take part in it, but blood upset her no less than it did Dora.' Savinkov was opposed to an attempt on Admiral Dubassov in the Petersburg–Moscow express because: 'If there were the least mistake, the explosion could take place in the carriage and kill strangers.' Later Savinkov, 'in the name of terrorist conscience', will deny, with indignation, having made a child of sixteen take part in an attempted assassination. At the moment of escaping from a Czarist prison, he decided to shoot any officers who might attempt to prevent his flight, but to kill himself rather than turn his revolver on an ordinary soldier. It is the same with Voinarovsky, who does not hesitate to kill men but who confesses that he had never hunted in that he finds 'the occupation barbarous' and who declares in his turn: 'If Dubassov is accompanied by his wife, I shall not throw the bomb.'

Such a degree of self-abnegation, accompanied by such profound consideration for the lives of others, allows the supposition that these fastidious assassins lived out the rebel destiny in its most contradictory form. It is possible to believe that they too, while recognizing the inevitability of violence, nevertheless admitted to themselves that it is unjustifiable. Necessary and inexcusable, that is how murder appeared to them. Mediocre minds, confronted with this terrible problem, can take refuge by ignoring one of the terms of the dilemma. They are content, in the name of formal principles, to find all direct violence inexcusable and then to sanction that diffuse form of violence which takes place on the scale of world history. Or they will console themselves, in the name of history, with the thought that violence is necessary and will add murder to murder, to the point of making of history nothing but a continuous violation of everything, in man, which protests against injustice. This defines the two aspects of contemporary nihilism, the bourgeois and the revolutionary.

But the extremists, with whom we are concerned, forgot nothing. From their earliest days they were incapable of justifying what they nevertheless found necessary and conceived the idea of offering themselves as a justification and of replying by personal sacrifice to the question they asked themselves. For them, as for all rebels before them, murder was identified with suicide. A life is paid for by another life, and from these two sacrifices springs the promise of a value. Kaliayev, Voinarovsky, and the others believe in the equal value of human lives. Therefore they do not value any idea above human life, although they kill for the sake of ideas. To be precise, they live on the plane of their idea. They justify it, finally, by incarnating it to the point of death. We are again confronted with a concept of rebellion which, if not religious, is at least metaphysical. Other men to come consumed with the same devouring faith as these, will find their methods sentimental and refuse to admit that any one life is the equivalent of another. They will then put an abstract idea above human life, even if they call it history, to which they themselves have submitted in advance and to which they will decide, quite arbitrarily, to submit everyone else as well. The problem of rebellion will no longer be resolved by arithmetic, but by estimating probabilities. Confronted with the possibility that the idea may be realized in the future, human life can be everything or nothing. The greater the faith that the estimate places in this final realization, the less the value of human life. At the ultimate limit, it is no longer worth anything at all.

We shall have occasion to examine this limit, by which we mean the period of State terrorism and of the philosophical executioners. But, meanwhile, the rebels of 1905, at the frontier on which they stand united, teach us, to the sound of exploding bombs, that rebellion cannot lead, without ceasing to be rebellion, to consolation and to the comforts of dogma. Their only apparent victory is to triumph, at least over solitude and negation. In the midst of a world which they deny and which rejects them, they try, one after another, like all courageous men, to reconstruct a brotherhood of man. The love they bear for one another which brings them happiness even in the desert of a prison, which extends to the great mass of their enslaved and silent fellow-men, gives the measure of their distress and of their hopes. To realize this love, they must first kill; to inaugurate the reign of innocence, they must accept a certain degree of culpability. This contradiction will only be resolved for them at the very last moment. Solitude and chivalry, renunciation and hope will only be surmounted by the willing acceptance of death. Already Jeliabov, who organized the attempt on Alexander II in 1881 and was arrested forty-eight hours before the murder, had asked to be executed at the same time as the real perpetrator of the attempt. 'Only the cowardice of the government', he said, 'could account for the erection of one gallows instead of two.' Five were erected, one of which was for a woman he loved. But Jeliabov died smiling, while Ryssakov, who had broken down during his interrogations, was dragged to the scaffold, half-mad with fear.

Jeliabov did this because of a sort of guilt which he did not want to accept and from which he knew he would suffer, like Ryssakov, if he remained alone after having committed or been the cause of a murder. At the foot of the gallows, Sofia Perovskaya kissed the man she loved and two other friends, but turned her back on Ryssakov, who died solitary and damned by the new religion. For Jeliabov, death in the midst of his comrades coincided with his justification. He who kills is only guilty if he consents to go on living or if, to remain alive, he betrays his comrades. To die, however, cancels out both the guilt and the crime itself. Thus Charlotte Corday shouts at Fouquier-Tinville: 'Oh the monster, he takes me for an assassin!' It is the agonizing and fugitive discovery of a human value which stands half-way between innocence and guilt, between reason and irrationality, between history and eternity. At the moment of this discovery, but only then, these desperate people experienced a strange feeling of peace, the peace of final victory. In his cell, Polivanov says that it would have been 'easy and sweet' for him to die. Voinarovsky writes that he has conquered the fear of death. 'Without a single muscle in my face twitching, without saying a word, I shall climb on the scaffold . . . And this will not be an act of violence perpetrated on myself, it will be the perfectly natural result of all that I have lived through.' Very much later, Lieutenant Schmidt will write before being shot: 'My death will consummate everything and my cause, crowned by my death, will emerge irreproachable and perfect.' And Kaliayev, condemned to the gallows after having played prosecutor to the tribunal, declares firmly: 'I consider my death as a supreme protest against a world of blood and tears,' and again writes: 'From the moment when I found myself behind bars, I never for one moment wanted to stay alive in any way whatsoever.' His wish is granted. On 10 May, at two o'clock in the morning, he walks towards the only justification he recognizes. Entirely dressed in black, without an overcoat, and wearing a felt hat, he climbs the scaffold. To Father Florinsky, who offers him the crucifix, the condemned man, turning his face from the figure of Christ, only answers: 'I already told you that I have finished with life and that I am prepared for death.'

The ancient value lives once more, at the culmination of nihilism and at the very foot of the gallows. It is the reflection, historic on this occasion, of the 'we are' which we found at the termination of our analysis of the rebel mind. It is privation and at the same time enlightened conviction. It is this that shone with such mortal radiance on the astonished countenance of Dora Brilliant at the thought of he who died for himself and for eternal friendship; it is this that drives Sazonov to suicide in prison as a protest and 'to earn respect for his comrades'; and this, again, which exonerates Nechayev on the day when he is asked to denounce his comrades by a general whom he knocks to the ground with a single blow. By means of this, the terrorists, while simultaneously affirming the world of men, place themselves above this world, thus demonstrating for the last time in our history that real rebellion is a creator of values.

Thanks to them, 1905 marks the highest peak of revolutionary momentum. But from then on a decline sets in. Martyrs do not build churches; they are the mortar, or the alibi. They are followed by the priests and bigots. The revolutionaries to come will not demand an exchange of lives. They will consent to risk death, but will also agree to preserve themselves as far as they can for the sake of serving the revolution. Thus they will accept for themselves the whole burden of guilt. The acceptance or humiliation – that is the true characteristic of twentieth-century revolutionaries, who place the revolution and the Church of man above themselves. Kaliayev proves, on the contrary, that though the revolution is a necessary means, it is not a sufficient end. In this way he elevates man instead of degrading him. It is Kaliayev and his Russian and German comrades who, in the history of the world, really oppose Hegel* who first recognizes universal recognition as necessary and then as insufficient. Appearances did not suffice for him. If the entire world had been willing to acknowledge and recognize him, a doubt would still have remained in Kaliayev's mind: he needed approval, and the approbation of the

---

* Two very different species of men. One kills only once and pays with his life. The other justifies thousands of crimes and consents to be rewarded with honours.

whole world would not have sufficed to silence the doubt which even a hundred enthusiastic acclamations give rise to in the mind of any honest man. Kaliayev doubted to the bitter end, but this doubt did not prevent him from acting; it is for that reason that he is the purest image of rebellion. He who accepts to die, to pay for a life with a life, no matter what his negations may be, affirms, by doing so, a value which surpasses him in his aspect of an individual in the historic sense. Kaliayev dedicates himself to history until death and, at the moment of dying, places himself above history. In a certain way, it is true, he prefers himself to history. But what should his preference be? Himself, whom he kills without hesitation, or the value which he incarnates and makes immortal? The answer is not difficult to guess. Kaliayev and his comrades triumphed over nihilism.

THE PATH OF CHIGALEV

But this triumph is to be short-lived: it coincides with death. Nihilism, provisionally, survives its victors. In the very bosom of the Revolutionary Socialist party, political cynicism continues to wend its way to victory. The party leader who sends Kaliayev to his death, Azev, plays a double game and denounces the revolutionaries to the Okhrana while planning the deaths of ministers and Grand Dukes. The concept of provocation reinstates the 'all is permitted' and again identifies history and absolute values. This particular form of nihilism, after having influenced individualistic socialism, goes on to contaminate so-called scientific socialism which appears in Russia during the eighteen-eighties. The joint legacy of Nechayev and Marx will give birth to the totalitarian revolution of the twentieth century. While individual terrorism hunted down the last representatives of divine right, State terrorism was getting ready to destroy divine right definitively, at the very root of human society. The technique of the seizure of power for the realization of ultimate ends takes the first step towards the exemplary affirmation of these ends.

Lenin, in fact, borrows from Tkachev, a comrade and spiritual brother of Nechayev, a concept of the seizure of power that he found 'majestic' and which he himself recapitulated thus: 'absolute secrecy, meticulous care in the choice of members, creation of professional revolutionaries'. Tkachev, who died insane, makes the transition from nihilism to militant socialism. He claimed to have created a Russian Jacobinism and yet only borrowed from the Jacobins their technique of action since he, too, denied every principle and every virtue. An enemy of art and ethics, he only reconciles the rational and the irrational in tactics. His aim is to achieve human equality by seizure of the power of the State. Secret organizations, revolutionary alliances, dictatorial powers for revolutionary leaders, these were the themes that defined the concept, if not the realization, of 'the apparatus' which was to enjoy so great and efficacious a success. As for the method itself, it is possible to form a fair idea of it when one learns that Tkachev proposed to suppress and eliminate all Russians over the age of twenty-five, as incapable of assimilating the new ideas. A really inspired method, and one which was to prevail in the techniques of the modern super-State, where the fanatical education of children is carried on in the midst of a terrorized adult population. Caesarian Socialism undoubtedly condemns individual terrorism to the extent that it revives values incompatible with the predominance of historic reason. But it will restore terror on the level of the State – with the creation of an ultimate divine humanity as its sole justification.

We have come full circle here and rebellion, cut off from its real roots, unfaithful to man in having surrendered to history, now contemplates the subjection of the entire universe. It is at this point that era of Chigalevism begins – proclaimed, in *The Possessed*, by Verkhovensky the nihilist who claims the right to choose dishonour. His is an unhappy and implacable mind and he chooses the will to power which, in fact, alone is capable of reigning over a history which has no other significance but itself. Chigalev, the philanthropist, is his guarantor; love of mankind will, henceforth, justify the enslavement of man. Possessed by the idea of equality, Chigalev, after long consideration, arrived at the despairing conclusion that only one system is possible even though it is a system of despair. 'Beginning with the premise of unlimited freedom, I arrive at unlimited despotism.' Complete freedom, which is the negation of everything, can only exist and justify itself by the creation of new values identified with the entire human race. If the creation of these values is postponed, humanity will tear itself to pieces. The shortest route to these new standards passes by way of total dictatorship. 'One-tenth of humanity will have the right to individuality and will exercise unlimited authority over the other nine-tenths. The latter will lose their individuality and will become like a flock of sheep; compelled to passive obedience, they will be led back to original innocence and, so to speak, to the primitive paradise where, nevertheless, they must work.' It is the government by philosophers of which the utopians dream; philosophers of this type, quite simply, believe in nothing. The Kingdom has come, but it negates real rebellion, and is only concerned with the reign of 'the Christs of Violence' – to use the expression of an enthusiastic writer extolling the life and death of Ravachol. 'The Pope on high', says Verkhovensky bitterly, 'with us around him, and beneath us Chigalevism.'

The totalitarian theocrats of the twentieth century and State terrorism are thus announced. The new aristocracy and the Grand Inquisitors reign today, by making use of the rebellion of the oppressed, over one part of our history. Their reign is cruel, but they excuse their cruelty, like the Satan of the romantics, by claiming that it is hard for them to bear. 'We reserve desire and suffering for ourselves, for the slaves there is Chigalevism.' A new and somewhat hideous race of martyrs is now born. Their martyrdom consists of consenting to inflict suffering on others; they become the slaves of their own domination. For man to become god, the victim must bow down before the executioner. That is why both victim and executioner are equally despairing. Neither slavery nor power will any longer coincide with happiness, the masters will be morose and the slaves sullen. Saint-Just was right – it is a terrible thing to torment the people. But how can one avoid tormenting men, if one has decided to make them gods? Just as Kirilov, who kills himself in order to become God, accepts seeing his suicide made use of by Verkhoven-sky's 'conspiracy', so man's deification by man breaks the bounds which rebellion, despite everything, reveals and thereby irrevocably commits itself to the labyrinth of tactics and terror from which history has not yet emerged.

State Terrorism and Irrational Terror

ALL modern revolutions have ended in a reinforcement of the power of the State. Seventeen eighty-nine brings Napoleon; 1848 Napoleon III; 1917 Stalin; the Italian disturbances of the twenties, Mussolini; the Weimar Republic, Hitler. These revolutions, particularly after the First World War had liquidated the vestiges of divine right, still proposed, with increasing audacity, to build the city of humanity and of authentic freedom. The growing omnipotence of the State sanctioned this ambition on every occasion. It would be erroneous to say that this was bound to happen. But it is possible to examine how it did happen; and perhaps the lesson will automatically follow.

Apart from a few explanations which are not the subject of this essay, the strange and terrifying growth of the modern State can be considered as the logical conclusion of inordinate technical and philosophical ambitions, foreign to the true spirit of rebellion, but which, nevertheless, gave birth to the revolutionary spirit of our time. The prophetic dream of Marx and the over-inspired predictions of Hegel or of Nietzsche ended by conjuring up, after the city of God had been razed to the ground, either a rational or an irrational State, but one which in both cases was founded on terror.

In actual fact, the Fascist revolutions of the twentieth century do not merit the title of revolution. They lacked the ambition of universality. Mussolini and Hitler, of course, tried to build an empire and the National-Socialist ideologists were bent, explicitly, on world domination. But the difference between them and the classic revolutionary movement is that, of the nihilist inheritance, they chose to deify the irrational, and the irrational alone, instead of deifying reason. In this way they renounced their claim to universality. And yet Mussolini is a disciple of Hegel and Hitler of Nietzsche; and both illustrate, historically, some of the prophecies of German ideology. In this respect they belong to the history of rebellion and of nihilism.

They were the first to construct a State on the concept that everything was meaningless and that history was only written in terms of the hazards of force. The consequences were not long in appearing.

As early as 1914 Mussolini proclaimed the 'holy religion of anarchy', and declared himself the enemy of every form of Christianity. As for Hitler, his professed religion unhesitatingly juxtaposed the God-Providence and Valhalla. Actually his god was an argument at a political meeting and a manner of reaching an impressive climax at the end of speeches. As long as he was successful, he chose to believe that he was inspired. In the hour of defeat, he considered himself betrayed by his people. Between the two nothing intervened to announce to the world that he would ever have been capable of thinking himself guilty in regard to any principle. The only man of superior culture who gave Nazism even an appearance of being a philosophy, Ernst Junger, even went so far as to choose the actual formulae of nihilism: 'The best answer to the betrayal of life by the spirit, is the betrayal of the spirit by the spirit, and one of the great and cruel pleasures of our times is to participate in the work of destruction.'

Men of action, when they are without faith, have never believed in anything but action. For Hitler, the insupportable paradox lay precisely in wanting to found a stable order on perpetual change and on negation. Rauschning, in his *Revolution of Nihilism*, was right in saying that the Hitlerian revolution was dynamic to the utmost degree. In Germany, shaken to its foundations by a war without precedent, by defeat, and by economic distress, values no longer existed. Although one must take into consideration what Goethe called 'the German destiny of making everything difficult', the epidemic of suicides which affected the entire country, between the two wars, indicates a great deal about the state of mental confusion. To those who despair of everything reason cannot provide a faith, but only passion, and in this case it must be the same passion that lay at the root of the despair, namely humiliation and hatred. There was no longer any standard of values, both common to and superior to the German people, in the name of which it would have been possible for them to judge one another. The Germany of 1933 thus agreed to adopt the degraded values of a mere handful of men and tried to impose them on an entire civilization. Deprived of the morality of Goethe, Germany chose, and submitted to, the ethics of the gang.

Gangster morality is an inexhaustible round of triumph and revenge, defeat and resentment. When Mussolini extolled 'the elementary forces of the individual', he announced the exaltation of the dark powers of blood and instinct, the biological justification of all the worst things produced by the instinct of domination. At the Nuremberg trials, Frank emphasized 'the hatred of form' which animated Hitler. It is true that this man was nothing but an elemental force in motion, directed and rendered more effective by extreme cunning and by a relentless tactical clairvoyance.

Even his physical appearance, which was thoroughly mediocre and commonplace, was no limitation: it established him firmly with the masses. Action alone kept him alive. For him, to exist was to act. That is why Hitler and his régime could not dispense with enemies. They could only define themselves, frenetic dandies* that they were, in relation to their enemies and only assume their final form in the bloody battle which was to be their downfall. The Jews, the Free-masons, the plutocrats, the Anglo-Saxons, the bestial Slavs succeeded one another in their propaganda and their history as a means of bolstering up, each time a little higher, the blind force which was stumbling headlong towards its end. Perpetual strife demanded perpetual stimulants.

Hitler was history in its purest form. 'Evolution', said Junger, 'is far more important than living.' Thus he preaches complete identification with the stream of life, on the lowest level and in defiance of all superior reality. A régime which invented a biological foreign policy was obviously acting against its own best interests. But at least it obeyed its own particular logic. Rosenberg speaks pompously of life in the following terms: 'The style of a column on the march, and it is of little importance towards what destination and

* It is well known that Goering sometimes entertained dressed as Nero and with his face made up.

for what ends this column is marching.' Though later the column will strew ruins over the pages of history and will devastate its own country, it will at least have had the gratification of living. The real logic of this dynamism was either total defeat or a progress from conquest to conquest and from enemy to enemy, until the eventual establishment of the empire of blood and action. It is very unlikely that Hitler ever had any conception, except in the most elementary fashion, of this empire. Neither by culture, nor even by instinct or tactical intelligence, was he equal to his destiny. Germany collapsed as a result of having engaged in a struggle for empire with the concepts of provincial politics. But Junger had grasped the import of this logic and had formulated it in definite terms. He had a vision of 'a technological world empire', of a 'religion of anti-Christian technology', of which the faithful and the militants would have themselves been the priests because (and here Junger rejoins Marx), by his human structure, the worker is universal. 'The Statutes of a new authoritarian régime take the place of a change in the social contract. The worker is removed from the sphere of negotiation, from pity, and from literature and elevated to the sphere of action. Legal obligations are transformed into military obligations.' It can be seen that the empire is simultaneously the factory and the barracks of the world, where Hegel's soldier-worker reigns as a slave. Hitler was halted relatively soon on the way to the realization of this empire. But even if he had gone still farther, we would only have witnessed the more and more extensive deployment of an irresistible dynamism and the increasingly violent enforcement of cynical principles which alone would be capable of serving this dynamism.

Speaking of such a revolution, Raushchning says that it has nothing to do with liberation, justice, and inspiration: it is 'the death of freedom, the triumph of violence, and the enslavement of the mind'. Fascism is an act of contempt, in fact. Inversely, every form of contempt, if it intervenes in politics, prepares the way for, or establishes, Fascism. It must be added that Fascism cannot be anything else but an expression of contempt without denying itself. Junger drew the conclusion from his own principles that it was better to be criminal than bourgeois. Hitler, who was endowed with less literary talent but, on this occasion, with more coherence, knew that to be either one or the other was a matter of complete indifference, from the moment that one ceased to believe in anything but success. Thus he authorized himself to be both at the same time. 'Fact is all,' said Mussolini. And Hitler added: 'When the race is in danger of being oppressed ... the question of legality only plays a secondary role.' Moreover, in that the race must always be menaced in order to exist, there is never any legality. 'I am ready to sign anything, to agree to anything. ... As far as I am concerned, I am capable, in complete good faith, of signing treaties today and of dispassionately tearing them up tomorrow if the future of the German people is at stake.' Before he declared war, moreover, Hitler made the statement to his generals that no one was going to ask the victor if he had told the truth or not. The leitmotive of Goering's defence at the Nuremberg trials returned time and again to this theme, 'the victor will always be the judge and the vanquished will always be the accused'. That is a point that can certainly be argued. But then it is hard to understand Rosenberg when he said during the Nuremberg trials that he had not foreseen that the Nazi myth would lead to murder. When the English prosecuting counsel observes that 'from *Mein Kampf* the road led straight to the gas chambers at Maidanek', he touches on the real subject of the trial, the historic responsibilities of Western nihilism and the only one which, nevertheless, was not really discussed at Nuremberg, for reasons only too apparent. A trial cannot be conducted by announcing the general culpability of a civilization. Only the actual deeds which, at least, stank in the nostrils of the entire world were brought to judgement.

Hitler, in any event, invented the perpetual motion of conquest without which he would have been nothing at all. But the perpetual enemy is perpetual terror, this time on the level of the State. The State is identified with the 'apparatus', that is to say with the sum-total of mechanisms of conquest and repression. Conquest directed towards the interior of the country is called repression or propaganda ('the first step on the road to hell', according to Frank) – directed towards the exterior, it creates the army. All problems are thus military, posed in terms of power and efficiency. The supreme commander determines policy and also deals with all the main problems of administration. This principle, axiomatic as far as strategy is concerned, is applied to civil life in general. One leader, one people, signifies one master and millions of slaves. The political intermediaries who are, in all societies, the guarantors of freedom, disappear to make way for a booted and spurred Jehovah who rules over the silent masses or, which comes to the same thing, over masses who shout words of command at the top of their lungs. There is no organ of conciliation or mediation interposed between the leader and the people, nothing in fact but the apparatus, in other words the party, which is the emanation of the leader and the tool of his will to oppress. In this way the first and sole principle of this degraded form of mysticism is born, the *Führerprinzip*, which restores idolatry and a debased deity to the world of nihilism.

Mussolini, who was a Latin and, therefore, by nature a jurist, contented himself with reasons of State, which he transformed, with a great deal of rhetoric, into the absolute. 'Nothing beyond the State, above the State, against the State. Everything to the State, for the State, in the State.' The Germany of Hitler gave his false reasoning its real expression, which was that of a religion. 'Our divine mission', a Nazi newspaper says during a party congress, 'was to lead everyone back to his origins, back to the common Mother. It was truly a divine mission.' The origins of this are to be found in a primitive baying to the moon. Who is the god in question? An official party declaration answers that: 'All of us, here below, believe in Adolf Hitler, our Fuhrer . . . and (we confess) that National Socialism is the only faith which can lead our people to salvation.' The commandments of the leader, standing in the burning bush of searchlights, on a Sinai of planks and flags, therefore comprise both law and virtue. If the superhuman microphones give orders only once for a crime to be committed, then the crime is handed down from chief to sub-chief until it reaches the slave who receives orders without being able to pass them on to anybody. One of the Dachau executioners weeps in prison and says, 'I only obeyed orders. The Fuhrer and the Reichsführer, alone, planned all this and then they ran away. Gluecks received orders from Kaltenbrunner and, finally, I received orders to carry out the shootings. I have been left holding the bag because I was only a little *Hauptscharführer* and because I couldn't hand it on any lower down the line. Now they say that I am the assassin.' Goering, during the trial, proclaimed his loyalty to the Führer and said that 'there was still a code of honour in that accursed life'. Honour lay in obedience which was often confused with crime. Military law punishes disobedience by death and its honour is servitude. When all the world has become military, then crime consists in not killing if military orders insist on it.

Orders, unfortunately, seldom insist on good deeds. Pure doctrinal dynamism cannot be directed towards good, but only towards efficaciousness. As long as enemies exist, terror will exist; and there will be enemies as long as dynamism exists to insure that: 'All the influences liable to undermine the sovereignty of the people, as exercised by the Führer with the assistance of the party . . . must be eliminated.' Enemies are heretics and must be converted by preaching or, in other words, by the Gestapo. The result is that man, if he is a member of the party, is no more than a tool in the hands of the Führer, a cog in the apparatus, or, if he is the enemy of the Führer, a waste product of the machine. The impetus towards irrationality of this movement, born of rebellion, now even goes so far as to propose subjugating all that makes man more than a cog in the machine; in other words, rebellion itself. The romantic individualism of the German revolution finally peters out in the world of inanimate objects. Irrational terror transforms men into matter, 'planetary bacilli', according to Hitler's formula. This formula proposes the destruction, not only of the individual, but of the universal possibilities of the individual, of reflection, solidarity, and the urge to absolute love. Propaganda and torture are the direct means of bringing about disintegration; more destructive still are systematic degradation, joint culpability with the cynical criminal and forced complicity. He who kills or tortures will only experience the shadow of victory: he will be unable to feel that he is innocent. Thus, he must create guilt in his victim so that, in a world that has no direction, universal guilt will authorize no other course of action but the use of force and give its blessing to nothing but success. When the concept of innocence disappears from the mind of the innocent victim himself, the value of power establishes a definitive rule over a world in despair. That is why an unworthy and cruel condemnation to penitence reigns in this world where only the stones are innocent. The condemned are compelled to hang one another. Even the innocent cry of maternity is stifled, as in the case of the Greek mother who was forced by an officer to choose which of her three sons was to be shot. This is the final realization of freedom: the power to kill and degrade saves the servile soul from utter emptiness. The hymn of German freedom is sung, to the music of a prisoners' orchestra, in the camps of death.

The crimes of the Hitler régime, among them the massacre of the Jews, are without precedent in history because history gives no other example of a doctrine of such total destruction being able to seize the levers of command of a civilized nation. But above all, for the first time in history, the rulers of a country have used their immense power to establish a mystique beyond the bounds of any ethical considerations. This first attempt to found a Church on nothingness was paid for by complete annihilation. The destruction of Lidice demonstrates clearly that the systematic and scientific aspect of the Nazi movement really hides an irrational drive which can only be interpreted as a drive of despair and arrogance. Until then, there were supposedly only two possible attitudes towards a village which was considered rebellious. Either calculated repression and cold-blooded execution of hostages, or a savage and necessarily brief sack by enraged soldiers. Lidice was destroyed by both methods simultaneously. It illustrates the ravages of that irrational form of reason which is the only value that can be found in the whole story. Not only were all the houses burned to the ground, the hundred and seventy-four men of the village shot, the two hundred and three women deported, and the three hundred children transferred elsewhere to be educated in the religion of the Führer, but special teams spent months at work levelling the terrain with dynamite, destroying the very stones, filling in the village pond and, finally, diverting the course of the river. After that, Lidice was really nothing more than a mere possibility according to the logic of the movement. To make assurance doubly sure, the cemetery was emptied of its dead who might have been a perpetual reminder that once something existed in this place.

The nihilist revolution, which is expressed historically in the Hitlerian religion, thus only aroused an insensate passion for nothingness which ended by turning against itself. Negation, this time without and despite Hegel, has not been creative. Hitler presents the example which is perhaps unique in history of a tyrant who has left absolutely no trace of his activities. For himself, for his people, and for the world, he was nothing but the epitome of suicide and murder. Seven million Jews assassinated, seven million Europeans deported or killed, ten million war victims are, perhaps, not sufficient to allow history to pass judgement: history is accustomed to murderers. But the very destruction of Hitler's final justification, by which we mean the German nation, henceforth makes this man, whose presence in history for years on end haunted the minds of millions of men, into an inconsistent and contemptible phantom. Speer's deposition at the Nuremberg trials showed that Hitler, although he could have stopped the war before the point of total disaster, really wanted universal suicide and the material and political destruction of the German nation. The only value for him remained, until the bitter end, success. Since Germany had lost the war, she was cowardly and treacherous and she deserved to die. 'If the German people are incapable of victory, they are unworthy to live.' Hitler, therefore, decided to drag them with him to the grave and to make his death an apotheosis, when the Russian cannons were already splitting apart the walls of his palace in Berlin. Hitler, Goering, who wanted to see his bones placed in a marble tomb, Goebbels, Himmler, Ley, killed themselves in dugouts or in cells. But their deaths were deaths for nothing, and they themselves were like a bad dream, a puff of smoke which vanishes. Neither efficacious nor exemplary, they consecrate the bloodthirsty vanity of nihilism. 'They thought they were free,' Frank cries hysterically; 'didn't they know that no one escapes from Hitlerism?' They did not know: nor did they know that the negation of everything is in itself a form of servitude and that real freedom is an inner submission to a value which defies history and its successes.

But the Fascist mystics, even though they aimed at gradually dominating the world, really never had pretensions to a universal empire. At the very most, Hitler, astonished at his own victories, was diverted from the provincial origins of his movement towards the indefinite dream of an empire of the Germans that had nothing to do with the universal city. Russian Communism, on the contrary, by its very origins, openly aspires to world empire. That is its strength, its deliberate significance, and its importance in our history. Despite appearances, the German revolution had no hope of a future. It was only a primitive impulse whose ravages have been greater than its real ambitions. Russian Communism, on the contrary, has appropriated the metaphysical ambition which this book describes, the erection, after the death of God, of a city of man finally deified. The name revolution, to which Hitler's adventure had no claim, was once deserved by Russian Communism, and although it apparently deserves it no longer it claims that one day it will deserve it forever. For the first time in history, a doctrine and a movement supported by an empire in arms has, as its purpose, definitive revolution and the unification of the world. It remains for us to examine this intention in detail. Hitler, at the height of his madness, wanted to fix the course of history for a thousand years. He thought himself on the point of doing so, and the realist philosophers of the conquered nations were preparing to acknowledge this and to excuse it, when the battle of Britain and Stalingrad threw him back on the path of death and set history once more on the march. But, as indefatigable as history itself, the claim of the human race to divinity is once more brought to life with more seriousness, more efficiency, and more reason under the auspices of the rational state as it is to be found in Russia.

State Terrorism and Rational Terror

MARX, in nineteenth-century England, in the midst of the terrible sufferings caused by the transition from an agricultural economy to an industrial economy, had plenty of material for constructing a striking analysis of primitive capitalism. As for Socialism, apart from the lessons, which for the most part contradicted its doctrines, that it could draw from the French Revolution, it was obliged to speak in the future tense and in the abstract. Thus it is not astonishing that it could blend in its doctrine the most valid critical method with a Utopian messianism of highly dubious value. The unfortunate thing is that its critical method which, by definition, should have been adjusted to reality, has found itself further and further separated from facts to the exact extent that it wanted to remain faithful to the prophecy. It was thought, and this is already an indication of the future, that what was conceded to truth could be taken from messianism. This contradiction is perceptible in Marx's lifetime. The doctrine of the *Communist Manifesto* is no longer strictly correct twenty years later, when *Das Kapital* appears. *Das Kapital* nevertheless, remained incomplete, because Marx was influenced at the end of his life by a new and prodigious mass of social and economic facts to which the system had to be adapted anew. These facts concerned, in particular, Russia, which he had spurned up till then. We now know that the Marx-Engels Institute in Moscow ceased, in 1935, the publication of the complete works of Marx while more than thirty volumes still remained unpublished: doubtless the content of these volumes was not 'Marxist' enough.

Since Marx's death, in any case, only a minority of disciples have remained faithful to his method. The Marxists who have made history have, on the contrary, appropriated the prophecy and the apocalyptic aspects of his doctrine in order to realize a Marxist revolution, in the exact circumstances under which Marx had foreseen that a revolution could not take place. It can be said of Marx that the greater part of his predictions came into conflict with facts as soon as his prophecies began to become an object of increasing faith. The reason is simple; the predictions were short term and could be controlled. Prophecy functions on a very long-term basis and has, as one of its properties, a characteristic which is the very source of strength of all religions: the impossibility of proof. When the predictions failed to come true, the prophecies remained the only hope: with the result that they alone rule over our history. Marxism and its successors will be examined here from the angle of prophecy.

THE BOURGEOIS PROPHECY

Marx is simultaneously a bourgeois and a revolutionary prophet. The latter is better known than the former. But the former explains many things in the career of the latter. A messianism of Christian and bourgeois origin, which was both historic and scientific, influenced his revolutionary messianism, which sprang from German ideology and the French rebellions.

In contrast to the ancient world, the unity of the Christian and Marxist world is astonishing. The two doctrines have in common a vision of the world which completely separates them from the Greek attitude. Jaspers defines this very well: 'it is a Christian way of thinking to consider that the history of man is strictly unique.' The Christians were the first to consider human life and the course of events as a history which is unfolding from a fixed beginning towards a definite end, in the course of which man gains his salvation or earns his punishment. The philosophy of history springs from a Christian representation, which is surprising to a Greek mind. The Greek idea of evolution has nothing in common with our idea of historic evolution. The difference between the two is the difference between a circle and a straight line. The Greeks imagine the history of the world as cyclical. Aristotle, to give a definite example, did not believe that he was living after the time of the Trojan war. Christianity was obliged, in order to penetrate the mediterranean world, to hellenize itself, which caused its doctrine to become simultaneously more flexible. But its originality lay in introducing into the ancient world two ideas which had never before been associated, the idea of history and the idea of punishment. In its concept of mediation, Christianity is Greek. In its idea of history, Christianity is Judaic and will be found again in German ideology.

It is easier to understand this dissimilarity by underlining the hostility of historic methods of thought toward nature, which they considered as an object not for contemplation but for transformation. For the Christian, as for the Marxist, nature must be subdued. The Greeks are of the opinion that it is better to obey it. The love of the ancients for the cosmos was completely unknown to the first Christians who, moreover, awaited with impatience an imminent end of the world. Hellenism, in association with Christianity, then produces the admirable efflorescence of the Albigensian heresy on the one hand, and on the other Saint Francis. But with the Inquisition and the destruction of the Albigensian heresy, the Church again parts company with the world and with beauty, and gives back to history its pre-eminence over nature. Jaspers is again right in saying: 'It is the Christian attitude that gradually empties the world of its substance . . . since the substance resided in a conglomeration of symbols.' These symbols are those of the drama of the divinity which unfolds throughout time. Nature is only the setting for this drama. The delicate equilibrium between humanity and nature, man's consent to the world, which gives ancient thought its distinction and its refulgence, was first shattered for the benefit of history by Christianity. The entry into this history of the nordic peoples, who have no tradition of friendship with the world, precipitated this trend. From the moment that the divinity of Christ is denied, or that thanks to the efforts of German ideology, He only symbolizes the man-god, the concept of mediation disappears and a Judaic world reappears. The implacable god of war rules again; all beauty is insulted as the source of idle pleasures, nature itself is enslaved. Marx, from this point of view, is the Jeremiah of the god of history and the Saint Augustine of the revolution. That this explains the really reactionary aspects of his doctrine can be demonstrated by a simple comparison with his one contemporary who was an intelligent theorist of reaction.

Joseph de Maistre refutes Jacobinism and Calvinism, two doctrines which summed up for him 'everything bad that has been thought for three centuries', in the name of a Christian philosophy of history. To counter schisms and heresies, he wanted to recreate 'the robe without a seam' of a really Catholic Church. His aim – and this can be seen at the period of his masonic adventures – is the universal Christian city. Maistre dreams of a protoplastic Adam, or the Universal Man, of Fabre D'Olivet, who will be the rallying-point of individual soul and of the Adam Kadmon of the Cabalists, who preceded the fall and who must now be brought to life again. When the Church has reclaimed the world, she will endow this first and last Adam with a body. In the *Soirées in Saint Petersburg* there is a mass of formulae on this subject which bears a striking resemblance to the messianic formulae of Hegel and Marx. In both the terrestrial and celestial Jerusalem that Maistre imagines 'all the inhabitants pervaded by the same spirit will pervade one another and will reflect one another's happiness'. Maistre does not go so far as to deny personal survival after death; he only dreams of a mysterious unity reconquered in which, 'evil having been annihilated, there will be no more passion nor self-interest', and where 'man will be reunited with himself when his double standard will be obliterated and his two centres unified.'

In the city of absolute knowledge, where the eyes of the mind and the eyes of the body became as one, Hegel also reconciled contradictions. But Maistre's vision again coincides with Marx who proclaims 'the end of the quarrel between essence and existence, between freedom and necessity'. Evil, for Maistre, who is an *ancien régime* reactionary, is less explicit on this point than Marx. Meanwhile he was awaiting a great religious revolution of which 1789 was only the 'appalling preface'. He quotes Saint John who asks that we *build* truth, which is exactly the programme of the modern revolutionary mind, and Saint Paul who announces that 'the last enemy

159

who must be destroyed is death'. Humanity marches, through crimes, violence, and death, towards this final consummation which will justify everything. The earth for Maistre is nothing but 'an immense altar on which all the living must be sacrificed, without end, without limit, without respite, until the end of time, until the extinction of evil, until the death of death'. However, his fatalism is active as well as passive. 'Man must act as if he were capable of all things and resign himself as if he were capable of nothing.' We find in Marx the same sort of creative fatalism. Maistre undoubtedly justifies the established order. But Marx justifies the order which is established in his time. The most eloquent eulogy of capitalism was made by its greatest enemy. Marx is only anti-capitalist in so far as capitalism is out of date. Another order must be established which will demand, in the name of history, a new conformity. As for the means, they are the same for Marx as for Maistre: political realism, discipline, force. When Maistre adopts Boussuet's bold idea that 'the heretic is he who has personal ideas', in other words ideas which have no reference either to a social or religious tradition, he provides the formula for the most ancient and the most modern of conformities. The Solicitor-General, pessimistic bard of the executioner, then proceeds to proclaim the coming of our diplomatic public prosecutors.

It goes without saying that these resemblances do not make Maistre a Marxist, nor Marx a traditional Christian. Marxist atheism is absolute. But nevertheless it does reinstate the supreme being. From this angle, socialism is therefore an enterprise for the deification of man and has assumed some of the characteristics of traditional religions. This reconciliation, in any case, is instructive as concerns the Christian origins of all types of historic messianism, even revolutionary messianism. The only difference lies in a change of symbols. With Maistre, as with Marx, the end of time realizes Vigny's ambitious dream, the reconciliation of the wolf and the lamb, the procession of criminal and victim to the same altar, the reopening or opening of a terrestrial paradise. For Marx, the laws of history reflect material reality; for Maistre they reflect divine reality. But for the former, matter is the substance; for the latter, the substance of his god is incarnate here below. Eternity separates them at the beginning, but the doctrines of history end by reuniting them in a realistic conclusion.

Maistre hated Greece (it also irked Marx, who found any form of beauty under the sun completely alien) of which he said that it had corrupted Europe by bequeathing it its spirit of division. It would have been more appropriate to say that Greek thought was the spirit of unity, precisely because it could not do without intermediaries, and because it was, on the contrary, quite unaware of the historic spirit of totality which was invented by Christianity and which, cut off from its religious origins, threatens the life of Europe today. 'Is there a fable, a form of madness, a vice which has not a Greek name, a Greek emblem, or a Greek mask?' Apart from outraged puritanism, this passionate denunciation expresses the spirit of modernity at variance with the ancient world and in direct continuity with authoritarian socialism, which is about to deconsecrate Christianity and incorporate it in a Church bent on conquest.

Marx's scientific materialism is itself of bourgeois origin. Progress, the future of science, the cult of technology and of production are bourgeois myths which in the nineteenth century became dogma. We note that the *Communist Manifesto* appeared in the same year as Renan's *Future of Science*. This profession of faith, which would cause considerable consternation to a contemporary reader, nevertheless gives the most accurate idea of the almost mystic hopes aroused in the nineteenth century by the expansion of industry and the surprising progress made by science. This hope is the hope of bourgeois society itself – the final beneficiary of technical progress.

The idea of progress is contemporary to the age of enlightenment and to the bourgeois revolution. Of course, certain sources of its inspiration can be found in the seventeenth century: the quarrel between the Ancients and the Moderns already introduced into European ideology the perfectly absurd conception of an artistic form of progress. In a more serious fashion, the idea of a science which steadily increases its conquests can also be derived from

Cartesian philosophy. But Turgot, in 1750, is the first person to give a clear definition of the new faith. His treatise on the progress of the human mind basically recapitulates Bossuet's universal history: except that the idea of progress is substituted for the divine will. 'The total mass of the human race, by alternating stages of calm and agitation, of good and evil, always marches, though with dragging footsteps, towards greater and greater perfection.' This optimistic statement will furnish the basic ingredient of the rhetorical observations of Condorcet, the official theorist of progress, which he linked with the progress of the State and of which he was also the official victim in that the enlightened State forced him to poison himself. Sorel was perfectly correct in saying that the philosophy of progress was exactly the philosophy to suit a society eager to enjoy the material prosperity derived from technical progress. When we are assured that tomorrow, in the natural order of events, will be better than today, we can enjoy ourselves in peace. Progress, paradoxically, can be used to justify conservatism. A draft drawn on confidence in the future, it allows the master to have a clear conscience. The slave and those whose present life is miserable and who can find no consolation in the heavens, are assured that at least the future belongs to them. The future is the only kind of property that the masters willingly concede to the slaves.

These reflections are not, as we can see, out of date. But they are not out of date because the revolutionary spirit has resumed this ambiguous and convenient theme of progress. Of course, it is not the same kind of progress; Marx cannot pour enough scorn on bourgeois rational optimism. His concept of reason, as we shall see, is different. But arduous progress towards a future of reconciliation nevertheless defines Marx's thought. Hegel and Marxism destroyed the formal values which lighted, for the Jacobins, the straight road of this optimistic version of history. Nevertheless they preserved this idea of the march forward of history, which was simply confounded by them with social progress and declared necessary. Thus they continued on the path of nineteenth-century bourgeois thought. Tocqueville, enthusiastically succeeded by Pecqueur (who influenced

Marx), had solemnly proclaimed that: 'The gradual and progressive development of equality is both the past and the future of the history of man.' To obtain Marxism, substitute the term 'level of production' for 'equality' and imagine that in the final stage of production a transformation takes place and a reconciled society is achieved.

As for the necessity of evolution, Auguste Comte, with the law of three stages of man which he formulates in 1822, gives the most systematic definition of it. Comte's conclusions are curiously like those finally accepted by scientific socialism. Positivism demonstrates, with considerable clarity, the repercussions of the ideological revolution of the nineteenth century, of which Marx is one of the representatives, and which consisted of relegating to the end of history the Garden of Eden and the Revelation which tradition had always placed at the beginning. The positivist era which was bound to follow the metaphysical era and the theological era was to mark the advent of a religion of humanity. Henri Gouhier gives an exact definition of Comte's enterprise when he says that his concern was to discover a man without any traces of God. Comte's primary aim, which was to substitute, everywhere, the relative for the absolute, was quickly transformed, by force of circumstances, into the deification of the relative and into preaching a new religion which is both universal and without transcendence. Comte saw, in the Jacobin cult of reason, an anticipation of positivism and considered himself, with perfect justification, as the real successor of the revolutionaries of 1789. He continued and enlarged the scope of this revolution by suppressing the transcendence of principles and by systematically founding the religion of the species. His formula 'set aside God in the name of religion' meant nothing else but this. Inaugurating a mania which has since enjoyed a great vogue, he wanted to be the Saint Paul of this new religion and replace the Catholicism of Rome by the Catholicism of Paris. We know that he wanted to see, in all the cathedrals, 'the statue of deified humanity on the former altar of God'. He calculated with considerable accuracy that they would be preaching positivism in Notre-Dame before 1860. This calculation was not as ridiculous as it seems. Notre-Dame, in a state of siege, still resists: but the religion of humanity was effectively preached towards the end of the nineteenth century and Marx, despite the fact that he had not read Comte, was one of its prophets. Marx only understood that a religion which did not embrace transcendence should properly be called politics. Comte knew it too, after all, or at least he understood that his religion was primarily a form of social idolatry and that it implied political realism,* the negation of individual rights and the establishment of despotism. A society whose scientists would be priests, two thousand bankers and technicians ruling over a Europe of one hundred and twenty million inhabitants where private life would be absolutely identified with public life, where absolute obedience 'of action, of thought, and of feeling' would be given to the high priest who would reign over everything, such was Comte's Utopia which announces what might be called the horizontal religions of our times. Convinced of the enlightening powers of science, Comte forgot to provide a police force. Others will be more practical; the religion of humanity will be effectively founded on the blood and suffering of humanity.

Finally, if we add to these observations that Marx owes to the bourgeois economists the idea, which he claims exclusively as his own, of the part played by industrial production in the development of humanity, and that he took the essentials of his theory of work-value from Ricardo, an economist of the bourgeois industrial revolution, our right to say that his prophecy is bourgeois in content will doubtless be recognized. These comparisons only aim to show that Marx, instead of being, as the fanatical Marxists of our day would have it, the beginning and the end of the prophecy, on the contrary, participates in human nature: he is an heir before he is a pioneer. His doctrine, which he wanted to be a realist doctrine, was actually realistic during the period of the religion of science, of Darwinian evolutionism, of the steam engine, and the textile industry. A hundred years later, science has encountered relativity, uncertainty, and hazard; the economy must take into account electricity, metal-

* 'Everything which develops spontaneously is necessarily legitimate, for a certain time.'

lurgy, and atomic production. The inability of pure Marxism to assimilate its successive discoveries was shared by the bourgeois optimist of Marx's time. It renders ridiculous the Marxist pretension of maintaining that truths one hundred years old are unalterable without ceasing to be scientific. Nineteenth-century messianism, whether it is revolutionary or bourgeois, has not resisted the successive developments of this science and this history, which to different degrees they have deified.

THE REVOLUTIONARY PROPHECY

Marx's prophecy is also revolutionary in principle. In that all human reality has its origins in the fruits of production, historic evolution is revolutionary because the economy is revolutionary. At each level of production the economy arouses the antagonisms which destroy, to the profit of a superior level of production, the corresponding society. Capitalism is the last of these stages of production because it produces the conditions in which every antagonism will be resolved and where there will be no more economy. On that day our history will become pre-history. This representation is the same as Hegel's, but in another perspective. The dialectic is considered from the angle of the spirit. Marx, of course, never spoke himself about dialectical materialism. He left to his heirs the task of extolling this logical monstrosity. But he says, at the same time, that reality is dialectic and that it is economic. Reality is a perpetual process of evolution, propelled by the fertile impact of perpetual antagonisms which are resolved each time into a superior synthesis which, itself, creates its opposite and again causes history to advance. What Hegel affirmed concerning reality advancing towards the spirit, Marx affirms concerning economy on the march towards a classless society; everything is both itself and its opposite, and this contradiction compels it to become something else. Capitalism, because it is bourgeois, reveals itself as revolutionary and prepares the way for communism.

Marx's originality lies in affirming that history is simultaneously dialectic and economic. Hegel, more extreme, affirmed that it was both matter and spirit. Moreover, it could only be matter to the extent that it was spirit and vice versa. Marx denies the spirit as the definitive substance and affirms historic materialism. We can immediately remark, with Berdaieff, on the impossibility of reconciling the dialectic with materialism. There can only be a dialectic of the mind. But even materialism itself is an ambiguous idea. Even only to form this word, it must be admitted that there is something more in the world than matter alone. For even stronger reasons, this criticism applies to historic materialism. History is distinguished from nature precisely by the fact that it transforms, by means of will, science, and passion. Marx, then, is not a pure materialist, for the obvious reason that there is neither a pure nor absolute materialism. So far is it from being pure or absolute that it recognizes that if weapons can secure the triumph of theory, theory can equally well give birth to weapons. Marx's position would be more properly called historic determinism. He does not deny thought; he imagines it absolutely determined by exterior reality. 'For me, the process of thought is only the reflection of the process of reality transported and transposed to the mind of man.' This particularly clumsy definition has no meaning. How and by what can an exterior process be 'transported to the mind', and this difficulty is as nothing compared to that of then defining 'the transposition' of this process. But Marx used the short-sighted philosophy of his time. What he wishes to say can be defined on other planes.

For him, man is only history, and in particular the history of the means of production. Marx, in fact, remarks that man differs from animals in that he produces his own means of subsistence. If he does not first eat, if he does not clothe himself or take shelter, he does not exist. This *primum vivere* is his first determination. The little that he thinks at this moment is in direct relation to these inevitable necessities. Marx then demonstrates that this dependence is both invariable and inevitable. 'The history of industry is the open book of man's essential faculties.' His personal generalization consists of inferring from this affirmation, which is on the whole acceptable, that economic dependence is unique and suffices to explain everything which still remains to be demonstrated. We can admit that economic determination plays a highly important role in the genesis of human thoughts and actions without drawing the conclusion, as Marx does, that the German rebellion against Napoleon is explained only by the lack of sugar and coffee. Moreover, pure determinism is absurd in itself. If it were not, then one single affirmation would suffice to lead, from consequence to consequence, to the entire truth. If this is not so, then either we have never made a single true affirmation – not even the one stated by determinism – or we simply happen occasionally to say the truth, but without any consequences, and determinism is then false. However, Marx had his reasons, which are foreign to pure logic, for resorting to so arbitrary a simplification.

To put economic determinations at the root of all human action is to sum man up in terms of his social relations. There is no such thing as a solitary man, that is the indisputable discovery of the nineteenth century. An arbitrary deduction then leads to the statement that man only feels solitary in society for social reasons. If, in fact, the solitary mind must be explained by something which is outside man, then man is on the road to some form of transcendence. On the other hand, society has only man as its source of origin; if, in addition, it can be affirmed that society is the creator of man, it would seem as though one had achieved the total explanation which would allow the final banishment of transcendence. Man would then be, as Marx wanted, 'author and actor of his own history'. Marx's prophecy is revolutionary because he completes the movement of negation begun by the philosophy of illumination. The Jacobins destroyed the transcendence of a personal god, but replaced it by the transcendence of principles. Marx institutes contemporary atheism by destroying the transcendence of principles as well. Marx destroys, even more radically than Hegel, the transcendence of reason and hurls it into the stream of history. Even before their time, history was a regulating principle, now it is triumphant. Marx goes further than Hegel and pretends to consider him as an idealist (which he is not, at least no more than Marx is a materialist) to the precise extent that the reign of the mind restores in a certain way, a supra-historic value. *Das Kapital* returns to the dialectic of mastery and servitude, but replaces a consciousness of self by economic autonomy and the final reign of the absolute Spirit through the advent of communism. 'Atheism is humanism mediated by the suppression of religion, communism is humanism mediated by the suppression of private property.' Religious alienation has the same origin as economic alienation. Religion can only be disposed of by achieving the absolute liberty of man in regard to his material determinations. The revolution is identified with atheism and with the reign of man.

That is why Marx is brought to the point of putting the emphasis on economic and social determination. Its most profitable undertaking has been to reveal the reality which is hidden behind the formal values of which the bourgeois of his time made a great show. His theory of mystification is still valid, because it is in fact universally true, and is equally applicable to revolutionary mystification. The freedom of which Monsieur Thiers dreamed was the freedom of privilege consolidated by the police; the family, extolled by the conservative newspapers, was supported by social conditions in which men and women were sent down the mines, attached to a communal rope; morality prospered on the prostitution of the working classes. That the demands of honesty and intelligence were put to egoistic ends by the hypocrisy of a mediocre and grasping society was a misfortune that Marx, the incomparable eye-opener, denounced with a vehemence quite unknown before him. This indignant denunciation brought other excesses in its train which require quite another denunciation. But, above all, we must recognize and state that the denunciation was born in the blood of the abortive Lyon rebellion of 1834 and in the despicable cruelty of the Versailles moralists in 1871. 'The man who has nothing is nothing.' If this affirmation is actually false, it was very nearly true in the optimist society of the nineteenth century. The extreme irresponsibility brought about by the economy of prosperity was to compel Marx to give first place to social and economic relationships and to magnify still more his prophecy of the reign of man.

It is now easier to understand the purely economic explanation of history offered by Marx. If principles are deceptive, only the reality of poverty and work is true. If it is then possible to demonstrate that this suffices to explain the past and the future of mankind, then principles will be destroyed forever and with them the society which profits by them. This in fact is Marx's ambition.

Man is born into a world of production and social relations. The unequal opportunities of different lands, the more or less rapid improvements in the means of production and the struggle for life have rapidly created social inequalities which have been crystallized into antagonisms between production and distribution; and, consequently, into class struggles. These struggles and antagonisms are the motive power of history. Slavery, in ancient times, and feudal bondage were stages on a long road which led to the artisanship of the Middle Ages, when the producer was master of the means of production. At this moment the opening of world trade routes and the discovery of new outlets demanded a less provincial form of production. The contradiction between the method of production and the new demands of distribution already announces the end of the régime of small-scale agricultural and industrial production. The industrial revolution, the invention of steam, and competition for outlets inevitably led to the expropriation of the small proprietor and to the introduction of large-scale production. The means of production are then concentrated in the hands of those who are able to buy them; the real producers, the workers, now only dispose of the strength of their arms which can be sold to the 'man with the money'. Thus bourgeois capitalism is defined by the separation of the producer from the means of production. From this conflict a series of inevitable consequences are going to spring which allow Marx to predicate the end of social antagonisms.

At first sight there is no reason why the firmly established principle of a dialectical class struggle should suddenly cease to be true. It is always true or it has never been true. Marx says plainly that there will be no more classes after the revolution than there were social distinctions after 1789. But social distinctions disappeared without classes disappearing, and there is nothing to prove that classes will not give way to some other form of social antagonism. The essential point of the Marxist prophecy lies, nevertheless, in this affirmation.

We know the Marxist scheme. Marx, following in the footsteps of Adam Smith and Ricardo, defines the value of all commodities in terms of the amount of work necessary to produce them. The amount of work is itself a commodity, sold by the proletarian to the capitalist, of which the value is defined by the quantity of work which produces it; in other words, by the value of the consumer's good necessary for its maintenance. The capitalist, in buying this commodity, thereby undertakes to pay sufficient for he who sells it – in other words, the worker – to feed and perpetuate himself. But at the same time he acquires the right to make the latter work as long as he can. He can work for a very much longer time than is necessary to pay for his subsistence. In a twelve-hour day, if half of the time suffices to produce a value equivalent to the value of the products of subsistence, the other six hours are hours not paid for, a plus-value, which constitutes the capitalist's own profit. Thus the capitalist's interest lies in prolonging to the maximum the hours of work or, when he can do so no longer, of increasing the worker's output to the maximum. The first type of coercion is a matter of oppression and cruelty. The second is a question of the organization of labour. It leads first to the division of labour, and finally to the utilization of the machine, which contributes to the dehumanization of the worker. Besides, competition for foreign markets and the necessity for larger and larger investments in raw materials, produce phenomena of concentration and accumulation. First, small capitalists are absorbed by big capitalists who can maintain, for example, unprofitable prices for a long period. A larger and larger part of the profits is finally invested in new machines and accumulated in the fixed assets of capital. This double movement first of all hastens the ruin of the middle classes, who are absorbed into the proletariat, and then proceeds to concentrate, in an increasingly small number of hands, the riches which are produced uniquely by the proletariat. Thus the proletariat increases in size in proportion to its increasing ruin. Capital is now concentrated in the hands of only a very few masters whose growing power is based on robbery. Moreover, these masters are shaken to their foundations by successive crises, overwhelmed by the contradictions of the system, and can no longer even assure mere subsistence to their slaves who then come to depend on private or public charity. A day comes, inevitably, when a huge army of oppressed slaves find themselves face to face with a handful of despicable masters. That day is the day of revolution. 'The ruin of the bourgeoisie and the victory of the proletariat are equally inevitable.'

This henceforth famous description does not yet give an account of the end of all antagonisms. After the victory of the proletariat, the struggle for life might well give birth to new antagonisms. Two ideas then intervene, one of which is economic, the identity of the development of production and the development of society, and the other, purely systematic, the mission of the proletariat. These two ideas reunite in what might be called Marx's activist passiveness.

The same economic evolution which in effect concentrates capital in a very few hands, makes the antagonism both more violent and, to a certain extent, unreal. It seems that, at the highest point of development of the productive forces, the slightest stimulus would lead to the proletariat finding itself alone in possession of the means of production, already snatched from the grasp of private ownership and concentrated in one enormous mass which, henceforth, would be held in common. When private property is concentrated in the hands of one single owner, it is only separated from collective ownership by the existence of one single man. The inevitable result of private capitalism is a kind of State capitalism which will then only have to be put to the service of the community to give birth to a society where capital and labour, henceforth indistinguishable, will produce, in one identical advance towards progress, both justice and abundance. It is in consideration of this happy outcome that Marx has always extolled the revolutionary role played, unconsciously it is true, by the bourgeoisie. He spoke of the 'historic rights' of capitalism, which he called a source both of progress and of misery. The historic mission and the justification of capitalism are, in his eyes, to prepare the ideal conditions for a superior mode of production. This mode of production is not, in itself, revolutionary; it will only be the crowning point of the revolution. Only the fundamental principles of bourgeois production are revolutionary. When Marx affirms that humanity only sets itself problems that it can solve, he is simultaneously demonstrating that the germ of the solution of the revolutionary problem is to be found, in principle, in the capitalist system itself. Therefore he recommends tolerating the bourgeois State, and even helping to build it, rather than returning to a less industrialized form of production. The proletariat 'can and must accept the bourgeois revolution as a condition of the working-class revolution'.

Thus Marx is the prophet of production and we are justified in thinking that on this precise point, and on no other, he ignored reality in favour of the system. He never ceased defending Ricardo, the economist of production in the manner of Manchester, against those who accused him of wanting production for production's sake ('He was absolutely right!' Marx exclaims) and of wanting it without any consideration for mankind. 'That is precisely his merit', Marx replies, with the same airy indifference as Hegel. What in fact does the sacrifice of individual men matter as long as it contributes to the salvation of all mankind! Progress resembles 'that horrible pagan god who only wished to drink nectar from the skulls of his fallen enemies'. But at least it is progress, which will cease to inflict torture after the industrial apocalypse when the day of reconciliation comes.

But if the proletariat cannot avoid this revolution nor avoid being put in possession of the means of production, will it at least know how to use them for the benefit of all? Where is the guarantee that, in the very bosom of the revolution, orders, classes, and antagonism will not arise? The guarantee lies in Hegel. The proletariat is forced to use its wealth for the universal good. It is not the proletariat, it is the universal in opposition to the particular, in other words to capitalism. The antagonism between capital and the proletariat is the last phase of the struggle between the particular and the universal, the same struggle which animated the historic tragedy of master and slave. At the end of the visionary design constructed by Marx, the proletariat will unite all classes and only discard a handful of masters, perpetrators of 'notorious crime', who will be justly destroyed by the revolution. What is more, capitalism, by driving the proletariat to the final point of degradation, gradually delivers it from every determination that might separate it from other men. It has nothing, neither property nor morality nor country. Therefore it clings to nothing but the species of which it is henceforth the naked and implacable representative. In affirming itself it affirms everything and everyone. Not because members of the proletariat are gods, but simply because they have been reduced to the most abjectly inhuman condition. 'Only the proletariat, totally excluded from this affirmation of their personality, are capable of realizing the complete affirmation of self.'

That is the mission of the proletariat: to bring forth supreme dignity from supreme humiliation. Through its suffering and its struggles, it is Christ in human form redeeming collective sin from alienation. It is, primarily, the multiform bearer of total negation and then the herald of definitive affirmation. 'Philosophy cannot realize itself without the disappearance of the proletariat, the proletariat cannot be itself without the realization of philosophy,' and again: 'The proletariat can only exist on the basis of world history . . . Communist action can only exist as historic reality on the planetary scale.' But this Christ is, at the same time, an avenger. According to Marx, he carries out the sentence that private property passed on itself. 'All the houses, in our times, are marked with a mysterious red cross. The judge is history, the executioner is the proletariat.' Thus the fulfilment is inevitable. Crisis will succeed crisis,* the degradation of the proletariat will become more and more profound, its existence will endure until the time of the universal crisis when the world of change will vanish and when history, by the supreme act of violence,

* Every ten or eleven years, Marx predicted. But the period between the recurrence of the cycles will gradually shorten.

will cease to be violent any longer. The kingdom of ends without means will have come.

We can see that this fatalism could be driven (as happened to Hegelian thought) to a sort of political quietism by Marxists, like Kautsky, for whom it was as little within the power of the proletariat to create the revolution as within the power of the bourgeois to prevent it. Even Lenin, who was to choose the activist aspect of the doctrine, wrote in 1905, in the style of an act of excommunication: 'It is a reactionary way of thinking to try to find salvation in the working class in any other way but in the top-heavy development of capitalism.' It is not in the nature of economics, according to Marx, to make leaps in the dark and it must not be encouraged to gallop ahead. It is completely false to say that the socialist reformers remained faithful to Marx on this point. On the contrary, fatalism excludes all reforms, in that there would be a risk of mitigating the catastrophic aspect of the outcome. The logic of such an attitude leads to the approval of everything that tends to increase working-class poverty. The worker must be given nothing so that one day he can have everything.

And yet Marx saw the danger of this particular form of quietism. Power either does not wait or else it waits indefinitely. A day comes when it must be seized and it is the exact definition of this day which remains of doubtful clarity to all readers of Marx. On this point he never stops contradicting himself. He remarked that society was 'historically compelled to pass through a period of dictatorship by the working classes'. As for the nature of this dictatorship, his definitions are contradictory. We are sure that he condemned the State in no uncertain terms saying that its existence and the existence of servitude are inseparable. But he protested against Bakunin's nevertheless judicious observation of finding the idea of provisional dictatorship contrary to what is known as human nature. Marx thought, it is true, that the dialectical verities were superior to psychological verities. What does the dialectic say? That 'the abolition of the State has no meaning except among communists where it is an inevitable result of the suppression of classes, the disappearance of which necessarily leads to the disappearance of the need for a power organized by one class for the oppression of another'. According to the sacred formula the government of people was then to be replaced by the administration of affairs. The dialectic was therefore explicit and only justified the existence of the proletarian State for the period necessary for the destruction or integration of the bourgeois class. But, unfortunately, the prophecy and its attitude of fatalism allowed other interpretations. If it is certain that the kingdom will come, what does time matter? Suffering is never provisional for the man who does not believe in the future. But one hundred years of suffering are fleeting in the eyes of the man who prophesies, for the hundred and first year, the Eternal City. In the perspective of the Marxist prophecy, nothing matters. In any event, when the bourgeois class has disappeared, the proletariat will establish the rule of the universal man at the summit of production, by the very logic of productive development. What does it matter that this should be accomplished by dictatorship and violence? In this New Jerusalem, echoing with the roar of miraculous machinery, who will still remember the cry of the victims?

The golden age, postponed until the end of history and coincident, to add to its attractions, with an apocalypse, therefore justifies everything. The prodigious ambitions of Marxism must be considered and its inordinate doctrines evaluated, in order to understand that hope on such a scale leads to the inevitable neglect of problems which therefore appear to be secondary. 'Communism in so far as it is real appropriation of the human essence by man and for man, in so far as it is the return of man to himself as a social being, in other words as a human being, a complete conscious return which preserves all the values of the inner movement, this communism, being absolute naturalism, coincides with humanism: it is the real end of the quarrel between man and nature, between man and man, between essence and existence, between externalization and the affirmation of self, between liberty and necessity, between the individual and the species. It solves the mystery of history and is aware of having solved it.' It is only the language here that aims at being scientific. Basically, where is the difference from Fourier who announces 'fertile deserts, sea water made drinkable and tasting of violets, eternal spring . . .'? The eternal springtime of mankind is foretold to us in the language of an Encyclical letter. What can man without God want and hope for, if not the kingdom of man? This explains the exaltation of all Marxist disciples. 'In a society without suffering, it is easy to ignore death,' says one of them. However, and this is the real condemnation of our society, fear of death is a luxury which is felt far more by the idler than the worker who is stifled by his own occupation. But every kind of socialism is Utopian, most of all scientific socialism. Utopia replaces God by the future. Then it proceeds to identify the future with ethics; the only values are those which serve this particular future. For that reason Utopias have almost always been coercive and authoritarian. Marx, in so far as he is a Utopian, does not differ from his frightening predecessors and one part of the teaching more than justifies his successors.

It has undoubtedly been correct to emphasize the ethical demands which form the basis of the Marxist dream. It must, in all fairness, be said, before examining the check to Marxism, that in them lie the real greatness of Marx. The very core of his theory was that work is profoundly dignified and unjustly despised. He rebelled against the degradation of work to the level of a commodity and of the worker to the level of an object. He reminded the privileged that their privileges were not divine and that property was not an eternal right. He gave a bad conscience to those who had no right to a clear one and denounced, with unparalleled profundity, a class whose crime is not so much having had power as having used it to advance the ends of a mediocre society deprived of any real nobility. To him we owe the idea which is the despair of our times – but in this case despair is worth more than any hope – that when work is a disgrace, it is not life, even though it occupies every moment of a life. Who, despite the pretensions of this society, can sleep in it in peace, when they know that it derives its mediocre pleasures from the work of millions of dead souls? By demanding for the worker real riches, which are not the riches of money but of leisure and creation, he has reclaimed, despite all appearance to the contrary, the dignity of man. In doing so, and this can be said with conviction, he never wanted the additional degradation which has been imposed on man in his name. One of his phrases, which for once is clear and trenchant, forever denies his triumphant disciples the greatness and the humanity which once were his: 'An end which requires unjust means is not a just end.'

But Nietzsche's tragedy is again discovered here. The aims, the prophecies are generous and universal, but the doctrine is restrictive and the reduction of every value to historic terms leads to the direst consequences. Marx thought that historic ends, at least, would prove to be moral and rational. That was his Utopia. But Utopia, at least in the form he knew it, is destined to serve cynicism of which he wanted no part. Marx destroys all transcendence, then carries out, by himself, the transition from fact to duty. But his concept of duty has no other origin but fact. The demand for justice ends in injustice if it is not primarily based on an ethical justification of justice: without this, crime itself one day becomes a duty. When good and evil are reintegrated in time and confused with events, nothing is any longer good or bad, but only either premature or out of date. Who will decide on the opportunity, if not the opportunist? Later, say the disciples, you shall judge. But the victims will not be there to judge. For the victim, the present is the only value, rebellion the only action. Messianism, in order to exist, must construct a defence against the victims. It is possible that Marx did not want this, but in this lies his responsibility which must be examined, that he incurred by justifying, in the name of the revolution, the henceforth bloody struggle against all forms of rebellion.

THE CHECK TO THE PROPHECY

Hegel haughtily brings history to an end in 1807; the disciples of Saint-Simon believe that the revolutionary convulsions of 1830 and 1848 are the last; Comte dies in 1857 preparing to climb into the pulpit and preach positivism to a humanity returned at last from the path of error. With the same blind romanticism, Marx, in his turn, prophesies the classless society and the solution of the mystery of historic events. Slightly more circumspect, however, he does not fix the date. Unfortunately, his prophecy also described the march of history up to the hour of fulfillment; it predicted the trends of events. The events and the facts, of course, have forgotten to arrange themselves according to the synthesis; and this already explains why it has been necessary to rally them by force. But above all, the prophecies from the moment that they begin to betray the living hopes of millions of men, cannot with impunity remain indeterminate. A time comes when deception transforms patient hope into furious disillusionment and when the ends, affirmed with the mania of obstinacy, demanded with ever-increasing cruelty, lead to the adoption of other means.

The revolutionary movement, at the end of the nineteenth and beginning of the twentieth centuries, lived, like the early Christians, in the expectation of the end of the world and the advent of the proletarian Christ. The passages from Marx already cited give a fair idea of the burning hope which inspired the revolutionary spirit of the time. Despite partial set-backs, this faith never ceased to increase up to the moment when it found itself, in 1917, face to face with the partial realization of its dreams. 'We are fighting for the gates of Heaven,' cried Liebknecht. In 1917 the revolutionary world really believed that it had arrived before those gates. Rosa Luxembourg's prophecy was being realized. 'The revolution will rise resoundingly tomorrow to its full height and, to your consternation, will announce with the sound of all its trumpets; I was, I am, I shall be.' The Spartakus movement believed that it had achieved the definitive revolution because, according to Marx himself, the latter would come to pass after the Russian revolution had been consummated by a Western revolution. After the revolution of 1917, a Soviet Germany would, in fact, have opened the gates of Heaven. But the Spartakus movement is crushed, the French general strike of 1920 fails, the Italian revolutionary movement is strangled. Liebknecht then recognizes that the time is not ripe for revolution. 'The period did not rebel.' But also, and now we grasp how defeat can excite vanquished faith to the point of religious trance: 'At the crash of economic collapse of which the rumblings can already be heard, the sleeping soldiers of the proletariat will awake as at the fanfare of the Last Judgement and the corpses of the victims of the struggle will arise and demand an accounting from those who are loaded down with curses.' While awaiting these events, Liebknecht and Rosa Luxembourg are assassinated and Germany rushes toward servitude. The Russian revolution remains isolated, living according to its own system, still far from the celestial gates, with an apocalypse to organize. The Advent is again postponed. Faith is intact, but it totters beneath an enormous load of problems and discoveries which Marxism had not foreseen. The new religion is once more confronted with Galilee: to preserve its faith, it must deny the sun and humiliate free man.

What does Galilee say, in fact, at this moment? What are the errors, demonstrated by history itself, of the prophecy? We know that the economic revolution of the contemporary world refutes a certain number of the postulates of Marx. If the revolution is to occur at the end of two parallel movements, the indefinite shrinking of capital and the indefinite expansion of the proletariat, it will not occur or ought not to occur. Capital and proletariat have both been equally unfaithful to Marx. The tendency observed in industrial England of the nineteenth century has, in certain cases, changed its course, and in others become more complex. Economic crises which should have occurred with increasing frequency have, on the contrary, become more sporadic: capitalism has learned the secrets of planned production and has contributed, on its own part, to the growth of the Moloch State. Moreover, with the introduction of companies in which stock could be held, capital, instead of becoming increasingly concentrated, has given rise to a new category of small-holders whose very last desire would certainly be to encourage strikes. Small enterprises have been, in many cases, destroyed by competition as Marx foresaw. But the complexity of modern production has generated a multitude of small factories around great enterprises. In 1938 Ford was able to announce that five thousand two hundred independent workshops supplied him with their products. Of course large industries inevitably assimilated these enterprises to a certain extent. But the essential thing is that these small industrialists form an intermediary social layer which complicates the scheme that Marx imagined. Finally, the law of concentration has proved absolutely false in the case of agricultural economy, which was treated with considerable frivolity by Marx. The hiatus is important here. In one of its aspects, the history of socialism in our times can be considered as the struggle between the proletarian movement and the peasant class. This struggle continues, on the historical plane, the nineteenth-century ideological struggle between authoritarian socialism and libertarian socialism, of which the peasant and artisan origins are quite evident. Thus Marx had, in the ideological material of his time, the elements for a study of the peasant problem. But his desire to systematize made him oversimplify everything. This particular simplification was to prove expensive for the kulaks who constituted more than five million historic exceptions to be brought, by death and deportation, within the Marxist pattern.

The same desire for simplification diverted Marx from the phenomenon of the nation in the very century of nationalism. He believed that through commerce and exchange, through the very victory of the proletariat, the barriers would fall. But it was national barriers which brought about the fall of the proletarian ideal. The struggle between nations has been proved at least as important, as a means of explaining history, as the class struggle. But nations cannot be entirely explained by economics; therefore the system ignored them.

The proletariat, on its part, did not toe the line. First of all, Marx's fear is confirmed: reforms and trade unions brought about a rise in the standard of living and an amelioration in working conditions. These improvements are very far from constituting an equitable settlement of the social problem. But the miserable condition of the English textile workers, in Marx's time, far from becoming general and even deteriorating, as he would have liked, has on the contrary been alleviated. Marx would not complain about this today, the equilibrium having been re-established by another error in his predictions. It has, in fact, been possible to prove that the most efficacious revolutionary or trade union asset has always been the existence of a working-class élite who have not been sterilized by hunger. Poverty and degeneration have never ceased to be what they were before Marx's time, and what he did not want to admit that they were despite all his observations: factors contributing to servitude not to revolution. One-third of working-class Germany was unemployed in 1933. Bourgeois society was then obliged to provide a means of livelihood for these unemployed, thus bringing about the situation which Marx said was essential for revolution. But it is not a good thing that future revolutionaries should be put in the situation of expecting to be fed by the State. This unnatural habit leads to others, which are even less good, and which Hitler made into doctrine.

Finally, the proletariat did not increase in numbers indefinitely. The very conditions of industrial production, which every Marxist is called upon to encourage, improved, to a considerable extent, the conditions of the middle class* and even created a new social stratum, the technicians. The ideal, so dear to Lenin, of a society in which the engineer would at the same time be a labourer is in conflict with the facts. The principal fact is that technology, like science, has reached such a degree of complication that it is not possible for a single man to understand the totality of its principles and applications. It is almost impossible, for instance, for a physicist today to have a complete understanding of the biological science of the times. Even within the realms of physics he cannot claim to be equally familiar with every branch of the subject. It is the same thing with technology. From the moment that productivity, which is considered

* From 1920 to 1930, in a period of intense productivity, the number of metallurgical workers decreased in the U.S.A., while the number of salesmen, working for the same industry, almost doubled.

by both bourgeois and Marxist as a benefit in itself, is developed to enormous proportions the division of labour, which Marx thought could have been avoided, became inevitable. Every worker has been brought to the point of performing a particular function without knowing the over-all plan into which his work will fit. Those who coordinate individual work have formed, by their very function, a class whose social importance is decisive.

It is only fair to point out that this era of technocracy announced by Burnham was described, about twenty years ago, by Simone Weil in a form that can be considered complete, without drawing Burnham's unacceptable conclusions. To the two traditional forms of oppression known to humanity – oppression by armed force and by wealth – Simone Weil adds a third – oppression by occupation. 'One can abolish the opposition between the buyer and the seller of work', she wrote, 'without abolishing the opposition between those who dispose of the machine and those of whom the machine disposes.' The Marxist plan to abolish the degrading opposition of intellectual work to manual work has come into conflict with the demands of production which, elsewhere, Marx exalted. Marx undoubtedly foresaw, in *Das Kapital*, the importance of the 'manager' on the level of maximum concentration of capital. But he did not believe that this concentration of capital could survive the abolition of private property. Division of labour and private property, he said, are identical expressions. History has demonstrated the contrary. The ideal régime based on collective property could be defined, according to Lenin, as justice plus electricity. In the final analysis it is only electricity, without justice.

The idea of a mission by the proletariat has not, so far, been able to formulate itself in history: that sums up the check to the Marxist prophecy. The failure of the second International has proved that the proletariat was influenced by other things as well as its economic condition and that, contrary to the famous formula, it was patriotic. The majority of the proletariat accepted or submitted to the war and collaborated, willy-nilly, in the nationalist excesses of the times. Marx intended that the working classes before they triumphed should have acquired legal and political acumen. His error only lay in believing that extreme poverty, and particularly industrial poverty, could lead to political maturity. Moreover, it is quite certain that the revolutionary capacity of the masses was curtailed by the decapitation of the libertarian revolution, during and after the Commune. After all, Marxism easily dominated the working-class movement from 1872 on, undoubtedly because of its own strength, but also because the only socialist tradition which could have opposed it had been drowned in blood: there were practically no Marxists amongst the insurgents of 1871. This automatic purification of revolution has been continued, through the activities of police States, until our times. More and more, revolution has found itself delivered into the hands of its bureaucrats and doctrinaires on the one hand, and to enfeebled and bewildered masses on the other. When the revolutionary élite are guillotined and when Talleyrand is left alive, who will oppose Bonaparte? But to these historic reasons are added economic necessities. The passages by Simone Weil on the condition of the factory worker must be read in order to realize to what degree of moral exhaustion and silent despair the rationalization of labour can lead. Simone Weil is right in saying that the worker's condition is doubly inhumane in that he is first deprived of money and then of dignity. Work in which one can have an interest, creative work, even though it is badly paid, does not degrade life. Industrial socialism has done nothing essential to alleviate the condition of the workers because it has not touched on the very principle of production and the organization of labour, which it has, on the contrary, extolled. It went so far as to offer the worker a historic justification of his lot of much the same value as a promise of celestial joy to someone who works himself to death; never did it attempt to give him the joy of creation. The political form of society is no longer in question at this level, but the beliefs of a technical civilization on which capitalism and socialism are equally dependent. Any ideas which do not advance the solution of this problem hardly touch on the misfortunes of the worker.

Only through the interplay of economic forces, so much admired by Marx, has the proletariat been able to reject the historic mission with which Marx had rightly charged it. His error can be excused because, confronted with the debasement of the ruling classes, a man who has the future of civilization at heart instinctively looks for an élite as a replacement. But this instinctive search is not, in itself alone, creative. The revolutionary bourgeoisie seized power in 1789 because they already had it. At this period legality, as Jules Monnerot says, was lagging behind the facts. The facts were that the bourgeoisie were already in possession of the posts of command and of the new power – money. The proletariat were not at all in the same position, having only their poverty and their hopes and being kept in their condition of misery by the bourgeoisie. The bourgeois class debased itself by a mania for production and material power, while the very organization of this mania made the creation of an élite impossible. But criticism of this organization and the development of rebel conscience could, on the contrary, forge a reserve élite. Only revolutionary trade-unionism, under Pelloutier and Sorel, embarked on this course and wanted to create, by professional and cultural education, new cadres for which a world without honour was calling and still calls. But that could not be accomplished in a day and the new masters were already on the scene, interested in making immediate use of human unhappiness for the sake of happiness in the distant future, rather than in relieving as much and as soon as possible the sufferings of millions of men. The authoritarian socialists deemed that history was going too slowly and that it was necessary, in order to hurry it on, to entrust the mission of the proletariat to a handful of doctrinaires. For that very reason they have been the first to deny this mission. Nevertheless it exists, not in the exclusive sense which Marx gives it, but in the sense that a mission exists for any human group which knows how to derive pride and fecundity from its labours and its sufferings. However, so that it can manifest itself, a risk must be taken and confidence put in working-class freedom and spontaneity. On the contrary, authoritarian socialism has confiscated this living freedom for the benefit of an ideal freedom, which is yet to come. In so doing, whether it wished to or not, it reinforced the attempt at enslavement begun by industrial capitalism. By the combined action of these two factors and during a hundred and fifty years, except in the Paris of the Commune which was the last refuge of rebel revolution, the proletariat has had no other historic mission but to be betrayed. The workers fought and died to give power to the military or to intellectuals who dreamed of becoming military and who would enslave them in their turn. This struggle, however, has been the source of their dignity, a fact which is recognized by all who have chosen to share their aspirations and their misfortunes. But this dignity has been acquired in opposition to the whole clan of old and new masters. At the very moment when they dare to make use of it, it denies them. In one sense, it announces their eclipse.

The economic predictions of Marx have, therefore, been at least called in question by reality. What remains true, in his vision of the economic world, is the establishment of a society more and more determined by the rhythm of production. But he shared this concept, in the enthusiasm of his period, with bourgeois ideology. The bourgeois illusions concerning science and technical progress, shared by the authoritarian socialists, gave birth to the civilization of the machine-tamers which can, through the stresses of competition and the desire for domination, be divided into enemy blocs but which on the economic plane is subject to identical laws: the accumulation of capital and nationalized and continually increasing production. The political difference, which concerns the degree of omnipotence of the State, is appreciable, but can be reduced by economic evolution. Only the difference in ethical concepts – formal virtue as opposed to historic cynicism – seems substantial. But the imperative of production dominates both universes and makes them, on the economic plane, one world.

In any event, if the economic imperative can no longer be denied, its consequences are not what Marx imagined. Economically speaking capitalism becomes oppressive through the phenomenon of accumulation. It is oppressive through being what it is, it accumulates in order to increase what it is, to exploit it all the more, and accordingly to accumulate still more. At that moment accumulation would only be necessary to a very small extent in order to guarantee social benefits. But the revolution, in its turn, becomes industrialized and realizes when accumulation is an attribute of technology itself, and not of capitalism, that the machine finally conjures up the machine. Every form of collectivity, fighting for survival, is forced to accumulate instead of distributing its revenues. It accumulates in order to increase and by doing so increases its power. Whether bourgeois or socialist, it postpones justice for a later date, for the benefit of power alone. But power opposes other forms of power. It arms and rearms because others are arming and rearming. It does not stop accumulating and will never cease to do so until the day, perhaps, when it will reign alone on earth. Moreover, for that to happen, it must pass through a war. Until that day the proletariat will only receive the bare minimum for its subsistence. The revolution compels itself to construct, at a great expenditure in human lives, the industrial and capitalist intermediary which its own system demands. Revenue is replaced by human labour. Slavery then becomes the general condition and the gates of Heaven remain locked. Such is the economic law governing a world which lives by the cult of production, and the reality is even more bloody than the law. Revolution, in the impasses where it has been led by its bourgeois opponents and its nihilist supporters, is nothing but slavery. Unless it changes its principles and its path, it can have no other final result but servile rebellions, crushed by bloodshed, or the hideous prospect of atomic suicide. The will to power, the nihilist struggle for domination and authority have done considerably more than sweep away the Marxist Utopia. This has become in its turn an historic fact destined to be put to use like all the other historic facts. This idea, which was to dominate history, has become lost in history; the mastery of every means has been reduced to a means in itself and cynically manipulated for the most banal and bloody ends. The uninterrupted development of production has not ruined the capitalist régime to the benefit of the revolution. It has equally been the ruin of both bourgeois and revolutionary society to the benefit of an idol, a Gorgon's head, contorted by dreams of unbridled power.

How could a so-called scientific socialism conflict, to such a point, with facts ? The answer is easy: it was not scientific. On the contrary, its defeat resulted from a method ambiguous enough to wish to be simultaneously determinist and prophetic, dialectic and dogmatic. If the mind is only the reflection of events, it cannot anticipate their progress, except by hypothesis. If Marxist theory is determined by economics, it can describe the past history of production, and not its future which remains in the realms of probability. The task of historic materialism can only be to establish a method of criticism of contemporary society; it is only capable of making suppositions, unless it abandons its scientific attitude, about the society of the future. Moreover, is it not for this reason that its most important work is called *Capital* and not *Revolution* ? Marx and the Marxists allowed themselves to prophesy the future and the triumph of communism to the detriment of their postulates and of their scientific method.

This prediction cannot be scientific, on the contrary, unless they stop prophesying definitively. Marxism is not scientific: at the best, it has scientific prejudices. It brought out into the open the profound difference between scientific reasoning, that fruitful instrument of research, of thought, and even of rebellion, and historic reasoning, which German ideology invented by its negation of all principles. Historic reasoning is not a type of reasoning which can within the framework of its own functions pass judgement on the world. While pretending to judge it, it really determines its course. Essentially a part of events, it directs them and is simultaneously pedagogic and all-conquering. Moreover, its more abstruse descriptions conceal the most simple truths. If man is reduced to being nothing but a character in history, he has no other choice but to subside into the sound and fury of a completely irrational history or to endow history with the form of human reason. Therefore the history of contemporary nihilism is nothing but a prolonged endeavour to give order, by human forces alone and simply by force, to a history no longer endowed with order. This pseudo-reasoning ends by identifying itself with cunning and strategy, while waiting to culminate in the ideological Empire. What part could science play in this concept ?

Nothing is less determined on conquest than reason. History is not made with scientific scruples, we are even condemned to not making history from the moment when we claim to act with scientific objectivity. Reason does not preach, or if it does, it is no longer reason. That is why historic reason is an irrational and romantic form of reason, which sometimes recalls the false logic of the insane and the mystic affirmation of the Word, of former times.

The only really scientific aspect of Marxism is to be found in its preliminary rejection of myths and in its exposure of the crudest kind of interests. But in this respect Marx is not more scientific in his attitude than La Rochefoucauld; and that is just the attitude that he abandons when he embarks on prophecy. Therefore it is not surprising that, to make Marxism scientific and to preserve this fiction which is very useful in this century of science, it has been a necessary first step to render science Marxist through terror. The progress of science, since Marx, has roughly consisted of replacing determinism and the rather crude mechanism of its period by a doctrine of provisional probability. Marx wrote to Engels that the Darwinian theory constituted the very foundation of their method. For Marxism to remain infallible, it has therefore been necessary to deny all biological discoveries made since Darwin. As it happens that all discoveries since the sudden mutations established by De Vries have consisted of introducing, contrary to the doctrines of determinism, the idea of hazard into biology, it has been necessary to entrust Lyssenko with the task of disciplining chromosomes and of demonstrating once again the truth of the most elementary determinism. That is ridiculous: to put the police force under Flaubert's Monsieur Homais would be no more ridiculous and this is the twentieth century. As far as that is concerned, the twentieth century has also witnessed the denial of the principle of indeterminism in science, of limited relativity, of the quantum theory,* and, finally, of every general tendency of contemporary science. Marxism is only scientific today in defiance of Heisenborg, Bohr, Einstein, and all the greatest minds of our time.

* Roger Callois remarks that Stalinism objects to the quantum theory but does not hesitate to make use of atomic science which is derived from it.

After all there is really nothing mysterious about the principle which consists of using scientific reasoning to the advantage of a prophecy. This has already been named the principle of authority and it is this that guides the Churches when they wish to subject living reason to dead faith and freedom of the intellect to the maintenance of temporal power. Finally, there remains of Marx's prophecy – henceforth in conflict with its two principles, economy and science – only the passionate annunciation of an event which will take place in the very far future. The only recourse of the Marxists consists of saying that the delays are simply longer than was imagined and that one day, far away in the future, the end will justify all. And so the problem which is posed is of another order. If the struggle waged by one or two generations throughout a period of economic evolution which is, perforce, beneficial, suffices to bring about a classless society, then the necessary sacrifice becomes comprehensible to the man with a militant turn of mind; the future for him has a concrete aspect – the aspect of his grandchild for instance. But if, when the sacrifice of several generations has proved insufficient, we must then embark on an infinite period of universal strife one thousand times more destructive than before, then the conviction of faith is needed in order to accept the necessity of killing and dying. This new faith is no more founded on pure reason than was the faith of the ancients.

In what terms is it possible to imagine this end of history? Marx did not fall back on Hegel's terms. He said, rather obscurely, that communism was only a necessary aspect of the future of humanity, and did not comprise the entire future. But either communism does not terminate the history of contradictions and suffering, or it does terminate it, and it is no longer possible to imagine the continuation of history except as an advance towards this perfected form of society. Thus a mystic idea is arbitrarily introduced into a description which claims to be scientific. The final disappearance of political economy – the favourite theme of Marx and Engels – indicates the end of all suffering. Economics, in fact, coincide with pain and suffering in history, which disappear with the disappearance of history. We arrive at last in the Garden of Eden.

We come no nearer to solving the problem by declaring that it is not a question of the end of history, but of a leap into the midst of a different history. We can only imagine this other history in terms of our own history: for man they are both one and the same thing. Moreover, this other history poses the same dilemma. Either it is not the solution of all contradictions and we suffer, die and kill for almost nothing, or it is the solution of contradictions and therefore, to all intents and purposes, terminates our history.

Can it be said, therefore, that this city of ends has a meaning? It has, in terms of the sacred universe, once the religious postulate has been admitted. The world was created, it will have an end; Adam left Eden, humanity must come to it. It has no meaning, in the historic universe, if the dialectical postulate is admitted. The dialectic correctly applied cannot and must not have a stop. The antagonistic terms of an historical situation can negate each other and then be surmounted in a new synthesis. But there is no reason why this new synthesis should be better than the original situation. Or rather there is no reason for supposing that, if one arbitrarily imposes an end to the dialectic, one therefore applies a judgement based on outside values. If the classless society is going to terminate history, then capitalist society is, in effect, superior to feudal society to the extent that it brings the advent of this classless society still nearer. But if the dialectic postulate is admitted at all, it must be admitted entirely. Just as aristocratic society has been succeeded by a society without an aristocracy but with classes, it must be concluded that the society of classes will be succeeded by a classless society, but animated by a new antagonism still to be defined. A movement which is refused a beginning cannot have an end. 'If socialism', says an anarchist essayist 'is an eternal evolution, its means are its end.' More precisely, it has no ends, it only has means which are guaranteed by nothing unless by a value foreign to evolution. In this sense, it is correct to remark that the dialectic is not and cannot be revolutionary. It is only from our point of view nihilist – an absolutist movement which aims at denying everything which is not itself.

There is no reason, therefore, in this universe to imagine the end of history. However, that is the only justification for the sacrifices demanded of humanity in the name of Marxism. But it has no other reasonable basis but a *petitio principii* which introduces into history – a kingdom which was meant to be unique and self-sufficient – a value foreign to history. Since that value is, at the same time, foreign to ethics, it is not, properly speaking, a value on which one can base one's conduct, it is a dogma without foundation that can be adopted only as the desperate effort to escape of a mind which is being stifled by solitude or by nihilism, or a value which is going to be imposed by those whom dogma profits. The end of history is not an exemplary or a perfectionist value: it is an arbitrary and terroristic principle.

Marx recognized that all revolutions before his time had failed. But he claimed that the revolution announced by him must succeed definitively. Up to now, the workers' movement has lived on this affirmation which has been continually belied by acts and of which it is high time that the falsehood should be calmly denounced. In proportion as the prophecy was postponed, the affirmation of the coming of the final kingdom, which could only find the most feeble support in reason, became an article of faith. The sole value of the Marxist world henceforth resides, despite Marx, in a dogma imposed on an entire ideological empire. The kingdom of ends is used, like the ethics of eternity and the Kingdom of Heaven, for purposes of social mystification. Elie Halèvy declared himself unqualified to say if socialism was going to lead to the universalization of the Swiss republic or to European Caesarism. Nowadays we are better informed. The prophecies of Nietzsche, on this point at least, are justified. Marxism is, henceforth, to win fame, in defiance of its own teachings and, by an inevitable process of logic, by intellectual Caesarism – which we must now finally describe. The last representative of the struggle of justice against grace, it takes over, without having wanted to do so, the struggle of justice against truth. How to live without grace – that is the question that dominates the nineteenth century. 'By justice,' answered all those who did not want to accept absolute nihilism. To the people who despaired of the Kingdom of Heaven, they promised the kingdom of men. The preaching of the

City of humanity increased in fervour up to the end of the nineteenth century when it became really visionary in tone and placed scientific certainties in the service of Utopia. But the kingdom has retreated into the distance, gigantic wars have ravaged the oldest of countries of Europe, the blood of rebels has bespattered walls, and total justice has approached not a step nearer. The question of the twentieth century – for which the terrorists of 1905 died and which tortures the contemporary world – has gradually been specified: how to live without grace and without justice?

Only nihilism, and not rebellion, has answered that question. Up to now, only nihilism has spoken, returning once more to the theme of the romantic rebels: 'Frenzy'. Frenzy, in terms of history, is called power. The will to power came to take the place of the will to justice, pretending at first to be identified with it and then relegating it to a place somewhere at the end of history, waiting until such time as nothing remains on earth to dominate. Thus the ideological consequence has triumphed over the economic consequence: the history of Russian communism gives the lie to every one of its principles. Once more we find, at the end of this long journey, metaphysical rebellion, which, this time, advances to the clash of arms and the whispering of passwords, forgetful of its real principles, burying its solitude in the bosom of armed crowds, covering the emptiness of its negations with obstinate scholasticism, still directed towards the future which it has made its only god, but separated from it by a multitude of nations to overthrow and continents to dominate. With action as its unique principle, and with the kingdom of man as an alibi, it has already begun, in the east of Europe, to construct its own armed camp, face to face with other armed camps.

THE KINGDOM OF ENDS

Marx never dreamed of such a terrifying apotheosis. Nor, indeed, did Lenin although he took a decisive step towards establishing a military empire. As good a strategist as he was a mediocre philosopher, he first of all posed himself the problem of the seizure of power. Let us note, immediately, that it is absolutely false to talk, as is often done, of Lenin's Jacobinism. Only his idea of units of agitators and revolutionaries is Jacobin. The Jacobins believed in principles and in virtue; they died because they had to deny them. Lenin only believes in the revolution and in the virtue of expediency. 'One must be prepared for every sacrifice, to use if necessary every stratagem, ruse, illegal method, to be determined to conceal the truth, for the sole purpose of penetrating the labour unions and of accomplishing, despite everything, the communist task.' The struggle against formal morality, inaugurated by Hegel and Marx, is found again in Lenin with his criticism of inefficacious revolutionary attitudes. Complete dominion was the aim of this movement.

If we examine the two works written at the beginning and at the end of his career as an agitator, one is struck by the fact that he never ceased to fight mercilessly against the sentimental forms of revolutionary action. He wanted to abolish the morality of revolutionary action because he believed, correctly, that revolutionary power could not be established while still respecting the ten commandments. When he appears, after his first experiences, on the stage of history where he was to play such an important role, to see him take the world so freely and so naturally as it had been shaped by the ideology and the economy of the preceding century, one would imagine him to be the first man of a new era. Completely impervious to anxiety, to nostalgia, to ethics, he takes command; looks for the best method of making the machine run and decides that certain virtues are suitable for the driver of history's chariot and that others are not. He gropes a little at first and hesitates as to whether Russia should first pass through the capitalist and industrial phase. But this comes to the same as doubting whether the revolution can take place in Russia. He himself is Russian and his task is to make the Russian Revolution. He jettisons economic fatalism and embarks on action. He roundly declares, from 1902 on, that the workers will never elaborate an independent ideology on their own. He denies the spontaneity of the masses. Socialist doctrine supposes a scientific basis which only the intellectuals can give it. When he says that all distinctions between workers and intellectuals must be effaced, what he means is that it is impossible to be proletarian and know better than the proletariat what their interests are. He then congratulates Lassalle for having carried on a tenacious struggle against the spontaneity of the masses. 'Theory', he says, 'should subordinate spontaneity.' In plain language, that means that revolution needs leaders and theorists.

He attacks both reformism, which he considers guilty of dissipating revolutionary strength, and terrorism, which he thinks is only an exemplary and inefficacious attitude. The revolution, before being either economic or sentimental, is military. Until the day that the revolution breaks out, revolutionary action is identified with strategy. Autocracy is its enemy, whose main source of strength is the police force which is nothing but a corps of professional political soldiers. The conclusion is simple. 'The struggle against the political police demands special qualities, in fact, demands professional revolutionaries.' The revolution will have its professional army as well as the masses which can be conscripted when needed. This corps of agitators must be organized long before the mass is organized. A network of agents is the expression that Lenin uses, thus announcing the reign of the secret society and of the realist monks of the revolution: 'We are the young Turks of the revolution,' he said, 'with something of the Jesuit added.' From that moment the proletariat no longer has a mission. It is only one powerful means, among others, in the hands of the revolutionary ascetics.

The problem of the seizure of power brings in its train the problem of the State. *The State and the Revolution* (1917), which deals with this subject, is the strangest and most contradictory of pamphlets. Lenin employs in it his favourite method, which is the method of authority. With the help of Marx and Engels, he begins by taking a stand against any kind of reformism which would claim to utilize the bourgeois State – that organism of domination of one class over another. The bourgeois State owes its survival to the police and to the army because it is primarily an instrument of oppression. It reflects both the irreconcilable antagonism of the classes and the forcible subjugation of this antagonism. This authority of fact is only worthy of contempt. 'Even the head of the military power of a civilized State must envy the head of the clan whom patriarchal society surrounded with voluntary respect not with respect imposed by the truncheon.' Moreover, Engels has firmly established that the concept of the State and the concept of a free society are irreconcilable. 'Classes will disappear as ineluctably as they appeared. With the disappearance of classes the State will inevitably disappear. The society which reorganizes production on the basis of the free and equal association of the producers will relegate the machine of State to the place it deserves: to the museum of antiquities, side by side with the spinning-wheel and the bronze axe.'

Doubtless this explains why inattentive readers have ascribed the reason for writing *The State and the Revolution* to Lenin's anarchistic tendencies and have regretted the peculiar posterity of a doctrine so severe about the army, the police, the truncheon, and bureaucracy. But Lenin's points of view, in order to be understood, must always be considered in terms of strategy. If he defends, so very energetically, Engels' thesis about the disappearance of the bourgeois State, it is because he wants, on the one hand, to put an obstacle in the way of the pure 'economism' of Plekhanov and Kautsky and, on the other, to demonstrate that Kerensky's government is a bourgeois government which must be destroyed. One month later, moreoever, he does destroy it.

It was also necessary to answer those who objected to the fact that the revolution itself had need of an administrative and repressive apparatus. There again, Marx and Engels are largely used to prove, authoritatively, that the proletarian State is not a State organized on the lines of other States, but a State which, by definition, is in the process of withering away. 'As soon as there is no longer a social class which must be kept oppressed . . . a State ceases to be necessary. The first act by which the [proletarian] State really establishes itself as the representative of an entire society – the seizure of the society's means of production – is, at the same time, the last real act of the State. For

the government of people is substituted the administration of things.
... The State is not abolished, it perishes.' The bourgeois State is
first suppressed by the proletariat. Then, but only then, the proletarian State fades away. The dictatorship of the proletariat is
necessary – first, to crush or suppress what remains of the bourgeois
class; secondly, to bring about the socialization of the means of production. Once these two tasks are accomplished, it immediately begins
to wither away.

Lenin, therefore, begins from the firm and indisputable principle
that the State dies as soon as the socialization of the means of production is achieved, and the exploiting class has consequently been
suppressed. Yet, in the same pamphlet, he ends by justifying the
preservation, even after the socialization of the means of production
and, without any predictable end, of the dictatorship of a revolutionary fraction over the rest of the people. The pamphlet, which
makes continuous reference to the experiences of the Commune,
flatly contradicts the contemporary federalist and anti-authoritarian
ideas which produced the Commune: and it is equally opposed to the
optimistic forecasts of Marx and Engels. The reason for this is clear;
Lenin had not forgotten that the Commune failed. As for the means
of such a surprising demonstration, they were even more simple:
with each new difficulty encountered by the revolution, the State as
described by Marx is endowed with a supplementary prerogative. Ten
pages farther on, without any kind of transition, Lenin in effect
affirms that power is necessary to crush the resistance of the exploiters
'and also to direct the great mass of the population, peasantry, lower
middle classes, and semi-proletariat, in the management of the
Socialist economy'. The shift here is undeniable, the provisional
State of Marx and Engels is charged with a new mission which risks
prolonging its life indefinitely. Already we can perceive the contradiction of the Stalinist régime in conflict with its official philosophy.
Either this régime has realized the classless Socialist society and the
maintenance of a formidable apparatus of repression is not justified in
Marxist terms, or it has not realized the classless society and has
therefore proved that Marxist doctrine is erroneous and, in particular,

that the socialization of the means of production does not mean the disappearance of classes. Confronted with its official doctrine, the régime is forced to choose: the doctrine is false or the régime has betrayed it. In fact, together with Nechayev and Tkachev, it is Lassalle, the inventor of State Socialism, whom Lenin has caused to triumph in Russia, to the detriment of Marx. From this moment on, the history of the interior struggles of the party, from Lenin to Stalin, is summed up in the struggle between the workers' democracy and military and bureaucratic dictatorship; in other words, between justice and expediency.

There is a moment's doubt about whether Lenin is not going to find a kind of means of conciliation when we hear him praising the measures adopted by the Commune: elected, revocable functionaries remunerated like workers, and replacement of industrial bureaucracy by direct workers' management. We even catch a glimpse of a federalist Lenin who praises the institution and representation of the Communes. But it becomes rapidly clear that this federalism is only extolled to the extent that it signifies the abolition of Parliamentarianism. Lenin, in defiance of every historic truth, calls it centralism and immediately puts the accent on the idea of the dictatorship of the proletariat, while reproaching the anarchists for their intransigence concerning the State. At this point, a new affirmation, based on Engels, is introduced which justifies the continuation of the dictatorship of the proletariat after Socialization, after the disappearance of the bourgeois class, and even after control by the masses has finally been achieved. The preservation of authority will now have as limits those that are prescribed for it by the very conditions of production. For example, the final withering away of the State will coincide with the moment when accommodation can be provided for all, free of charge. It is the higher phase of communism: 'to each according to his needs'. Until then, the State will continue.

How rapid will be the development towards this higher phase of communism when each shall receive according to his needs ? 'That, we do not and cannot know. . . . We have no gifts which allow us to solve these questions.' 'For the sake of greater clarity', Lenin affirms with his customary arbitrariness, 'it has never been vouchsafed to any communist to guarantee the advent of the higher phase of communism.' It can be said that, at this point, freedom definitely died. From the rule of the masses and the concept of the proletarian revolution we first pass on to the idea of a revolution made and directed by professional agents. The relentless criticism of the State is then reconciled with the necessary, but provisional, dictatorship of the proletariat, embodied in its leaders. Finally, it is announced that the end of this provisional condition cannot be foreseen and that, what is more, no one has ever presumed to promise that there will be an end. After that, it is logical that the autonomy of the Soviets should be contested, Makhno betrayed, and the sailors of Kronstadt crushed by the party.

Undoubtedly, many of the affirmations of Lenin, who was a passionate lover of justice, can still be opposed to the Stalinist régime: mainly, the notion of the withering away of the State. Even if it is admitted that the proletarian State cannot disappear before many years have passed, it is still necessary, according to Marxist doctrine, that it should tend to disappear and become less and less restrictive so that it can call itself proletarian. It is certain that Lenin believed this trend to be inevitable and that, in this particular sense, he has been ignored. For more than thirty years the proletarian State has shown no signs of progressive anaemia: on the contrary, it seems to be enjoying increasing strength. Meanwhile, in a lecture at the Sverdlov University two years later, under the pressure of outside events and interior realities, Lenin spoke with a precision which left little doubt about the indefinite continuation of the proletarian super-State. 'With this machine, or rather this weapon [the State], we shall crush every form of exploitation, and when there are no longer any possibilities of exploitation left on earth, no more people owning land or factories, no more people gorging themselves under the eyes of others who are starving, when such things become impossible, then and only then shall we cast this machine aside. Then, there will be neither State nor exploitation. Therefore as long as there exists on earth, and no longer in a specific society, one single oppressed person and one proprietor, the State will continue to exist. It also will be obliged to increase in strength during this period, so as to vanquish one by one the injustices, the governments responsible for injustice, the obstinately bourgeois nations, and the people who are blind to their own interests. And when, on an earth which has finally been subdued and purged of enemies, the final iniquity shall have been drowned in the blood of the just and the unjust, then the State, which has reached the limit of all power, a monstrous idol covering the entire earth, will be discreetly absorbed into the silent city of Justice.'

Under the easily predictable pressure of adverse imperialism, the imperialism of justice was born, in reality, with Lenin. But imperialism, even the imperialism of justice, has no other end but defeat or world empire. Until then, it has no other means but injustice. From now on the doctrine is definitively identified with the prophecy. For the sake of justice in the far-away future, it authorizes injustice throughout the entire course of history and becomes the type of mystification which Lenin detested more than anything in the world. It contrives the acceptance of injustice, crime, and falsehood by the promise of a miracle. Still greater production, still more power, uninterrupted labour, incessant suffering, permanent war, and then a moment will come when universal bondage in the totalitarian empire will be miraculously changed into its opposite: free leisure in a universal republic. Pseudo-revolutionary mystification has now acquired a formula: all freedom must be crushed in order to conquer the empire and one day the empire will be the equivalent of freedom. And so the way to unity passes through totality.

TOTALITY AND TRIAL

Totality is, in effect, nothing other than the ancient dream of unity common to both believers and rebels, but projected horizontally on to an earth deprived of God. To renounce every value, therefore, amounts to renouncing rebellion in order to accept the empire and slavery. Criticism of formal values cannot pass over the concept of freedom. Once the impossibility has been recognized of creating, by means of the forces of rebellion alone, the free individual of whom the romantics dreamed, freedom itself has also been incorporated in the movement of history. It has become freedom fighting for existence, which, in order to exist, must create itself. Identified with the dynamism of history, it cannot play its proper role until history comes to a stop, in the realization of the Universal City. Until then, every one of its victories will lead to an antithesis which will render it pointless. The German nation frees itself from its oppressors but at the price of the freedom of every German. The individuals under a totalitarian régime are not free, even though man in the collective sense is free. Finally, when the empire delivers the entire human species, freedom will reign over herds of slaves who at least will be free in relation to God and, in general, to every kind of transcendence. The dialectic miracle, the transformation of quantity into quality is explained here: it is the decision to call total servitude freedom. Moreover, as in all the examples cited by Hegel and Marx, there is no objective transformation, but only a subjective change of denomination. In other words, there is no miracle. If the only hope of nihilism lies in thinking that millions of slaves can one day constitute a humanity which will be freed forever, then history is nothing but a desperate dream. Historic thought was to deliver man from subjection to a divinity; but this liberation demanded of him the most absolute subjection to historical evolution. Then man takes refuge in the concept of the permanence of the party in the same way that he formerly prostrated himself before the altar. That is why the era which dares to claim that it is the most rebellious that has ever existed only offers a choice of various types of conformity. The real passion of the twentieth century is servitude.

But total freedom is no more easy to conquer than individual freedom. To insure man's control of the world it is necessary to suppress, in the world and in man, everything that escapes the empire, everything that does not come under the reign of quantity: and this is an endless undertaking. The empire must embrace time, space, and people which comprise the three dimensions of history. It is simultaneously war, obscurantism, and tyranny, desperately affirming that one day it will be liberty, fraternity, and truth; the logic of its postulates obliges it to do so. There is undoubtedly in Russia today, and even in its communist doctrines, a truth which denies Stalinist ideology. But this ideology has its logic which must be isolated and exposed if we wish the revolutionary spirit to escape final disgrace.

The cynical intervention of the armies of the Western Powers against the Soviet Revolution demonstrated, among other things, to the Russian revolutionaries that war and nationalism were realities in the same category as the class struggle. Without an international solidarity of the working classes, a solidarity which would come into play automatically, no interior revolution could be considered likely to survive unless an international order were created. From then on it was necessary to admit that the Universal City could only be built on two conditions – either by almost simultaneous revolutions in every big country, or by the liquidation, through war, of the bourgeois nations: permanent revolution or permanent war. We know that the first point of view failed to establish itself. The revolutionary movements in Germany, Italy, and France marked the high point in revolutionary hopes and aspirations. But the crushing of these revolutions and the ensuing reinforcement of capitalist régimes has made war the reality of the revolution. Thus the philosophy of the age of enlightenment finally led to the Europe of the black-out. By the logic of history and of doctrine, the Universal City, which was to have been realized by the spontaneous insurrection of the oppressed, has been little by little replaced by the empire imposed by means of power. Engels, with the approval of Marx, dispassionately accepted this prospect when he wrote in answer to Bakunin's *Appeal to the Slavs*: 'The next world war will cause the disappearance from the surface of the globe, not only of reactionary classes and dynasties, but of whole races of reactionaries. That also is part of progress.' That particular form of progress, in Engels' mind, was destined to eliminate the Russia of the Czars. Today the Russian nation has reversed the direction of progress. War, cold and lukewarm, is the slavery imposed by world empire. But now that it has become imperialist, the revolution is in an impasse. If it does not renounce its false principles in order to return to the origins of rebellion, it only means the continuation, for several generations and until capitalism spontaneously decomposes, of a total dictatorship over hundreds of millions of men; or, if it wants to precipitate the advent of the Universal City, it only signifies the atomic war which it does not want and after which any city whatsoever will only be able to contemplate utter ruin. World revolution, by the very laws of the history it so imprudently deified, is condemned to police domination or to the bomb. At the same time, it finds itself confronted with yet another contradiction. The sacrifice of ethics and virtue, the acceptance of all the means that it constantly justified by the end it pursued, can only be accepted, if absolutely necessary, in terms of an end which is reasonably likely to be realized. The cold war supposes, by the indefinite prolongation of dictatorship, the indefinite negation of this end. The danger of war, moreover, makes this end highly unlikely. The extension of the empire over the face of the earth is an inevitable necessity for twentieth-century revolution. But this necessity confronts it with a final dilemma: to construct new principles for itself or to renounce justice and peace whose definitive reign it always wanted.

While waiting to dominate space, the empire sees itself also compelled to reign over time. In denying every last truth, it is compelled to go to the point of denying the very lowest form of truth – the truth of history. It has transported revolution, which is still impossible on a world-wide scale, back into a past which it is determined to deny. Even that, too, is logical. Any kind of coherence, which is not purely economic, between the past and the future of humanity, supposes a constant which, in its turn, can lead to a belief in a human nature. The profound coherence that Marx, who was a man of culture, had perceived as existing between all civilizations, threatened to swamp his thesis and to bring to light a natural continuity, far broader in scope than economic continuity. Little by little, Russian communism has been forced to burn its bridges, to introduce a solution of continuity into the problem of historical evolution. The negation of every genius who proves to be a heretic (and almost all of them do), the denial of the benefits of civilization, of art – to the infinite degree in which it escapes from history – and the renunciation of vital traditions, has gradually forced contemporary Marxism within narrower and narrower limits. It has not sufficed for Marxism to deny or to silence the things, in the history of the world, which cannot be assimilated by its doctrine, nor to reject the discoveries of modern science. It has also had to rewrite history, even the most recent and the best known, even the history of the party and of the revolution. Year by year, sometimes month by month, *Pravda* corrects itself and rewritten editions of the official history books follow one another off the presses. Lenin is censored, Marx is not published. At this point a comparison with religious obscurantism is no longer even fair. The Church never went so far as to decide that the divine manifestation was embodied in two, then in four, or in three, and then again in two, persons. The acceleration of events which is part of our times also affects the fabrication of truth which, accomplished at this speed, becomes pure fantasy. As in the fairy story, in which all the looms of an entire town wove the empty air to provide clothes for the king, thousands of men, whose strange profession it is, rewrite a presumptuous version of history which is destroyed the same evening while waiting for the calm voice of a child to proclaim suddenly that the king is naked. This small voice, the voice of rebellion, will then be saying, what all the world can see already, that a revolution which, in order to last, is condemned to deny its universal vocation, or to renounce itself in order to be universal, is living by false principles.

Meanwhile, these principles continue to dominate the lives of millions of men. The dream of empire, held in check by the realities of time and space, gratifies its desires on humanity. People are not only hostile to the empire as individuals: in that case the traditional methods of terror would suffice. They are hostile to it in so far as human nature, to date, has never been able to live by history alone and has always escaped from it by some means. The empire supposes a negation and a certainty: the certainty of the infinite malleability of man and the negation of human nature. Propaganda techniques serve to measure the degree of this malleability and try to make reflection and conditioned reflex coincide. Propaganda makes it possible to sign a pact with those who for years have been designated as the mortal enemy. Even more, it allows the psychological effect thus obtained to be reversed and the people, once again, to be aligned against this same enemy. The experiment has not yet been brought to an end, but its principle is logical. If there is no human nature, then the malleability of man is, in fact, infinite. Political realism, on this level, is nothing but unbridled romanticism, a romanticism of expediency.

In this way it is possible to explain why Russian Marxism rejects, in its entirety and even though it knows very well how to make use of it, the world of the irrational. The irrational can serve the empire as well as refute it. The irrational escapes calculation and calculation alone must reign in the empire. Man is only an interplay of forces who can be rationally influenced. A few thoughtless Marxists were rash enough to imagine that they could reconcile their doctrine with Freud's for example. Their eyes were opened for them quickly enough. Freud is a heretic thinker and a '*petit bourgeois*' because he brought to light the unconscious and bestowed on it at least as much reality as on the super or social ego. This unconscious mind can therefore define a human nature, which is quite separate from the historic ego. Man, on the contrary, must be explained in terms of the social and rational ego and as an object of calculation. Therefore, it has been necessary to enslave, not only each individual life, but also the most irrational and the most solitary event of all, the expectancy of which accompanies man throughout his entire life. The empire, in its convulsive effort to found a definitive kingdom, strives to integrate death.

A living man can be enslaved and reduced to the historic condition of an object. But if he dies in refusing to be enslaved, he reaffirms the existence of another kind of human nature which refuses to be classified as an object. That is why the accused is never produced and killed before the eyes of the world unless he consents to say that his death is just and unless he conforms to the empire of objects. One must die dishonoured or no longer exist – neither in life nor in death. In the latter event, the victim does not die, he disappears. If he is punished, his punishment would be a silent protest and might cause a fissure in the totality. But the culprit is not punished, he is simply replaced and thus helps to construct the machine of empire. He is transformed into a cog in the machinery of production, so indispensable that in the long run he will not be used in production because he is guilty, but considered guilty because production has need of him. The concentration camp system of the Russians has, in fact, accomplished the dialectical transition from the government of people to the administration of objects, but by confusing people with objects.

Even the enemy must collaborate in the common endeavour. Beyond the confines of the empire there is no salvation. This is, or will be, the empire of friendship. But this friendship is the befriending of objects, for the friend cannot be preferred to the empire. The friendship of people – and there is no other definition of it – is specific solidarity, to the point of death, against everything that is not part of the kingdom of friendship. The friendship of objects is friendship in general, friendship with everything which supposes – when it is a question of self-preservation – mutual denunciation. He who loves his friend loves him in the present and the revolution only wants to love a man who has not yet appeared. To love is, in a certain way, to kill the perfect man who is going to be born of the revolution. In order that one day he may live he should from now on be preferred to anyone else. In the kingdom of humanity, men are bound by ties of affection: in the empire of objects, men are united by mutual accusation. The city which planned to be the city of fraternity becomes an ant-heap of solitary men.

On another plane, only a brute in a state of irrational fury can imagine that men should be sadistically tortured in order to obtain their consent. Such an act only accomplishes the subjugation of one man by another, in an outrageous coupling of bodies. The representative of rational totality is content, on the contrary, to allow the object to subdue the person in the soul of man. The highest mind is first of all reduced to the level of the lowest by the police technique of joint accusation. Then five, ten, twenty nights of insomnia will culminate in a false conclusion and will bring yet another dead soul into the world. From this point of view, the only psychological revolution known to our times since Freud's has been brought about by the N.K.V.D. and the political police in general. Guided by a determinist hypothesis which calculates the weak points and the degree of elasticity of the soul, these new techniques have once again thrust aside one of man's limits and have attempted to demonstrate that no individual psychology is original and that the common measure of all human character is matter. They have literally created the physics of the soul.

From that point on traditional human relations have been transformed. These progressive transformations characterize the world of rational terror in which, in different degrees, Europe lives. Dialogue and personal relations have been replaced by propaganda or polemic, which are two kinds of monologue. Abstraction, which belongs to the world of power and calculation, has replaced the real passions which are in the domain of the flesh and of the irrational. The ration coupon substituted for bread; love and friendship submitted to a doctrine and destiny to a plan; punishment considered the norm, and production substituted for living creation, quite satisfactorily describe this disembodied Europe, peopled with positive or negative symbols. 'How miserable', Marx exclaims, 'is a society which knows no better means of defence than the executioner.' But in Marx's day the executioner had not yet become a philosopher and at least made no pretence at universal philanthropy.

The ultimate contradiction of the greatest revolution that history ever knew does not, after all, lie entirely in the fact that it lays claim to justice despite an uninterrupted procession of violence and injustice. This is an evil common to all times and a product of servitude or mystification. The tragedy of this revolution is the tragedy of nihilism – it confounds itself with the drama of contemporary intelligence which, while claiming to be universal, is only responsible for a series of mutilations to men's minds. Totality is not unity. The state of siege, even when it is extended to the very boundaries of the earth, is not reconciliation. The claim to a universal city is only supported, in this revolution, by rejecting two-thirds of the world and the magnificent heritage of the centuries, by denying, to the advantage of history, both nature and beauty and by depriving man of the power of passion, doubt, happiness, and imaginative invention – in a word, of his greatness. The principles which men give to themselves end by overwhelming their noblest intentions. By dint of argument, incessant struggle, polemics, excommunications, persecutions conducted and suffered, the universal city of free and fraternal man is slowly diverted and gives way to the only universe in which history and expediency can, in fact, be elevated to the position of supreme judges: the universe of the trial.

Every religion revolves around the concepts of innocence and guilt. However, Prometheus, the first rebel, denies the right to punish. Zeus himself, Zeus above all, is not innocent enough to exercise this right. Thus rebellion, in its very first manifestation, refuses to recognize punishment as legitimate. But in his last incarnation, at the end of his exhausting journey, the rebel once more adopts the religious concept of punishment and places it at the centre of his universe. The supreme judge is no longer in the heavens; history itself acts as an implacable divinity. History, in one sense, is nothing but a protracted punishment since the real reward will only be granted at the end of time. We are far, it would seem, from Marxism and from Hegel, and even farther from the first rebels. Nevertheless, all purely historic thought leads to the brink of this abyss. To the extent to which Marx predicted the inevitable establishment of the classless city and to the extent to which he thus established the goodwill of history, every check to the advance toward freedom must be imputed to the ill-will of mankind. Marx reintroduced crime and punishment into the unchristian world, but only in relation to history. Marxism in one of its aspects is a doctrine of culpability on man's part and innocence on history's. His interpretation of history is that when it is deprived of power, it expresses itself in revolutionary violence; at the height of its power, it risked becoming legal violence, in other words, terror and trial.

In the universe of religion, moreover, the final judgement is postponed; it is not necessary for crime to be punished without delay or for innocence to be rewarded. In the new universe, on the other hand, the judgement pronounced by history must be pronounced immediately, for culpability coincides with the check to progress and with punishment. History has judged Bukarin in that it condemned him to death. It proclaims the innocence of Stalin: he is the most powerful man on earth. Tito is on trial, as was Trotsky, whose guilt only became clear to the philosophers of historical crime at the moment when the murderer's axe cracked his skull. Tito has been denounced but not yet struck down. When he has been struck down his guilt will be certain. Besides, Trotsky's and Tito's provisional innocence depended and depends to a large extent on geography; they were far removed from the arm of secular power. That is why those who can be reached by that arm must be judged without delay. The definitive judgement of history depends on an infinite number of judgements which will have been pronounced between now and then and which will finally be confirmed or invalidated. Thus there is the promise of mysterious absolutions on the day when the tribunal of the world will be established by the world itself. The accused, who will proclaim himself a contemptible traitor, will enter the Pantheon of mankind; those who maintain their innocence will be condemned to the hell of history. But who, then, will be the judge? Man himself, finally fulfilled in his divinity. Meanwhile, those who have understood the prophecy, and who alone are capable of reading in history the meaning with which they previously endowed it, will pronounce sentence – definitive for the guilty, provisional sentences for the judges. But it sometimes happens that those who judge, like Rajk, are judged in their turn. Must we believe that he no longer interpreted history correctly? His defeat and death, in fact, prove it. Then who guarantees that those who judge him today, will not be traitors tomorrow, hurled down from the height of their judgement seat to the concrete caves where history's damned suffer their agony? The guarantee lies in their infallible clairvoyance. What proof is there of that? Their uninterrupted success. The world of trial is a spherical world in which success and innocence authenticate each other and where every mirror reflects the same mystification.

Thus there will be an historic grace whose power alone can interpret events and which favours, or excommunicates, the subject of the empire. To guard against its caprices, the latter only has faith at his disposal – faith as defined in the *Spiritual Exercises* of Saint Ignatius: 'We should always be prepared so as never to err to believe that what I see as white is black, if the hierarchic Church defines it thus.' Only this active faith held by the representatives of truth can save the subject from the mysterious ravages of history. He is not yet free of the universe of trial to which he is bound by the historic sentiment of fear. But, without this faith, he runs a perpetual risk of becoming, without having wished to do so and with the best intentions in the world, an objective criminal.

The universe of trial finally culminates in this concept, at which point we have come full circle. At the end of this long insurrection, in the name of human innocence, there arises, by an inevitable perversion of fact, the affirmation of general culpability. Every man is a criminal who is unaware of being so. The objective criminal is, precisely, he who believed himself innocent. His actions he considered subjectively inoffensive, or even advantageous for the future of justice. But it is demonstrated to him that objectively his actions have been harmful to that future. Are we dealing with scientific objectivity here? ... No, but with historic objectivity. How is it possible to know, for example, if the future of justice is compromised by the unconsidered denunciation of present injustice? Real objectivity would consist of judging by results which can be scientifically observed and by facts and their general tendencies. But the concept of objective culpability proves that this curious kind of objectivity is only based on results and facts which will only become accessible to science in the year 2000, at the very earliest. Meanwhile, it is embodied in an interminable subjectivity which is imposed on others as objectivity: and that is the philosophic definition of terror. This type of objectivity has no definable meaning, but power will give it a content by decreeing that everything of which it does not approve is guilty. It will consent to say, or allow to be said, to philosophers who live outside the empire, that in this way it is taking a risk in regard to history, just as the objective culprit took a risk, though without knowing it. When victim and executioner have disappeared the matter will be judged. But this consolation is only of any value to the executioner, who has really no need of it. Meanwhile, the faithful are regularly bidden to attend strange feasts where, according to scrupulous rites, victims overwhelmed with contrition are offered as sacrifice to the end of history.

The express object of this idea is to prevent indifference in matters of faith. It is compulsory evangelization. The law, whose function it is to pursue suspects, fabricates them. By fabricating them, it converts them. In bourgeois society, for example, every citizen is supposed to approve the law. In objective society every citizen will be presumed to disapprove of it. Or at least he should always be ready to prove that he does not disapprove of it. Culpability no longer has any factual basis, it simply consists of absence of faith, which explains the apparent contradiction of the objective system. Under a capitalist régime, the man who says he is neutral is considered objectively to be favourable to the régime. Under the régime of the empire, the man who is neutral is considered hostile objectively to the régime. There is nothing astonishing about that. If a subject of the empire does not believe in the empire he is, of his own choice, nothing, historically speaking; therefore, he takes sides against history and is, in other words, a blasphemer. Even lip service paid to faith will not suffice; it must be lived and acted in order to be served properly and the citizen must be always on the alert to consent in time to the changes in dogma. At the slightest error potential culpability becomes in its turn objective culpability. Consummating its history in this manner, the revolution is not content with killing all rebellion. It insists on holding every man, even the most servile, responsible for the fact that rebellion ever existed and still exists under the sun. In the universe of the trial, conquered and completed at last, a race of culprits will endlessly shuffle towards an impossible innocence, under the grim regard of the Grand Inquisitors. In the twentieth century, power wears the mask of tragedy.

Rebellion and Revolution

THE revolution based on principles kills God in the person of His representative on earth. The revolution of the twentieth century kills what remains of God in the principles themselves, and consecrates historic nihilism. Whatever paths nihilism may proceed to take, from the moment that it decides to be the creative force of its period and ignores every moral precept, it begins to build the temple of Caesar. To choose history, and history alone, is to choose nihilism, contrary to the teachings of rebellion itself. Those who rush blindly to history in the name of the irrational, proclaiming that it is meaningless, encounter servitude and terror and finally emerge into the universe of concentration camps. Those who launch themselves into it, preaching its absolute rationality, encounter servitude and terror and emerge into the universe of the concentration camps. Fascism wants to establish the advent of the Nietzschean superman. It immediately discovers that God, if He exists, may well be this or that, but He is primarily the master of death. If man wants to become God, he arrogates to himself the power of life or death over others. The rational revolution, on its part, wants to realize the total man described by Marx. The logic of history, from the moment that it is totally accepted, gradually leads it, against its most passionate convictions, to mutilate man more and more, and to transform itself into objective crime. It is not legitimate to identify the ends of Fascism with the ends of Russian communism. The first represents the exaltation of the executioner by the executioner; the second, more dramatic in concept, the exaltation of the executioner by the victim. The former never dreamed of liberating all men, but only of liberating a few by subjugating the rest. The latter, in its most profound principle, aims at liberating all men by provisionally enslaving them all. It must be granted the grandeur of its intentions. But, on the other hand, it is legitimate to identify the means employed by both with political cynicism which they have drawn from the same source, moral nihilism. Everything has taken place as though the descendants of Stirner and of Nechayev were making use of the descendants of Kaliayev and Proudhon. The nihilists today are seated on thrones. Methods of thought which claim to give the lead to our world in the name of revolution have become, in reality, ideologies of consent and not of rebellion. That is why our period is the period of private and public techniques of annihilation.

The revolution, obedient to the dictates of nihilism, has in fact turned against its rebel origins. Man, who hated death and the god of death, who despaired of personal survival, wanted to free himself in the immortality of the species. But as long as the group does not dominate the world, as long as the species does not reign, it is still necessary to die. Time is pressing, therefore persuasion demands leisure and friendship a structure which will never be completed; thus, terror remains the shortest route to immortality. But these extremes simultaneously proclaim a longing for the primitive values of rebellion. The contemporary revolution which claims to deny every value is already, in itself, a standard for judging values. Man wants to reign supreme through the revolution. But why reign supreme if nothing has any meaning? Why wish for immortality if the aspect of life is so hideous? There is no method of thought which is absolutely nihilist except, perhaps, the method that leads to suicide, any more than there is absolute materialism. The destruction of man once more affirms man. Terror and concentration camps are the drastic means used by man to escape solitude. If men kill one another, it is because they reject mortality and desire immortality for all men. Therefore, in one sense, they commit suicide. But they prove, at the same time, that they cannot dispense with mankind; they satisfy a terrible hunger for fraternity. 'The human being needs happiness and, when he is unhappy, he needs another human being.' Those who reject the agony of living and dying wish to dominate. 'Solitude is power,' says Sade. Power, today, because for thousands of solitary people it signifies the suffering of others, bears witness to the need for others. Terror is the homage that the malignant recluse finally pays to the brotherhood of man.

But nihilism, if it does not exist, tries to do so; and that is enough to make the world a desert. This particular form of madness is what has given our times their forbidding aspect. The land of humanism has become the Europe we know, the land of inhumanity. But the times are ours and how can we disown them? If our history is our hell, then we cannot turn away. This horror cannot be escaped, but is assumed in order to be ignored, by the very people who accepted it with lucidity and not by those who, having provoked it, think that they have a right to pronounce judgement. Such a plant could, in fact, only thrive in the fertile soil of accumulated iniquities. In the last throes of a death struggle in which men are indiscriminately mingled through the folly of the times, the enemy remains the fraternal enemy. Even when he has been denounced for his errors, he can neither be despised nor hated; misfortune is, today, the common fatherland, and the only earthly kingdom which has fulfilled the promise.

The longing for rest and peace must, itself, be thrust aside; it coincides with the acceptance of iniquity. Those who weep for the happy periods which they encounter in history acknowledge what they want; not the alleviation but the silencing of misery. But on the contrary, let us sing the praises of our times when misery cries aloud and disturbs the sleep of the surfeited rich! Maistre has already spoken of the 'terrible sermon which the revolution preached to kings'. It preaches the same sermon today and in a still more urgent fashion, to the dishonoured élite of the times. This sermon must be heard. In every word and in every act, even though it be criminal, lies the promise of a value which we must seek out and bring to light. The future cannot be foreseen and it is possible that the renaissance is impossible. Even though the historic dialectic is false and criminal, the world, after all, can very well realize itself in crime and in pursuit of a false concept. This kind of resignation is, quite simply, rejected here: we must stake everything on the renaissance.

Nothing remains for us, moreover, but to be reborn or to die. If we are at the moment in history when rebellion has reached the point of its most extreme contradiction by denying itself, then it must either perish with the world it has created or find a new object of faith and a new impetus. Before going any farther, this contradiction must at least be stated in plain language. It is not a clear definition to say, like the existentialists, for example (who are also subjected for the moment to the cult of history and its contradictions),* that there is progress in the transition from rebellion to revolution and that the rebel is nothing if he is not revolutionary. The contradiction is, in reality, considerably more restricted. The revolutionary is simultaneously a rebel or he is not a revolutionary, but a policeman, or a bureaucrat, who turns against rebellion. But if he is a rebel he ends by taking sides against the revolution. So much so that there is absolutely no progress from one attitude to the other, but coexistence and endlessly increasing contradiction. Every revolutionary ends by becoming either an oppressor or a heretic. In the purely historical universe that they have chosen, rebellion and revolution end in the same dilemma: either police rule or insanity.

On this level, therefore, history alone offers no hope. It is not a source of values, but is still a source of nihilism. Can one, at least, create values in defiance of history, if only on the level of a philosophy based on eternity? That comes to the same as ratifying historic injustice and the sufferings of man. To slander the world leads to the nihilism defined by Nietzsche. Thought which is derived from history alone, like thought which rejects history completely, deprives man of the means and the reason for living. The former drives him to the extreme decadence of 'why live?' the latter to 'how to live?' History, necessary but not sufficient, is therefore only an occasional cause. It is not absence of values, nor values themselves, nor even the source of values. It is one occasion, among others, for man to prove the still confused existence of a value which allows him to judge history. Rebellion itself makes us the promise of such a value.

* Atheist existentialism at least wishes to create a morality. It is still to be defined. But the real difficulty lies in creating it without reintroducing into historic existence a value foreign to history.

Absolute revolution, in fact, supposes the absolute malleability of human nature and its possible reduction to the condition of a historic force. But rebellion, in man, is the refusal to be treated as an object and to be reduced to simple historical terms. It is the affirmation of a nature common to all men, which eludes the world of power. History, undoubtedly, is one of the limits of man's experience; in this sense the revolutionaries are right. But man, by rebelling, imposes in his turn a limit to history and at this limit the promise of a value is born. It is the birth of this value which the Caesarian revolution implacably combats today because it presages its final defeat and the obligation to renounce its principles. The fate of the world is not being played out at present, as it seemed it would be, in the struggle between bourgeois production and revolutionary production; their end-results will be the same. It is being played out between the forces of rebellion and those of the Caesarian revolution. The triumphant revolution must prove by means of its police, its trials, and its excommunications, that there is no such thing as human nature. Humiliated rebellion, by its contradictions, its sufferings, its continuous defeats, and its inexhaustible pride, must give its content of hope and suffering to this nature.

'I rebel, therefore we exist', said the slave. Metaphysical rebellion then added, 'we are alone', by which we still live today. But, if we are alone beneath the empty heavens, if we must die forever, how can we really exist? Metaphysical rebellion, then, tried to construct existence with appearances. After which purely historic thought came to say that to be was to act. We did not exist, but we should exist by every possible means. Our revolution is an attempt to conquer a new existence, by action which recognizes no moral strictures. That is why it is condemned to live only for history and in a reign of terror. Man is nothing, according to the revolution, if he does not obtain from history, willingly or unwillingly, unanimous approval. At this exact point, the limit is exceeded, rebellion is first betrayed and then logically assassinated for it has never affirmed – in its purest form – anything but the existence of a limit and the divided existence that we represent: it is not, originally, the total negation of all existence.

Quite the contrary, it says yes and no simultaneously. It is the rejection of one part of existence in the name of another part which it exalts. The more deeply felt the exaltation, the more implacable is the rejection. Then, when rebellion, in rage or intoxication, adopts the attitude of 'all or nothing' and the negation of all existence and all human nature, it is at this point that it denies itself completely. Total negation only justifies the concept of a totality that must be conquered. But the affirmation of a limit, a dignity, and a beauty common to all men only entails the necessity of extending this value to embrace everything and everyone and of advancing towards unity without denying the origins of rebellion. In this sense rebellion, in its primary aspect of authenticity, does not justify any purely historic concept. Rebellion's claim is unity, historic revolution's claim is totality. The former starts from a negative supported by an affirmative, the latter from absolute negation and is condemned to fabricate an affirmative which is dismissed until the end of time. One is creative, the other nihilist. The first is dedicated to creation so as to exist more and more completely, the second is forced to produce results in order to negate more and more completely. The historic revolution is always obliged to act in the hope, which is invariably disappointed, of one day really existing. Even unanimous approval will not suffice to create its existence. 'Obey', said Frederick the Great to his subjects, but when he died his words were, 'I am tired of ruling slaves.' To escape this absurd destiny, the revolution is and will be condemned to renounce, not only its own principles, but nihilism as well as purely historic values in order to rediscover the creative source of rebellion. Revolution, in order to be creative, cannot do without either a moral or metaphysical rule to balance the insanity of history. Undoubtedly, it has nothing but scorn for the formal and meretricious morality to be found in bourgeois society. But its folly has been to extend its scorn to every moral attitude. At the very sources of its inspiration and in its most profound transports is to be found a rule which is not formal but which, nevertheless, can serve as a guide. Rebellion, in fact, will say – and will say more and more explicitly – that revolution must try to act, not in order to come into existence at some future date, but in terms of the obscure existence which is already made manifest in the act of insurrection. This rule is neither formal nor subject to history, it is what can be best described by examining it in its pure state – in artistic creation. Before doing so, let us only note that to the 'I rebel, therefore we exist' and the 'we are alone' of the metaphysical rebellion, rebellion at grips with history adds that instead of killing and dying in order to produce the being that we are not, we have to live and let live in order to create what we are.

4

REBELLION AND ART

ART is an activity which exalts and denies simultaneously. 'No artist tolerates reality', says Nietzsche. That is true, but no artist can ignore reality. Artistic creation is a demand for unity and a rejection of the world. But it rejects the world on account of what it lacks and in the name of what it sometimes is. Rebellion can be observed here in its pure state and in its original complexities. Thus, art should give us a final perspective on the content of rebellion.

However, the hostility to art shown by all revolutionary reformers must be pointed out. Plato is moderately reasonable. He only calls in question the deceptive function of language and exiles the poets from his republic. Apart from that, he considers beauty more important than the world. But the revolutionary movement of modern times coincides with an artistic process which is not yet completed. The Reformation chooses morality and exiles beauty. Rousseau denounces art as a corruption of Nature by society. Saint-Just inveighs against the theatre and in the elaborate programme he composes for the 'Feast of Reason' he states that he would like Reason to be personified by someone 'virtuous rather than beautiful'. The French Revolution gave birth to no artists but only to a great journalist, Desmoulins, and to an under-the-counter writer, Sade. The only poet of the times was the guillotine. The only great prose writer took refuge in London and pleaded the cause of Christianity and legitimacy. A little later the followers of Saint-Simon demanded a 'socially useful' form of art. 'Art for progress' was a commonplace of the whole period and one which Hugo revived, without succeeding in making it sound convincing. Vallès alone brings to his malediction of art a tone of imprecation which gives it authenticity.

This tone is also employed by the Russian nihilists. Pisarev proclaims the deposition of aesthetic values, in favour of pragmatic values. 'I would rather be a Russian shoemaker than a Russian Raphael.' A pair of boots, in his eyes, is more useful than Shakespeare. The nihilist Nekrassov, a great and moving poet, nevertheless affirms that he prefers a piece of cheese to all of Pushkin. Finally, we are familiar with the excommunication of art pronounced by Tolstoy. Revolutionary Russia finally even turned its back on the marble statues of Venus and Apollo, still gilded by the Italian sun, that Peter the Great had had brought to his summer garden in St Petersburg. Suffering, sometimes, turned away from too painful expressions of happiness.

German ideology is no less severe in its accusations. According to the revolutionary interpreters of the *Phenomenology* there will be no art in reconciled society. Beauty will be lived and no longer only imagined. Reality, become entirely rational, will satisfy, completely on its own, every form of desire. The criticism of formal conscience and of escapist values naturally extends itself to embrace art. Art does not belong to all times; it is determined, on the contrary, by its period and expresses, says Marx, the privileged values of the ruling classes. Thus, there is only one revolutionary form of art which is, precisely, art dedicated to the service of the revolution. Moreover, by creating beauty outside the course of history, art impedes the only rational activity: the transformation of history itself into absolute beauty. The Russian shoemaker, once he is aware of his revolutionary role, is the real creator of definitive beauty. As for Raphael, he only created a transitory beauty which will be quite incomprehensible to the new man.

Marx asks himself, it is true, how the beauty created by the Greeks can still be beautiful for us. His answer is that this beauty is the expression of the naïve childhood of this world and that we have, in the midst of our adult struggles, a nostalgia for this childhood. But how can the masterpieces of the Italian Renaissance, how can Rembrandt, how can Chinese art still be beautiful in our eyes? What does it matter! The trial of art has been opened definitively and is continuing today with the embarrassed complicity of artists and intellectuals dedicated to calumniating both their art and their intelligence. We notice, in fact, that in the contest between Shakespeare and the shoemaker, it is not the shoemaker who maligns Shakespeare or beauty but, on the contrary, the man who continues to read Shakespeare and who does not choose to make shoes, which he could never make if it comes to that. The artists of our time resemble the repentant noblemen of nineteenth-century Russia; their bad conscience is their excuse. But the last emotion that an artist can experience, confronted with his art, is repentance. It is going far beyond simple and necessary humility to pretend to dismiss beauty, too, until the end of time, and meanwhile, to deprive all the world, including the shoemaker, of this additional bread of which one has taken advantage oneself.

This form of ascetic insanity, nevertheless, has its reasons which at least are of interest to us. They express, on the aesthetic level, the struggle, already described, between revolution and rebellion. In every rebellion is to be found the metaphysical demand for unity, the impossibility of capturing it and the construction of a substitute universe. Rebellion, from this point of view, is a fabricator of universes. This also defines art. The demands of rebellion are really, in part, aesthetic demands. All rebel thought, as we have seen, is either expressed in rhetoric or in a closed universe. The convents and isolated castles of Sade, the island or the lonely rock of the romantics, the solitary heights of Nietzsche, prison, the nation behind barbed wire, the concentration camps, the empire of free slaves all illustrate, after their own fashion, the same need for coherence and unity. In these sealed worlds, man can reign and have knowledge at last.

This is also the tendency of all the arts. The artist reconstructs the world to his plan. The symphonies of Nature know no organ point. The world is never quiet, even its silence eternally resounds with the same notes, in vibrations which escape our ears. As for those that we perceive, they carry sounds to us, occasionally a chord, never a melody. However, music exists in which symphonies are finished, where melody gives its form to sounds which by themselves have none, and where, finally, a particular arrangement of notes extracts, from natural disorder, a unity which is satisfying to the mind and the heart.

'I believe more and more', writes Van Gogh, 'that God must not be judged on this earth. The world is a study of God which has turned out badly.' Every artist tried to reconstruct this study and to give it the style it lacks. The greatest and most ambitious of all the arts, sculpture, is bent on capturing, in three dimensions, the fugitive face of man, and on restoring the unity of great style to the general disorder of gestures. Sculpture does not reject resemblance of which, indeed, it has need. But resemblance is not its first aim. What it is looking for, in its periods of greatness, is the gesture, the expression, or the empty stare which will sum up all the gestures and all the stares in the world. Its purpose is not to imitate, but to stylize and to imprison, in one significant expression, the fleeting ecstasy of the body or the infinite variety of human attitudes. Then, and only then, does it erect, on the pediments of riotous cities, the model, the type, the motionless perfection which will cool, for one moment, the fevered brow of man. The frustrated lover of love can finally gaze at the Greek caryatides and grasp what it is that triumphs, in the body and face of a woman, over every degradation.

The principle of painting is also to make a choice. 'Even genius', writes Delacroix, ruminating on his art, 'is only the gift of generalizing and choosing.' The painter isolates his subject, which is the first way of unifying it. Landscapes flee, vanish from the memory, or destroy one another. That is why the landscape painter or the painter of still life isolates in space and time things which normally change with the light, get lost in an infinite perspective or disappear under the impact of other values. The first thing that a landscape painter does is to square off his canvas. He eliminates as much as he includes. Similarly, subject painting isolates, both in time and space, an action which normally would become lost in another action. Thus the painter arrives at a point of stabilization. The really great creative artists are those who, like Piero della Francesca, give the impression that the stabilization has only just taken place, that the projection machine has suddenly stopped dead. All their subjects give the impression that, by some miracle of art, they continue to live, while ceasing to be mortal. Long after his death, Rembrandt's philosopher still meditates, between light and shade, on the same problem.

'How vain a thing is painting which beguiles us by the resemblance of objects which do not please us at all.' Delacroix, who quotes Pascal's celebrated remark, is correct in writing 'strange' instead of 'vain'. These objects do not please us at all because we do not see them; they are obscured and negated by a perpetual process of change. Who looked at the hands of the executioner during the Flagellation and the olive trees on the way to the Cross? But here we see them represented, transfigured by the incessant movement of the Passion and the agony of Christ, imprisoned in images of violence and beauty, cries out again, each day, in the cold rooms of museums. A painter's style lies in this blending of Nature and history, in this stability imposed on incessant change. Art realizes, without apparent effort, the reconciliation of the unique with the universal of which Hegel dreamed. Perhaps that is why periods, such as ours, which are bent on unity to the point of madness, turn to primitive arts, in which stylization is the most intense and unity the most provocative. The most abstract stylization is always found at the beginning and end of artistic movements; it demonstrates the intensity of negation and transposition which has given modern painting its disorderly impetus towards interpreting unity and existence. Van Gogh's admirable complaint is the arrogant and desperate cry of all artists. 'I can very well, in life, and in painting, too, do without God. But I cannot, suffering as I do, do without something that is greater than I am, which is my life – the power to create.'

But the artist's rebellion against reality, which is automatically suspect to the totalitarian revolution, contains the same affirmation as the spontaneous rebellion of the oppressed. The revolutionary spirit, born of total negation, instinctively feels that besides refusal, there was also in art a tendency to acquiescence; that there was a risk of contemplation counterbalancing action and beauty counteracting injustice, and that in certain cases, beauty itself was a form of injustice from which there was no appeal. Equally well, no form of art can survive on total denial alone. Just as all thought, and primarily that of non-signification, signifies something, so there is no art that has no signification. Man can allow himself to denounce the total injustice of the world and then demand a total justice which he alone will create. But he cannot affirm the total hideousness of the world. To create beauty, he must simultaneously reject reality and exalt certain of its aspects. Art disputes reality, but does not hide from it. Nietzsche could deny any form of transcendence, whether moral or divine, in saying that transcendence drove one to slander this world and this life. But perhaps there is a living transcendence, of which beauty carries the promise, which can make this mortal and limited world preferable to and more appealing than any other. Art thus leads us back to the origins of rebellion, to the extent that it tries to give its form to an elusive value which the future perpetually promises, but which the artist presents and wishes to snatch from the grasp of history. We shall understand this better in considering the art form whose precise aim is to dive into the stream of the ceaseless change of things in order to give it the style that it lacks; in other words, the novel.

REBELLION AND THE NOVEL

It is possible to separate the literature of consent which coincides, by and large, with ancient history and the classical period from the literature of rebellion which begins in modern times. We note the scarcity of fiction in the former. When it exists, with very few exceptions, it is not concerned with history but with fantasy (*Theagenus and Chariclea* or *Astraea*). These are fairy-tales not novels. In the latter period, on the contrary, the novel form is really developed – a form which has not ceased to thrive and extend its field of activity up to the present day, in conjunction with the critical and revolutionary movement. The novel is born simultaneously with the spirit of rebellion and expresses, on the aesthetic plane, the same ambition.

'Make-believe history, written in prose,' says Littré about the novel. Is it only that? In any case, a catholic critic has written: 'Art, whatever its aims, is always in sinful competition with God.' Actually, it is more correct to talk about competition with God, in connexion with the novel, than of competition with the State. Thibaudet expresses a similar idea when he says of Balzac: '*The Human Comedy* is the *Imitation* of God the Father.' The aim of great literature seems to be to create a closed universe or a perfect type. The West, in its great creative works, does not limit itself to retracing the steps of its daily life. It ceaselessly presents magnificently conceived images which inflame its imagination and sets off, hot foot, in pursuit of them.

After all, writing or even reading a novel are unusual activities. To construct a story by a new arrangement of actual facts has nothing inevitable or even necessary about it. Even if the ordinary explanation of the mutual pleasure of reader and writer were true, it would still be necessary to ask why it was incumbent on a large part of humanity to take pleasure and an interest in make-believe stories. Revolutionary criticism condemns the novel in its pure form as being simply a means of escape for an idle imagination. In everyday speech we find the term 'romance' used to describe an exaggerated description or lying account of some event. Not so very long ago it was a commonplace that young girls, despite all appearance to the contrary, were 'romantic', by which was meant that these idealized creatures took no account of everyday realities. In general, it has always been considered that the romantic was quite separate from life and that it enhanced it while, at the same time, betraying it. The simplest and most common way of envisaging the expression of romanticism is to see it as an escapist exercise. Common sense joins hands with revolutionary criticism.

But what are we escaping from by means of a novel? From a reality we consider too overwhelming? Happy people read novels, too, and it is an established fact that extreme suffering takes away the taste for literature. From another angle, the romantic universe of the novel certainly has less substance than the other universe where people of flesh and blood lay siege to us without respite. However, by what magic does Adolphe, for instance, seem a so much more familiar figure to us than Benjamin Constant, and Count Mosca than our professional moralists ? Balzac once terminated a long conversation about politics and the fate of the world by saying: 'And now let us get back to serious matters', meaning that he wanted to talk about his novels. The incontestable importance of the world of the novel, our insistence, in fact, on taking seriously the innumerable myths with which we have been provided, for the last two centuries, by the genius of writers, implies a sort of rejection of reality. But this rejection is not a mere escapist flight, and should be interpreted as the retreat of the soul which, according to Hegel, creates for itself in its deception a fictitious world in which ethics reign alone. However, the edifying novel is always far from being great literature; and the best of all romantic novels, *Paul et Virginie*, is a really heart-breaking book, and makes no concessions to consolation.

The contradiction is this: man rejects the world as it is, without accepting the necessity of escaping it. In fact, men cling to the world and by far the greater majority do not want to abandon it. Far from always wanting to forget it, they suffer, on the contrary, from not being able to possess it completely enough, strangers to the world they live in and exiled from their own country. Except for vivid moments of fulfilment, all reality for them is incomplete. Their actions escape them in the form of other actions, return, in unexpected guises, to judge them and disappear like the water Tantalus longed to drink, into some still undiscovered orifice. To know the whereabouts of the orifice, to control the course of the river, to understand life, at last, as destiny — these are their true aspirations. But this vision which in the realm of consciousness at least, will reconcile them with themselves, can only appear, if it ever does appear, at the fugitive moment which is death, and in which everything is consummated. In order to exist just once in the world, it is necessary never again to exist.

At this point is born the fatal envy, which so many men feel, of the lives of others. Seen from a distance, these existences seem to possess a coherence and a unity which they cannot have, in reality, but which seem evident to the spectator. He only sees the salient points of these lives without taking into account the details of corrosion. Thus we make these lives into works of art. In an elementary fashion we turn them into novels. In this sense, everyone tries to make his life a work of art. We want love to last and we know that it does not last; even if, by some miracle, it were to last a whole lifetime, it would still be incomplete. Perhaps, in this insatiable need for perpetuation, we should better understand human suffering, if we knew that it was eternal. It appears that great minds are, sometimes, less horrified by suffering than by the fact that it does not endure. In default of inexhaustible happiness, eternal suffering would at least give us a destiny. But we do not even have that consolation, and our worst agonies come to an end one day. One morning, after many dark nights of despair, an irrepressible longing to live will announce to us the fact that all is finished and that suffering has no more meaning than happiness.

The desire for possession is only another form of the desire to endure; it is this that comprises the impotent delirium of love. No human being, even the most passionately loved and passionately loving, is ever in our possession. On the pitiless earth where lovers are often separated in death and are always born divided, the total possession of another human being and absolute communion throughout an entire lifetime are impossible dreams. The desire for possession is insatiable, to such a point that it can survive even love itself. To love, therefore, is to sterilize the person one loves. The shame-faced suffering of the abandoned lover is not so much due to being no longer loved as to knowing that the other partner can and must love again. In the final analysis, every man devoured by the overpowering desire to endure and possess wishes that the people whom he has loved were either sterile or dead. This is real rebellion. Those who have not insisted, at least once, on the absolute virginity of human beings and of the world, who have not trembled with longing and impotence at the fact that it is impossible, and have then not been destroyed by trying to love half-heartedly, perpetually forced back upon their longing for the absolute, cannot understand the realities of rebellion and its ravening desire for destruction. But the lives of others always escape us and we escape them too; they are without firm contours. Life, from this point of view, is without style. It is only an impulse which endlessly pursues its form without ever finding it. Man, tortured by this, tries in vain to find the form which will impose certain limits between which he can be king. If only one single living thing had definite form, he would be reconciled.

There is not one human being who, above a certain elementary level of consciousness, does not exhaust himself in trying to find formulae or attitudes which will give his existence the unity it lacks. Appearance and action, the dandy and the revolutionary, all demand unity, in order to exist and in order to exist on this earth. As in those pathetic and miserable relationships which sometimes survive for a very long time because one of the partners is waiting to find the right word, action, gesture, or situation which will bring his adventure to an end on exactly the right note, so everyone proposes and creates for himself the final word. It is not sufficient to live, there must be a destiny which does not have to wait on death. It is therefore justifiable to say that man has an idea of a better world than this. But better does not mean different, it means unified. This passion which lifts the mind above the commonplaces of a dispersed world, from which it nevertheless detaches itself, is the passion for unity. It does not result in mediocre efforts to escape, however, but in the most obstinate demands. Religion or crime, every human endeavour in fact, finally obeys this unreasonable desire and claims to give life a form it does not have. The same impulse which can lead to the adoration of the heavens or the destruction of man, also leads to creative literature which derives its serious content at this source.

What, in fact, is a novel but a universe in which action is endowed with form, where final words are pronounced, where people possess one another completely and where life assumes the aspect of destiny? The world of the novel is only a rectification of the world we live in, in pursuance of man's deepest wishes. For the world is undoubtedly the same one we know. The suffering, the illusion, the love are the same.

The heroes speak our language, have our weaknesses and our strength. Their universe is neither more beautiful nor more enlightening than ours. But they, at least, pursue their destinies to the bitter end and there are no more fascinating heroes than those who indulge their passions to the fullest, Kirilov and Stavrogin, Madame Graslin, Julien Sorel, or the Prince de Clèves. It is here that we can no longer keep pace with them, for they complete things which we can never consummate.

Mme de La Fayette derived the *Princesse de Clèves* from the most harrowing experiences. Undoubtedly she is Madame de Clèves and yet she is not. Where lies the difference? The difference is that Mme de La Fayette did not go into a convent and that no one around her died of despair. No doubt she knew moments, at least, of agony in her unrivalled passion. But there was no dénouement, she survived her love and prolonged it by ceasing to live it, and finally no one, not even herself, would have known its pattern if she had not given it the ideal delineation of faultless prose.

Here we have an imaginary world, therefore, which is created from the rectification of the actual world – a world where suffering can, if it wishes, continue until death, where passions are never distracted, where people are prey to obsessions and are always present to each other. Man is finally able to give himself the alleviating form and limits which he pursues in vain in his own life. The novel makes destiny to measure. In this way man competes with creation and, provisionally, conquers death. A detailed analysis of the most famous novels would show, in different perspectives each time, that the essence of the novel lies in this perpetual alteration, always directed towards the same ends, that the artist makes in his own experience. Far from being moral or even purely formal, this alteration aims, primarily, at unity and thereby indicates a metaphysical need. The novel, on this level, is primarily an exercise of the intelligence in the service of nostalgic or rebellious sensibilities. It would be possible to study this quest for unity in the French analytical novel and in Melville, Balzac, Dostoyevsky, or Tolstoy. But a brief comparison between two attempts which stand at different poles of the world of the novel – the works of Proust and American fiction of the last few years – will suffice for our purpose.

The American novel* claims to find its unity in reducing man either to elementals or to his external reactions and to his behaviour. It does not choose feelings or passions of which to give a detailed description, such as we find in classic French literature. It rejects analysis and the search for a fundamental psychological motive which could explain and recapitulate the behaviour of a character. This is why the unity of this novel form is only the unity of the flash of recognition. Its technique consists of describing men by their outside appearances, in their most casual actions, of reproducing, without comment, everything they say down to their repetitions and finally by acting as if men were entirely defined by their daily automatisms. On this mechanical level men, in fact, seem exactly alike, which explains this peculiar universe in which all the characters appear interchangeable, even down to their physical peculiarities. This technique is only called realistic, thanks to a misapprehension. In addition to the fact that realism in art is, as we shall see, an incomprehensible idea, it is perfectly obvious that this fictitious world is not attempting a reproduction, pure and simple, of reality, but the most arbitrary form of stylization. It is born of a mutilation and of a voluntary mutilation performed on reality. The unity thus obtained is a degraded unity, a levelling off of human beings and of the world. It would seem that, for these writers, it is the inner life which deprives human actions of unity and which tears people away from one another. This is a partially legitimate suspicion. But rebellion, which is one of the sources of the art of fiction, can only find satisfaction in constructing unity on the basis of affirming this interior reality and not of denying it. To deny it totally is to refer oneself to the opinion of an imaginary man. Novels of violence are also love stories of which they have the formal conceits – in their own way, they edify. The life of the body, reduced to its essentials, paradoxically produces an abstract and gratuitous universe, continuously denied, in its turn, by reality. This type of

* We are referring, of course, to the 'tough' novel of the thirties and not to the admirable American efflorescence of the nineteenth century.

novel, purged of interior life, in which men seem to be observed behind a pane of glass, logically ends by giving itself, as its unique subject, the supposedly average man studied from the pathological point of view. In this way it is possible to explain the extraordinary number of 'innocents' who appear in this universe. The innocent is the ideal subject for such an enterprise since he can only be defined – and completely defined – by his behaviour. He is the symbol of the despairing world in which wretched automatons live in the most mechanically coherent way and which American novelists have presented as a heart rending but sterile protest.

As for Proust, his contribution has been to create, from an obstinate contemplation of reality, a closed world which belonged only to him and which indicated his victory over the transitoriness of things and over death. But he uses absolutely the opposite means. He upholds above everything, by a deliberate choice, a careful selection of unique experience which the writer chooses from the most secret recesses of his past. Immense empty spaces are thus discarded from life because they have left no trace in the memory. If the American novel is the novel of men without memory, the world of Proust is nothing but memory. It is only concerned with the most difficult and most exacting of memories, the memory which rejects the dispersion of the actual world and which derives, from the trace of a lingering perfume, the secret of a new and ancient universe. Proust chooses the interior life and, of the interior life, that which is more interior than life itself in preference to what is forgotten in the world of reality, in other words the purely mechanical and blind aspects of the world. But by his rejection of reality he does not deny reality. He does not commit the error, which would counter-balance the error of American fiction, of suppressing the mechanical. He unites, on the contrary, into a superior form of unity, the memory of the past and the immediate sensation, the twisted foot and the happy days of times past.

It is difficult to return to the places of one's early happiness. The young girls in the flower of their youth still laugh and chatter on the seashore, but he who watches them gradually loses his right to love them, just as those he has loved lose the power to be loved. This melancholy is the melancholy of Proust. It was powerful enough in him to cause a violent rejection of all existence. But his passion for faces and for the light, at the same time, attached him to life. He never admitted that the happy days of his youth were lost forever. He undertook the task of recreating them and of demonstrating, in the face of death, that the past could be regained at the end of time in the form of an imperishable present, both truer and richer than it was at the beginning. The psychological analysis of *Remembrance of Things Past* is nothing but a potent means to an end. The real greatness of Proust lies in having written *Time Regained* which bears the resemblance of the world of dispersion and which gives it a meaning on the very level of discord. His difficult victory, on the eve of his death, is to have been able to extract from the incessant flight of forms, by means of memory and intelligence alone, the tentative trembling symbols of human unity. The most definite challenge that a work of this kind can give to creation is to present itself as an entirety, as a closed and unified world. This defines an unrepentant work of art.

It has been said that the world of Proust was a world without a god. If that is true, it is not because God is never spoken of, but because the ambition of this world is to be absolute perfection and to give to eternity the aspect of man. *Time Regained*, at least in its aspirations, is eternity without God. Proust's work, in this regard, appears to be one of the most ambitious and most significant of man's enterprises against his mortal condition. He has demonstrated that the art of the novel can reconstruct creation itself, in the form that it is imposed on us and in the form in which we reject it. In one of its aspects at least, this art consists of choosing the creature in preference to his creator. But still more profoundly, it is allied to the beauty of the world or of its inhabitants against the powers of death and oblivion. It is in this way that his rebellion is creative.

REBELLION AND STYLE

By the treatment that the artist imposes on reality, he declares the intensity of his rejection of it. But what he retains of reality, in the universe that he creates, reveals the degree of consent that he gives to at least one part of reality – which he draws from the shadows of evolution to bring it to the light of creation. In the final analysis, if the rejection is total, reality is then completely banished and the result is a purely formal work. If, on the other hand, the artist chooses, for reasons often unconnected with art, to exalt crude reality, the result is then realism. In the first case, the primitive creative impulse in which rebellion and consent, affirmation and negation are closely allied, is adulterated to the advantage of rejection. It then represents formal escapism of which our period has furnished so many examples and of which the nihilist origin is quite evident. In this second case, the artist claims to give the world unity by withdrawing from it all privileged perspectives. In this sense, he confesses his need for unity, even a degraded form of unity. But he also renounces the first requirement of artistic creation. To deny the relative freedom of the creative mind more forcibly, he affirms the immediate totality of the world. The act of creation itself is denied in both these kinds of work. Originally, it only refused one aspect of reality while simultaneously affirming another. Whether it comes to the point of rejecting all reality or of affirming nothing but reality, it denies itself each time either by absolute negation or by absolute affirmation. It can be seen that, on the plane of aesthetics, this analysis coincides with the analysis we have sketched on the historic plane.

But just as there is no nihilism which ends by supposing a value, and no materialism which, being self-conceived, does not end by contradicting itself, so formal art and realist art are absurd concepts. No art can completely reject reality. The Gorgon is, undoubtedly, a purely imaginary creature; its face and the serpents that crown it are part of nature. Formalism can succeed in purging itself more and more of real content, but there is always a limit. Even pure geometry, where abstract painting sometimes ends, still derives its colour and its conformity to perspective from the exterior world. The only real formalism is silence. Moreover, realism cannot dispense with a minimum of interpretation and arbitrariness. Even the very best photographs betray reality – they result from an act of selection and impose a limit on something that has none. The realist artist and the formal artist try to find unity where it does not exist, in reality in its crudest state, or in imaginative creation which wants to expel all reality. On the contrary, unity in art appears at the limit of the transformation which the artist imposes on reality. It cannot dispense with either. This correction* which the artist imposes by his language and by a redistribution of elements derived from reality, is called style and gives the recreated universe its unity and its boundaries. It attempts, in the work of every rebel, and succeeds in the case of a few geniuses, to impose its laws on the world. 'Poets', said Shelley, 'are the unacknowledged legislators of the world.'

Romantic art, by its origins, cannot fail to illustrate this vocation. It can neither totally consent to reality nor turn aside from it completely. The purely imaginary does not exist and, even if it did exist in an ideal novel which would be purely disincarnate, it would have no artistic significance, in that the primary necessity for a mind in search of unity is that the unity should be communicable. From another point of view, the unity of pure reasoning is a false unity since it is not based on reality. The sentimental love story, the horror story, and the edifying novel deviate from art to the great or small extent that they disobey this law. Real literary creation, on the other hand, uses reality and only reality with all its warmth and its blood, its passion and its outcries. It simply adds something which transfigures reality.

Likewise, what is commonly called the realistic novel tries to be the reproduction of reality in its immediate aspects. To reproduce the

* Delacroix notes, and this is a penetrating observation, that it is necessary to correct the inflexible perspective which (in reality) falsifies the appearance of objects 'by virtue of precision'.

elements of reality without making any kind of selection would be, if such an undertaking could be imagined, nothing but a sterile repetition of creation. Realism should only be the means of expression of religious genius – Spanish art admirably illustrates this contention – or, at the other extreme, the artistic expressions of monkeys which are quite satisfied with mere imitation. In fact, art is never realistic though sometimes it is tempted to be. To be really realistic a description would have to be endless. Where Stendhal describes, in one phrase, Lucien Leuwen's entrance into a room, the realistic artist ought, logically, to fill several volumes with descriptions of characters and settings, still without succeeding in exhausting every detail. Realism is indefinite enumeration. By this it reveals that its real ambition is conquest, not of the unity, but of the totality of the real world. Now we understand why it should be the official aesthetic of a totalitarian revolution. But the impossibility of such an aesthetic has already been demonstrated. Realistic novels select their material, despite themselves, from reality, because the choice and the conquest of reality are absolute conditions of thought and expression. To write is already to choose. There is thus an arbitrary aspect to reality, just as there is an arbitrary aspect to the ideal, which makes a realistic novel an implicit problem novel. To reduce the unity of the world of fiction to the totality of reality can only be done by means of an *a priori* judgement which eliminates form, reality, and everything that conflicts with doctrine. Therefore, so-called socialist realism is condemned by the very logic of its nihilism to accumulate the advantages of the edifying novel and propaganda literature.

Whether the event enslaves the creator or whether the creator claims to deny the event completely, creation is nevertheless reduced to the degraded forms of nihilist art. It is the same thing with creation as with civilization: it presumes uninterrupted tension between form and matter, between evolution and the mind, and between history and values. If the equilibrium is destroyed the result is dictatorship or anarchy, propaganda or formal insanity. In either case creation, which coincides always with rational freedom, is impossible. Whether it succumbs to the intoxication of abstraction and formal obscurantism, or whether it appeals to the whip of the crudest and most ingenious realism, modern art, in its semi-totality, is an art of tyrants and slaves, not of creators.

A work in which the content overflows the form, in which the form drowns the content, only bespeaks an unconvinced and unconvincing unity. In this domain, as in others, any unity which is not a unity of style is a mutilation. Whatever may be the chosen point of view of an artist, one principle remains common to all creators: stylization, which supposes the simultaneous existence of reality and of the mind which gives reality its form. Through style, the creative reconstructs the world and always with the same slight distortion which is the mark of both art and protest. Whether it is the magnification of the microscope which Proust brings to bear on human experience or, on the contrary, the absurd insignificance with which the American novel endows its characters, reality is in some way artificial. The creative force, the fecundity of rebellion are contained in this distortion which represents the style and tone of a work. Art is an impossible demand given expression and form. When the most agonizing protest finds its most resolute form of expression, rebellion satisfies its real aspirations and derives, from this fidelity to itself, a creative strength. Despite the fact that this runs counter to the prejudices of the times, the greatest style in art is the expression of the most passionate rebellion. Just as genuine classicism is only romanticism subdued, genius is a rebellion which has created its own limits. That is why there is no genius, contrary to what we are taught today, in negation and pure despair.

This means, at the same time, that great style is not a mere formal virtue. It is a mere formal virtue when it is sought out for its own sake to the detriment of reality, but then it is not great style. It no longer invents, but imitates – like all academic works – while real creation is, in its own fashion, revolutionary. If stylization must be pushed very far, since it sums up the intervention of man and the desire for rectification which the artist brings to his reproduction of reality, it is nevertheless desirable that it should remain invisible so that the demand which gives birth to art should be expressed in its most extreme tension. Great style is invisible stylization or rather stylization incarnate. 'There is never any need', says Flaubert,'to be afraid of exaggeration in art.' But he adds that the exaggeration should be 'continuous and proportionate to itself'. When stylization is exaggerated and obvious, the work becomes nothing but pure nostalgia; the unity it is trying to conquer has nothing to do with concrete unity. On the other hand, when reality is delivered over to unadorned fact or to insignificant stylization, then the concrete is presented without unity. Great art, style, and the true aspect of rebellion lie somewhere between these two heresies.

CREATION AND REVOLUTION

In art, rebellion is consummated and perpetuated in the act of real creation, not in criticism or commentary. Revolution, in its turn, can only affirm itself in a civilization and not in terror or tyranny. The two questions posed, henceforth, by our times to a society caught in a dilemma – Is creation possible? Is the revolution possible? – are in reality only one question which concerns the renaissance of civilization.

The revolution and art of the twentieth century are tributaries of the same nihilism and live in the same contradiction. They deny what they affirm, however, even in their very actions, and both try to find an impossible solution through terror. The contemporary revolution believes that it is inaugurating a new world when it is really only the contradictory climax of the ancient world. Finally capitalist society and revolutionary society are one and the same thing to the extent that they submit themselves to the same means – industrial production – and to the same promise. But one makes its promise in the name of formal principles which it is quite incapable of incarnating and which are denied by the methods it employs. The other justifies its prophecy in the name of the only reality it recognizes and ends by mutilating reality. The society based on production is only productive, not creative.

Contemporary art, because it is nihilistic, also flounders between formalism and realism. Realism, moreover, is just as much bourgeois, when it is 'tough', as socialist when it becomes edifying. Formalism belongs just as much to the society of the past, when it takes the form of gratuitous abstraction, as to the society which claims to be the society of the future – when it becomes propaganda. Language destroyed by irrational negation becomes lost in verbal delirium; subject to determinist ideology it is summed up in the word of command. Half-way between the two lies art. If the rebel must simultaneously reject the frenzy of annihilation and the acceptance of totality, the artist must simultaneously escape from the passion for formality and the totalitarian aesthetic of reality. The world today is one, in fact, but its unity is the unity of nihilism. Civilization is only possible if, by renouncing the nihilism of formal principles and nihilism without principles, the world rediscovers the road to a creative synthesis. In the same way, in art, the time of perpetual commentary and reportage is at the point of death; it announces the advent of creative artists.

But art and society, creation and revolution must, to prepare for this event, rediscover the source of rebellion where refusal and acceptance, in unique and the universal, the individual and history balance each other in a condition of the most acute tension. Rebellion, in itself, is not an element of civilization. But it is a preliminary to all civilization. Rebellion alone, in the blind alley in which we live, allows us to hope for the future of which Nietzsche dreamed: 'Instead of the judge and the oppressor, the creator'. This formula certainly does not authorize the ridiculous illusion of a civilization controlled by artists. It only illuminates the drama of our times in which work, entirely subordinated to production, has ceased to be creative. Industrial society will only open the way to a new civilization by restoring to the worker the dignity of a creator; in other words, by making him apply his interest and his intelligence as much to the work itself as to what it produces. The type of civilization which is inevitable will not be able to separate, amongst classes as well as in the individual, the worker from the creator; any more than artistic creation dreams of form and foundation, history and the mind. In this way it will bestow on everyone the dignity which rebellion affirms. It would be unjust, and moreover Utopian, for Shakespeare to direct the shoemakers' union. But it would be equally disastrous for the shoemakers' union to ignore Shakespeare. Shakespeare without the shoemakers serves as an alibi for tyranny. The shoemaker without Shakespeare is absorbed by tyranny when he does not contribute to its propagation. Every act of creation denies, by its mere existence, the world of master and slave. The appalling society of tyrants and slaves in which we survive will only find its death and transfiguration on the level of creation.

But the fact that creation is necessary does not perforce imply that it is possible. A creative period in art is determined by the order of a particular style applied to the disorder of a particular time. It gives form and formulae to contemporary passions. Thus it no longer suffices, for a creative artist, to repeat, say, the words of Mme de La Fayette in a period when our morose princes have no more time for love. Today when collective passions have stolen a march on individual passions, the ecstasy of love can always be controlled by art. But the ineluctable problem is also to control collective passions and the historic struggle. The scope of art, despite the regrets of the plagiarists, has been extended from psychology to the human condition. When the passions of the times put the fate of the whole world at stake, creation wants to dominate the whole of destiny. But, at the same time, it maintains, in the face of totality, the affirmation of unity. In simple words, creation is then imperilled, first by itself, and then by the spirit of totality. To create, today, is to create dangerously.

Collective passions must, in fact, be lived through and experienced, at least relatively. At the same time that he experiences them, the artist is devoured by them. The result is that our period is rather the period of reportage than the period of the work of art. The exercise of these passions, finally, entails far greater chances of death than in the time of love and ambition, in that the only way of living collective passions is to be willing to die for them or by their hand. The greatest opportunity for authenticity is, today, the greatest defeat of art. If creation is impossible during wars and revolutions, then we shall have no creative artists, for war and revolution are our lot. The myth of unlimited production brings war in its train as inevitably as clouds announce a storm. Wars lay waste to the West and kill a genius or two. Hardly has it arisen from the ruins when the bourgeois system sees the revolutionary system advancing upon it. The genius has not even had time to be reborn; the war which threatens us will, perhaps, kill all those who might have been geniuses. If a creative classicism is, nevertheless, proved possible, we must recognize that, even though it is rendered illustrious by one name alone, it will be the work of an entire generation. The chances of defeat, in the century of destruction, can only be compensated for by the hazard of numbers; in other words, the chance that of ten authentic artists one, at least, will survive, take charge of the first utterances of his brother artists and succeed in finding in his life both the time for passion and the time for creation. The artist, whether he likes it or not, can no longer be a solitary, except in the melancholy triumph which he owes to all his fellow-artists. Rebellious art also ends by revealing the 'We are' and with it the way to a burning humility.

Meanwhile, the triumphant revolution, in the aberrations of its nihilism, menaces those who, in defiance of it, claim to maintain the existence of unity in totality. One of the implications of history today, and still more of the history of tomorrow, is the struggle between the artists and the new conquerors, between the witnesses to the creative revolution and the founders of the nihilist revolution. As to the outcome of the struggle, it is only possible to make inspired guesses. At least we know that it must, hereafter, be carried on to the bitter end. Modern conquerors can kill, but do not seem to be able to create. Artists know how to create but cannot really kill. Murderers are only very exceptionally found among artists. In the long run, therefore, art in our revolutionary societies must die. But then the revolution will have lived its allotted span. Each time that the revolution kills in a man the artist that he might have been, it attenuates itself a little more. If, finally, the conquerors succeed in moulding the world according to their laws, it will not prove that quality is king but that this world is hell. In this hell, the place of art will coincide with that of vanquished rebellion, a blind and empty hope in the pit of despair. Ernst Dwinger in his *Siberian Diary* mentions a German lieutenant – for years a prisoner in a camp where cold and hunger were almost unbearable – who constructed himself a silent piano with wooden keys. In the most abject misery, perpetually surrounded by a ragged mob, he composed a strange music which was audible to him alone. And for us who have been thrown into hell, mysterious melodies and the torturing images of a vanquished beauty will always bring us, in the midst of crime and folly, the echo of that harmonious insurrection which bears witness, throughout the centuries, to the greatness of humanity.

But hell can endure for only a limited period and life will begin again one day. History may perhaps have an end; but our task is not to terminate it but to create it, in the image of what we henceforth know to be true. Art, at least, teaches us that man cannot be explained by history alone and that he also finds a reason for his existence in the order of nature. For him, the great god Pan is not dead. His most distinctive act of rebellion, while it affirms the value and the dignity common to all men, obstinately claims, so as to satisfy its hunger for unity, an integral part of the reality whose name is beauty. One can reject all history and yet accept the world of the sea and the stars. The rebels who wish to ignore nature and beauty are condemned to banish from history everything with which they want to construct the dignity of existence and of labour. Every great reformer tries to create in history what Shakespeare, Cervantes, Molière, and Tolstoy knew how to create: a world always ready to satisfy the hunger for freedom and dignity which every man carries in his heart. Beauty, no doubt, does not make revolutions. But a day will come when revolutions will have need of beauty. The procedure of beauty, which is to resist the real while conferring unity upon it, is also the procedure of rebellion. Is it possible eternally to reject injustice without ceasing to acclaim the nature of man and the beauty of the world? Our answer is yes. This ethic, at once unsubmissive and loyal, is in any event the only one which lights the way to a truly realistic revolution. In upholding beauty, we prepare the way for the day of regeneration

when civilization will give first place – far ahead of the formal principles and degraded values of history – to this living virtue on which is
founded the common dignity of man and the world he lives in, and
which we now have to define in the face of a world which insults it.

5

THOUGHT AT THE MERIDIAN

REBELLION AND MURDER

FAR from this source of life, however, Europe and the revolution are being shaken to the core by a spectacular convulsion. During the last century, man cast off the fetters of religion. Hardly was he free, however, when he created new and utterly intolerable chains. Virtue dies but is born again, more exacting than ever. It preaches an ear-splitting sermon on charity to all comers and a form of love from a distance which makes a mockery of contemporary humanism. At this point of coagulation, it can only wreak havoc. A day comes when it becomes bitter, immediately adopts police methods, and, for the salvation of mankind, assumes the tawdry aspect of an inquisition. At the climax of contemporary tragedy, we therefore become intimates of crime. The sources of life and of creation seem exhausted. Fear paralyses a Europe peopled with phantoms and machines. Between two holocausts, scaffolds are installed in underground caverns where humanist executioners celebrate their new cult, in silence. What cry would ever trouble them? The poets themselves, confronted with the murder of their brother men, proudly declare that their hands are clean. The whole world absent-mindedly turns its back on these crimes; the victims have reached the extremity of their disgrace: they are a bore. In ancient times the blood of murder at least produced a religious horror and in this way sanctified the value of life. The real condemnation of the period we live in is, on the contrary, that it leads us to think that it is not bloodthirsty enough. Blood is no longer visible; it does not bespatter the faces of

our Pharisees visibly enough. This is the extreme of nihilism; blind
and savage murder becomes an oasis and the imbecile criminal seems
positively refreshing in comparison to our highly intelligent executioners.

Having believed for a long time that it could fight against God with
all humanity as its ally, the European mind then perceived that it must
also, if it did not want to die, fight against men. The rebels who
united against death and wanted to construct, on the foundation of
the human species, a triumphant immortality, are terrified at the
prospect of being obliged to kill in their turn. Nevertheless, if they
retreat they must accept death; if they advance they must accept
murder. Rebellion, cut off from its origins and cynically travestied,
oscillates, on all levels, between sacrifice and murder. The form of
justice that it advocated and which it hoped was impartial has
transpired to be summary. The kingdom of grace has been conquered,
but the kingdom of justice is crumbling too. Europe is dying of this
deception. Rebellion pleaded for the innocence of mankind and now
it has hardened its heart against its own culpability. Hardly does it
start off in search of totality when it receives as its portion the most
desperate sensations of solitude. It wanted to enter into communion
with mankind and now it has no other hope but to assemble, one by
one, throughout the years, the solitary men who fight their way towards unity.

Must we therefore renounce every kind of rebellion, whether we
accept, with all its injustices, a society which outlives its usefulness,
or whether we decide, cynically, to serve, against the interest of man,
the inexorable advance of history? After all if the logic of our
reflection should lead to a cowardly conformism it would have to be
accepted as certain families sometimes accept inevitable dishonour.
If it must also justify all the varieties of attempts against man, and
even his systematic destruction, it would be necessary to consent to
this suicide. The desire for justice would finally realize its ambition:
the disappearance of a world of tradesmen and police.

But are we still living in a rebellious world? Has not rebellion
become, on the contrary, the alibi of a new variety of tyrant? Can the

'We are' contained in the movement of rebellion, without shame and without subterfuge, be reconciled with murder? In assigning oppression a limit within which begins the dignity common to all men, rebellion defined a primary value. It put in the first rank of its frame of reference an obvious mutual complicity amongst men, a common texture, the solidarity of chains, a communication between human being and human being which makes men similar and united. In this way, it compelled the mind to take a first step in defiance of an absurd world. By this progress, it rendered still more acute the problem which it must now solve in regard to murder. On the level of the absurd, in fact, murder would only give rise to logical contradictions; on the level of rebellion it is mental laceration. For it is now a question of deciding if it is possible to kill someone, whose resemblance to ourselves we have at last recognized and whose identity we have just sanctified. When we have only just conquered solitude, must we then re-establish it definitively by legitimizing the act which isolates everything? To force solitude on a man who has just come to understand that he is not alone, is that not the definitive crime against man?

Logically, one should reply that murder and rebellion are contradictory. If a single master should, in fact, be killed, the rebel in a certain way is no longer justified in using the term 'community of men' from which he derived his justification. If this world has no higher meaning, if man is only responsible to man, it suffices for a man to remove one single human being from the society of the living to automatically exclude himself from it. When Cain kills Abel, he flees to the desert. And if the murderers are legion, then this legion lives in the desert and in the other kind of solitude called promiscuity.

From the moment that he strikes, the rebel cuts the world in two. He rebelled in the name of the identity of man with man and he sacrifices this identity by consecrating the difference in blood. His only existence, in the midst of suffering and oppression, was contained in this identity. The same movement, which intended to affirm it, thus brings an end to its existence. It can claim that some, or even all, are with it. But if one single human being is missing in the world of fraternity then this world is immediately depopulated. If we are not, then I am not and this explains the infinite sadness of Kaliayev and the silence of Saint-Just. The rebels, who have decided to gain their ends through violence and murder, have in vain replaced, in order to preserve the hope of existing, the 'we are' by a 'we shall be'. When the murderer and the victim have disappeared, the community will provide its own justification without them. The exception having lasted its appointed time, the rule will once more become possible. On the level of history, as in individual life, murder is thus a desperate exception or it is nothing. The disturbance that it brings to the order of things offers no hope of a future; it is an exception and therefore it can be neither utilitarian nor systematic as the purely historic attitude would have it. It is the limit that can only be reached but once and after which one must die. The rebel has only one way of reconciling himself with his act of murder if he allows himself to be led into performing it: to accept his own death and sacrifice. He kills and dies so that it shall be clear that murder is impossible. He demonstrates that, in reality, he prefers the 'We are' to the 'We shall be'. The calm happiness of Kaliayev is his prison, the serenity of Saint-Just when he walks towards the scaffold are explained in their turn. Beyond that farthest frontier, contradiction and nihilism begin.

NIHILISTIC MURDER

Irrational crime and rational crime, in fact, both equally betray the value brought to light by the movement of rebellion. Let us first consider the former. He who denies everything and assumes the authority to kill – Sade, the homicidal dandy, the Unique, Karamazov, the supporters of the ruthless criminal – lay claim to nothing short of total freedom and the unlimited deployment of human pride. Nihilism confounds creator and created in the same blind fury. Suppressing every principle of hope, it rejects the idea of any limit, and in blind indignation, which no longer even has a reason, ends with the conclusion that it is a matter of indifference to kill when the victim is in any case already condemned to death.

But its reasons – the mutual recognition of a common destiny and the communication of men between themselves – are always valid. Rebellion proclaims them and undertakes to serve them. In the same way it defines, contrary to nihilism, a rule of conduct which has no need to await the end of history or to explain its actions and which is, nevertheless, not formal. Contrary to Jacobin morality, it took the part of everything which escapes from rules and laws. It opened the way to a morality which, far from obeying abstract principles, only discovers them in the heat of battle and in the incessant movement of debate. Nothing justifies the assertion that these principles have existed eternally, nothing serves to declare that they will one day exist. But they do exist, in the very period in which we exist. With us they deny, throughout all history, servitude, falsehood, and terror.

There is, in fact, nothing in common between a master and a slave; it is impossible to speak and communicate with a person who has been reduced to servitude. Instead of the implicit and untrammelled dialogue through which we come to recognize our similarity and consecrate our destiny, servitude gives rise to the most terrible of silences. If injustice is bad for the rebel, it is not because it contradicts an eternal idea of justice, but because it perpetuates the silent hostility which separates the oppressor and the oppressed. It kills the small part of existence which can be realized on this earth through the mutual understanding of men. In the same way, since the man who lies shuts himself off from other men, falsehood is therefore proscribed and, on a slightly lower level, murder and violence, which impose definitive silence. The mutual understanding and communication discovered by rebellion can only survive in the free exchange of dialogue. Every ambiguity, every misunderstanding, leads to death; clear language and simple words are the only salvation from it.* The climax of every tragedy lies in the deafness of its heroes. Plato is right and not Moses and Nietzsche. Dialogue on the level of mankind is

* It is worth noting that the language peculiar to totalitarian doctrines is always a scholastic or administrative language.

less costly than the gospel preached by totalitarian régimes in the form of a monologue dictated from the top of a lonely mountain. On the stage as in reality, the monologue precedes death. Every rebel, by the movement which sets him in opposition to the oppressor, therefore pleads for life, undertakes to struggle against servitude, falsehood, and terror and affirms, in a flash, that these three afflictions are the cause of silence between men, obscure them from one another and prevent them from rediscovering themselves in the only value which can save them from nihilism – the long complicity between men at grips with their destiny.

In a flash – but that is time enough to say, provisionally, that the most extreme form of freedom, the freedom to kill, is not compatible with the motives of rebellion. Rebellion is in no way the demand for total freedom. On the contrary, rebellion puts total freedom up for trial. The object of its attack is exactly the unlimited power which authorizes a superior to violate the forbidden frontier. Far from demanding general independence, the rebel wants it to be recognized that freedom has its limits everywhere that a human being is to be found – the limit being precisely that human being's power to rebel. The most profound reason of rebellious intransigence is to be found here. The more aware rebellion is of demanding a justifiable limit, the more inflexible it becomes. The rebel demands undoubtedly a certain degree of freedom for himself; but in no case, if he is consistent, does he demand the right to destroy the existence and the freedom of others. He humiliates no one. The freedom he claims, he claims for all; the freedom he refuses, he forbids everyone to enjoy. He is not only the slave against the master, but also man against the world of master and slave. Therefore there is, thanks to rebellion, something more in history than the relation between mastery and servitude. Unlimited power is not the only law. It is in the name of another value that the rebel affirms the impossibility of total freedom while he claims for himself the relative freedom necessary to recognize this impossibility. Every human freedom, at its very roots, is therefore relative. Absolute freedom, which is the freedom to kill, is the only one which does not claim – at the same time as itself – the things which limit and obliterate it. Thus it cuts itself off from its roots and – abstract and malevolent shade – wanders haphazardly until such time as it imagines that it has found substance in some ideology.

It is then possible to say that rebellion, when it emerges into destruction, is illogical. Claiming the unity of the human condition, it is a force of life and not of death. Its most profound logic is not the logic of destruction; it is the logic of creation. Its movement, in order to be authentic, must never abandon any of the terms of the contradiction which sustains it. It must be faithful to the *yes* that it contains as well as to the *no* which nihilistic interpretations isolate in rebellion. The logic of the rebel is to want to serve justice so as not to add to the injustice of the human condition, to insist on plain language so as not to increase the universal falsehood, and to wager, in spite of human misery, for happiness. Nihilistic passion, adding to falsehood and injustice, destroys, in its fury, its ancient demands and thus deprives rebellion of its most cogent reasons. It kills, in the fond conviction that this world is dedicated to death. The consequence of rebellion, on the contrary, is to refuse to legitimize murder because rebellion, in principle, is a protest against death.

But if man were capable of introducing, entirely on his own, unity into the world, if he could establish the reign, by his own decree, of sincerity, innocence, and justice: he would be God himself. Equally, if he could accomplish all this, there would be no more reasons for rebellion. If rebellion exists, it is because falsehood, injustice, and violence are part of the rebel's condition. He cannot, therefore, absolutely claim not to kill or lie, without renouncing his rebellion and accepting, once and for all, evil and murder. But nor can he agree to kill and lie, since the inverse reasoning which would justify murder and violence would also destroy the reasons for his insurrection. Thus the rebel can never find peace. He knows what is good and, despite himself, does evil. The value which supports him is never given to him once and for all – he must fight to uphold it, unceasingly. Again the existence he achieves collapses if rebellion does not support him. In any case, if he is not always able not to kill, either directly or indirectly, he can put his conviction and passion to work at diminishing the chances of murder around him. His only virtue will lie in never yielding to the impulse to allow himself to be engulfed in the shadows which surround him and in obstinately dragging the chains of evil, with which he is bound, towards the light of good. If he is finally forced to kill, he will accept death himself. Faithful to his origins, the rebel demonstrates by sacrifice that his real freedom is not freedom from murder but freedom from his own death. At the same time, he achieves honour in metaphysical terms. Thus Kaliayev climbs the gallows and visibly designates to all his fellow-men the exact limit where the honour of man begins and ends.

HISTORIC MURDER

Rebellion also deploys itself in history, which demands not only exemplary choices, but also efficacious attitudes. Rational murder runs the risk of finding itself justified by history. The contradiction of rebellion, then, is reflected in an apparently insoluble antithesis, of which the two counterparts in politics are on the one hand the opposition between violence and non-violence, and on the other hand the opposition between justice and freedom. Let us try and define them in the terms of their paradox.

The positive value contained in the initial movement of rebellion supposes the renunciation of violence committed on principle. It consequently entails the impossibility of stabilizing a revolution. Rebellion is, incessantly, prey to this contradiction. On the level of history it becomes even more insoluble. If I renounce the project of making human identity respected, I abdicate in favour of oppression, I renounce rebellion and fall back on an attitude of nihilistic consent. Then nihilism becomes conservative. If I insist that human identity should be recognized as existing then I engage in an action which, to succeed, supposes a cynical attitude towards violence and denies this identity and rebellion itself. To examine the contradiction still further, if the unity of the world cannot come from on high, man must construct it on his own level, in history. History without a value to transfigure it is controlled by the law of expediency. Historic materialism, determinism, violence, negation of every form of freedom which does not coincide with expediency and the world of silent courage are the highly legitimate consequences of a pure philosophy of history. Only a philosophy of eternity, in the world today, could justify nonviolence. To absolute worship of history it would make the objection of the creation of history and of the historic situation it would ask from whence it had sprung. Finally, it would put the responsibility for justice in God's hands, thus consecrating injustice. Equally, its answers, in their turn, would insist on faith. The objection will be raised of evil, and of the paradox of an all-powerful and malevolent, or benevolent and sterile, God. The choice will remain open between grace and history, God or the sword.

What, then, should be the attitude of the rebel? He cannot turn away from the world and from history without denying the very principle of his rebellion, nor can he choose eternal life without resigning himself, in one sense, to evil. If, for example, he is not a Christian, he should go to the bitter end. But to the bitter end means to choose history absolutely and with it murder, if murder is essential to history: to accept the justification of murder is again to deny his origins. If the rebel makes no choice, he chooses the silence and slavery of others. If, in a moment of despair, he declared that he opts both against God and against history, he bears witness to pure freedom; in other words, to nothing. In our period of history and in the impossible condition in which he finds himself, of being unable to affirm a superior motive which does not have its limits in evil, his apparent dilemma is silence or murder – in either case, a surrender.

And it is the same again with justice and freedom. These two demands are already to be found at the beginning of the rebel movement, and are to be found again in the first impetus of revolution. The history of revolutions demonstrates, however, that they almost always conflict as though their mutual demands were irreconcilable. Absolute freedom is the right of the strongest to dominate. Therefore it prolongs the conflicts which profit by injustice. Absolute justice is achieved by the suppression of all contradiction: therefore it destroys freedom. The revolution to achieve justice, through freedom, ends by aligning them against one another. Thus there exists in every revolution, once the class which dominated up to then has been liquidated, a stage in which it gives birth, itself, to a movement of rebellion which indicates its limits and announces its chances of failure. The revolution, first of all, proposes to satisfy the spirit of rebellion which has given rise to it; then it is compelled to deny it, the better to affirm itself. There is, it would seem, an ineradicable opposition between the movement of rebellion and the attainments of revolution.

But these contradictions only exist in the absolute. They suppose a world and a method of thought without premeditation. There is, in fact, no conciliation possible between a god who is totally separated from history and a history purged of all transcendence. Their representatives on earth are, indeed, the yogi and the commissar. But the difference between these two types of men is not, as has been stated, the difference between ineffectual purity and expediency. The former chooses only the ineffectiveness of abstention and the second the ineffectiveness of destruction. Because both reject the conciliatory value that rebellion, on the contrary, reveals, they only offer us two kinds of impotence, both equally removed from reality, that of good and that of evil.

If, in fact, to ignore history comes to the same as denying reality, it is still alienating oneself from reality to consider history as a completely self-sufficient absolute. The revolution of the twentieth century believes that it can avoid nihilism and remain faithful to true rebellion, by replacing God by history. In reality, it fortifies the former and betrays the latter. History in its pure form furnished no value by itself. Therefore one must live by the principles of immediate expediency and keep silent or tell lies. Systematic violence, or imposed silence, selfishness or concerted falsehood become the inevitable rule. Purely historic thought is therefore nihilistic: it accepts wholeheartedly the evil of history and in this way is opposed to rebellion. It is useless for it to affirm, in compensation, the absolute rationality of history, for historic reason will never be fulfilled and will never have its full meaning or value until the end of history. In the meanwhile, it is necessary to act, and to act without a moral rule in order that the definitive rule should one day be realized. Cynicism as a political attitude is only logical as a function of absolute thought; in other words, absolute nihilism on the one hand, absolute rationalism on the other. As for the consequences, there is no difference between the two attitudes. From the moment that they are accepted, the earth becomes a desert.

In reality the purely historic absolute is not even conceivable. Jaspers' thought, for example, in its essentials, underlines the impossibility of man's grasping totality, since he lives in the midst of this totality. History, as an entirety, could only exist in the eyes of an observer outside it and outside the world. History only exists, in the final analysis, for God. Thus it is impossible to act according to plans embracing the totality of universal history. Any historic enterprise can therefore only be a more or less reasonable or justifiable adventure. It is, primarily, a risk. In so far as it is a risk it cannot be used to justify any excess or any ruthless and absolutist position.

If, on the other hand, rebellion could found a philosophy it would be a philosophy of limits, of calculated ignorance, and of risk. He who does not know everything cannot kill everything. The rebel, far from making an absolute of history, rejects and disputes it, in the name of a concept which he has of his own nature. He refuses his condition, and his condition to a large extent is historical. Injustice, the transience of time, death – all are manifest in history. In spurning them, history itself is spurned. Most certainly the rebel does not deny the history which surrounds him; it is in terms of this that he attempts the affirmation of himself. But confronted with it he feels like the artist confronted with reality; he spurns it without escaping from it. He has never succeeded in creating an absolute history. Even though he can participate, by the force of events, in the crime of history, he cannot necessarily legitimate it. Rational crime not only cannot be admitted on the level of rebellion, but also signifies the death of rebellion. To make this evidence more convincing, rational crime exercises itself, in the first place, on rebels whose insurrection contests a history which is henceforth deified.

The mystification peculiar to the mind which claims to be revolutionary today sums up and increases bourgeois mystification. It contrives, by the promise of absolute justice, the acceptance of perpetual injustice, of unlimited compromise, and of indignity. Rebellion itself only aspires to the relative and can only promise an assured dignity coupled with relative justice. It supposes a limit at which the community of man is established. Its universe is the universe of relative values. Instead of saying, with Hegel and Marx, that all is necessary, it only repeats that all is possible and that, at a certain point, on the farthest frontier, it is worth making the supreme sacrifice for the sake of the possible. Between God and history, the yogi and the commissar, it opens a difficult path where contradictions may exist and thrive. Let us consider the two contradictions, given as an example, in this way.

A revolutionary action which wishes to be coherent in terms of its origins should be embodied in an active consent to the relative. It should express fidelity to the human condition. Uncompromising as to its means, it should accept an approximation as far as its ends are concerned and, so that the approximation should become more and more accurately defined, it should demand absolute freedom of speech. Thus it would preserve the common existence which justifies its insurrection. In particular, it should preserve, as an absolute right, the permanent possibility to express one's thoughts. This defines a particular line of conduct in regard to justice and freedom. There is no justice in society without natural or civil rights as its basis. There are no rights without expression of those rights. If the rights are expressed without hesitation it is more than probable that, sooner or later, the justice which they postulate will come to the world. To conquer existence, we must start from the small amount of existence which we find in ourselves and not deny it from the very beginning. To silence the expression of rights until justice is established, is to silence it for ever since it will have no more occasion to speak if justice reigns forever. Once more, we thus confide justice into the keeping of those who alone have the ability to make themselves heard – those in power. For centuries, justice and existence as dispensed by those in power have been considered a favour. To kill freedom in order to establish the reign of justice, comes to the same as resuscitating the idea of grace without divine intercession and of restoring by a mystifying reaction the mystical body in its basest elements. Even when justice is not realized, freedom preserves the power to protest and guarantees human communication. Justice in a silent world, justice enslaved and mute, destroys mutual complicity and finally can no longer be justice. The revolution of the twentieth century has arbitrarily separated, for over-ambitious ends of conquest, two inseparable ideas. Absolute freedom mocks at justice. Absolute justice denies freedom. To be fruitful, the two ideas must find their limits in one another. No man considers that his condition is free if it is not at the same time just, nor just unless it is free. Freedom, precisely, cannot even be imagined without the power of saying clearly what is just and what is unjust, of claiming all existence in the name of a small part of existence which refuses to die. Finally there is a justice, although a very different kind of justice, in restoring freedom, which is the only imperishable value of history. Men are never really willing to die except for the sake of freedom: therefore they do not believe in dying completely.

The same reasoning can be applied to violence. Absolute non-violence is the negative basis of slavery and its acts of violence; systematic violence positively destroys the living community and the existence we receive from it. To be fruitful these two ideas must establish their limits. In history, considered as an absolute, violence finds itself legitimized; as a relative risk, it is the cause of a rupture in communication. It must therefore preserve, for the rebel, its provisional character of effraction and must always be bound, if it cannot be avoided, to a personal responsibility and to an immediate risk. Systematic violence is part of the order of things; in a certain sense, this is comforting. *Führerprinzip* or historic reason, whatever order may establish it, reigns over the universe of things, not the universe of men. Just as the rebel considers murder as the limit which he must, if he is so inclined, consecrate by his own death, so violence can only be an extreme limit which combats another form of violence, as, for example, in the case of an insurrection. If an excess of injustice renders the latter inevitable, the rebel rejects violence in advance, in the service of a doctrine or of a reason of State. Every historic crisis, for example, terminates in institutions. If we have no control over the institutions since we can define them, choose the ones for which we will fight, and thus bend our efforts towards their establishment. Authentic acts of rebellion will only consent to take up arms for institutions which limit violence, not for those which codify it. A revolution is not worth dying for unless it assures the immediate suppression of the death penalty; not worth going to prison for unless it refuses in advance to pass sentence without fixed terms. If rebel violence employs itself in the establishment of these institutions, announcing its aims as often as it can, it is the only way in which it can be really provisional. When the end is absolute, historically speaking, and when it is believed certain of realization, it is possible to go so far as to sacrifice others. When it is not, only one-self can be sacrificed, in the hazards of a struggle for the common dignity. Does the end justify the means? That is possible. But what will justify the end? To that question, which historic thought leaves pending, rebellion replies: the means.

What does such an attitude signify in politics? And, first of all, is it efficacious? We must answer without hesitation, that it is the only attitude that is efficacious today. There are two sorts of efficaciousness, that of the typhoon and that of the dew. Historic absolutism is not efficacious, it is efficient; it has seized and kept power. Once it is in possession of power, it destroys the only creative reality. Uncompromising and limited action, springing from rebellion, upholds the reality and only tries to extend it farther and farther. It is not said that this action cannot conquer. It is said that it runs the risk of not conquering and of dying. But either revolution will take this risk or it will confess that it is only the undertaking of a new set of masters, punishable by the same scorn. A revolution which is separated from honour betrays its origins which belong to the reign of honour. Its choice, in any case, is limited to material expediency and final annihilation, or to taking risks and thus to creation. The revolutionaries of the past went ahead as fast as they could and their optimism was complete. But today, the revolutionary spirit has grown in knowledge and clear-sightedness; it has behind it a hundred and fifty years of experience. Moreover, the revolution has lost its illusions of being a public holiday. It is, entirely on its own, a pro- digious calculation, which embraces the entire universe. It knows, even though it does not always say so, that it will be worldwide or that it will not be at all. Its chances are balanced against the risk of a universal war which, even in the case of victory, will only present it with an empire of ruins. It can remain faithful to its nihilism, and incarnate in the charnel houses the ultimate reason of history. Then it will be necessary to renounce everything except the silent music which will again transfigure the terrestrial hell. But the revolutionary spirit in Europe can also, for the first and last time, reflect upon its principles, ask itself what the deviation is which leads it from its path into terror and into war, and rediscover with the reasons of its rebellion, its faith in itself.

Moderation and Excess

THE errors of contemporary revolution are first of all explained by the ignorance or systematic misconception of the limit which seems inseparable from human nature and which rebellion accurately reveals. Nihilist thought, because it neglects this frontier, ends by precipitating itself into a uniformly accelerated movement. Nothing stops it any longer in its course and it reaches the point of justifying total destruction or indefinite conquest. We know at the end of this long inquiry into rebellion and nihilism that rebellion with no other limits but historical expediency signifies unlimited slavery. To escape this fate, the revolutionary mind, if it wants to remain alive, must therefore return again to the sources of rebellion and draw its inspiration from the only system of thought which is faithful to its origins; thought which recognizes limits. If the limit discovered by rebellion transfigures everything; if every thought, every action which goes beyond a certain point negates itself, there is in effect a measure by which to judge events and men. In history, as in psychology, rebellion is an irregular pendulum which swings in an erratic arc because it is looking for its most perfect and profound rhythm. But its irregularity is not total: it functions around a pivot. At the same time that it suggests a nature common to all men, rebellion brings to light the measure and the limit which are the very principle of this nature.

Every reflection today, whether nihilist or positivist, gives birth, sometimes without knowing it, to standards which science itself confirms. The quantum theory, relativity, the uncertainty of inter-relationships define a world which has no definable reality except on the scale of average greatness which is our own. The ideologies which guide our world were born in the time of absolute scientific discoveries on the grand scale. Our real knowledge, on the other hand, only justifies a system of thought based on relative greatness. 'Intelligence', says Lazare Bickel, 'is our faculty for not developing what

we think to the very end, so that we can still believe in reality.'
Approximative thought is the only creator of reality.

The very forces of matter, in their blind advance, impose their
own limits. That is why it is useless to want to reverse the advance of
technology. The age of the spinning-wheel is over and the dream of a
civilization of artisans is vain. The machine is only bad in the way
that it is now employed. Its benefits must be accepted even if its
ravages are rejected. The truck, driven day and night, does not
humiliate the driver, who knows it inside out and treats it with
affection and efficiency. The real and inhuman excess lies in the
division of labour. But, by dint of this excess, a day comes when a
machine capable of a hundred operations, operated by one man
creates one sole object. This man, on a different scale, will have
partially rediscovered the power of creation which he possessed in
the days of the artisan. The anonymous producer then draws nearer
to the creator. It is not certain, naturally, that industrial excess will
immediately take to this path. But it already demonstrates, by the
way that it functions, the necessity for moderation and gives rise to
reflections on the proper way to organize this moderation. Either this
value of limitation will be realized, or contemporary excesses will only
find their principle and peace in universal destruction.

This law of moderation equally well extends to all the contradictions of rebellious thought. The real is not entirely rational, nor is the
rational entirely real. As we have seen in regard to surrealism, the
desire for unity does not only demand that everything should be
rational. It also wishes that the irrational should not be sacrificed.
One cannot say that nothing has any meaning because, in doing so,
one affirms a value sanctified by an opinion; not that everything has a
meaning since the word 'everything' has no signification for us. The
irrational imposes limits on the rational which, in its turn, gives it
moderation. Something has a meaning, finally, which we must obtain
from meaninglessness. In the same way, it cannot be said that existence
takes place only on the level of essence. Where could one perceive
essence except on the level of existence and evolution? But nor can it
be said that being is only existence. Something that is always in the

process of development could not exist – there must be a beginning. Being can only prove itself in development and development is nothing without being. The world is not in a condition of pure stability; but it is only movement. It is both movement and stability. The historical dialectic, for example, is not in continuous pursuit of an unknown value. It revolves around the limit which is its prime value. Heraclitus, the inventor of the constant change of things, nevertheless set a limit to this perpetual process. This limit was symbolized by Nemesis, the goddess of moderation and the implacable enemy of the immoderate. A process of thought which wanted to take into account the contemporary contradictions of rebellion should seek its inspiration from this goddess.

As for the moral contradictions, they too begin to become soluble in the light of this conciliatory value. Virtue cannot separate itself from reality without becoming a principle of evil. Nor can it identify itself completely with reality without denying itself. The moral value brought to light by rebellion, finally, is no farther above life and history than history and life are above it. In actual truth, it assumes no reality in history until man gives his life for it or dedicates himself entirely to it. Jacobin and bourgeois civilization presumes that values are above history and its formal virtues then lay the foundation of a repugnant form of mystification. The revolution of the twentieth century decrees that values are intermingled with the movement of history and that their historic foundations justify a new form of mystification. Moderation, confronted with this irregularity, teaches us that at least one part of realism is necessary to every ethic: unadulterated virtue, pure and simple, is homicidal. That is why humanitarian cant has no more basis than cynical provocation. Finally, man is not entirely to blame, it was not he who started history; nor is he entirely innocent since he continues it. Those who go beyond this limit and affirm his total innocence end in the insanity of definitive culpability. Rebellion, on the contrary, sets us on the path of calculated culpability. Its sole but invincible hope is incarnated, in the final analysis, in innocent murderers.

At this limit, the 'We are' paradoxically defines a new form of individualism. 'We are' in terms of history, and history must reckon with this 'We are' which must, in its turn, keep its place in history. I have need of others who have need of me and of each other. Every collective action, every form of society supposes a discipline and the individual, without this discipline, is only a stranger, bowed down by the weight of an inimical collectivity. But society and discipline lose their direction if they deny the 'we are'. I alone, in one sense, support the common dignity that I cannot allow either myself or others to debase. This individualism is in no sense pleasure, it is perpetual struggle and, sometimes, unparalleled joy when it reaches the heights of intrepid compassion.

THOUGHT AT THE MERIDIAN

As for knowing if such an attitude can find political expression in the contemporary world, it is easy to evoke – and this is only an example – what is traditionally called revolutionary trade unionism. Cannot it be said that even this trade unionism is ineffectual? The answer is simple: it is this movement alone which, in one century, is responsible for the enormously improved condition of the workers from the sixteen-hour day to the forty-hour week. The ideological empire has turned socialism back on its tracks and destroyed the greater part of the conquests of trade unionism. It is because trade unionism started from a concrete basis, the basis of professional employment (which is to the economic order what the masses are to the political order), the living cell on which the organism builds itself, while the Caesarian revolution starts from doctrine and forcibly introduces reality into it. Trade unionism, like the masses, is the negation, to the benefit of reality, of bureaucratic and abstract centralism. The revolution of the twentieth century, on the contrary, claims to base itself on economics, but is primarily political and ideological. It cannot, by its very function, avoid terror and violence done to reality. Despite its pretensions, it begins in the absolute and attempts to mould reality. Rebellion, inversely, relies on reality to assist it in its perpetual struggle for truth. The former tries to realize itself from top to bottom, the latter from bottom to top. Far from being a form of romanticism, rebellion, on the contrary, takes the part of true realism. If it wants a revolution, it wants it on behalf of life not in defiance of it. That is why it relies primarily on the most concrete realities – on occupation, on the country village, where the living heart of things and of men are to be found. Politics, to satisfy the demands of rebellion, must submit to the eternal verities. Finally, when it causes history to advance and alleviates the sufferings of mankind, it does so without terror, if not without violence, and in the most dissimilar political conditions.

But this example goes farther than it seems. On the very day when the Caesarian revolution triumphed over the syndicalist and libertarian spirit, revolutionary thought lost, in itself, a counterpoise of which it cannot, without decaying, deprive itself. This counterpoise, this spirit which takes the measure of life, is the same which animates the long tradition that can be called solitary thought and in which, since the time of the Greeks, nature has always been weighed against evolution. The history of the first International when German socialism ceaselessly fought against the libertarian thought of the French, the Spanish, and the Italian, is the history of the struggle of German ideology against the Mediterranean mind. The masses against the State, concrete society against absolutist society, deliberate freedom against rational tyranny, finally, altruistic individualism against the colonization of the masses, are thus the contradictions which express, once again, the endless opposition of moderation to excess which has animated the history of the Occident since the time of the ancient world. The profound conflict of this century is, perhaps, not so much between the German ideologies of history and Christian political concepts, which in a certain way are accomplices, as between German dreams and Mediterranean traditions, between the violence of eternal adolescence and virile strength, between nostalgia, rendered more acute by knowledge and by books and courage reinforced and enlightened by the experience of life – in other words, between history and nature. But German ideology, in this sense, has come into an inheritance. It consummates two centuries of abortive struggle against Nature, first in the name of an historic god and then of a deified history. Christianity, no doubt, was only unable to conquer its catholicity by assimilating as much as it could of Greek thought. But when the Church dissipated its Mediterranean heritage, it placed the emphasis on history to the detriment of Nature, caused the Gothic to triumph over the Roman, and, destroying a limit in itself, has made increasing claims to temporal power and historic dynamism. When Nature ceases to be an object of contemplation and admiration it can then be nothing more than material for an action which aims at transferring it. These tendencies – and not the concepts of mediation which would have comprised the real strength of Christianity – are triumphing in modern times, to the detriment of Christianity itself, by an inevitable turn of events. That God should, in fact, be expelled from this historic universe and German ideology be born where action is no longer a process of perfection but pure conquest is an expression of tyranny.

But historic absolutism, despite its triumphs, has never ceased to come into collision with an irrepressible demand of human nature of which the Mediterranean, where intelligence is intimately related to the blinding light of the sun, guards the secret. Rebellious thought, that of the Commune or of revolutionary trade unionism, has never ceased to deny this demand in the face of bourgeois nihilism as well as of Caesarian socialism. Authoritarian thought, by means of three wars and thanks to the physical destruction of a revolutionary élite, has succeeded in submerging this libertarian tradition. But this barren victory is only provisional, the battle still continues. Europe has never been free of this struggle between darkness and light. It has only degraded itself by deserting the struggle and eclipsing day by night. The destruction of this equilibrium is, today, bearing its bitterest fruits. Deprived of our means of mediation, exiled from natural beauty, we are once again in the world of the Old Testament, crushed between a cruel Pharaoh and an implacable heaven.

In the common condition of misery, the eternal demand is heard again; Nature once more takes up the fight against history. Naturally, of course, it is not a question of despising anything, or of exalting one civilization at the expense of another, but of simply saying that it is a process of thought which the world today cannot do without for very much longer. There is, undoubtedly, in the Russian people something by which to endow Europe with the strength of sacrifice, and in America an absolutely essential power of production. But the youth of the world always find themselves standing on the same shore. Thrown into the unworthy melting-pot of Europe where, deprived of beauty and friendship, the proudest of races is gradually dying, we Mediterraneans live by the same light. In the depths of the European night, solar thought, civilization with a double face, awaits its dawn. But it already illuminates the paths of real mastery.

Real mastery consists of creating justice out of the prejudices of the time, initially out of the deepest and most malignant of them which would like to reduce man, after his deliverance from excess, to a barren wisdom. It is very true that excess can be a form of sanctity when it is paid for by the madness of Nietzsche. But is this intoxication of the soul which is exhibited on the scene of our culture always the madness of excess, the folly of attempting the impossible of which the brand can never be removed from he who has, once at least, abandoned himself to it? Has Prometheus ever had this fanatical or accusing aspect? No, our civilization survives in the complacency of cowardly or malignant minds – a sacrifice to the vanity of ageing adolescents. Lucifer also has died with God, and from his ashes has arisen a spiteful demon who does not even understand the object of his venture. In 1953, excess is always a comfort, and sometimes a career. Moderation, on the one hand, is nothing but pure tension. It smiles, no doubt, and our convulsionists, dedicated to elaborate apocalypses, despise it. But its smile shines brightly at the climax of an interminable effort: it is in itself a supplementary source of strength. Why do these petty-minded Europeans who show us an avaricious face, if they no longer have the strength to smile, claim that their desperate convulsions are examples of superiority?

The real madness of excess dies or creates its own moderation. It does not cause the death of others in order to create an alibi for itself.

In its most extreme manifestations, it finds its limit on which, like Kaliayev, it sacrifices itself if necessary. Moderation is not the opposite of rebellion. Rebellion in itself is moderation, and it demands, defends, and re-creates it throughout history and its eternal disturbances. The very origin of this value guarantees us that it can only be partially destroyed. Moderation, born of rebellion, can only live by rebellion. It is a perpetual conflict, continually created and mastered by the intelligence. It does not triumph either in the impossible or in the abyss. It finds its equilibrium through them. Whatever we may do, excess will always keep its place in the heart of man, in the place where solitude is found. We all carry within us our places of exile, our crimes, and our ravages. But our task is not to unleash them on the world; it is to fight them in ourselves and in others. Rebellion, the secular will not to surrender of which Barrès speaks, is still, today, at the basis of the struggle. Origin of form, source of real life, it keeps us always erect in the savage formless movement of history.

Beyond Nihilism

THERE does exist, therefore, a way of acting and of thinking, for man, which is possible on the level of moderation to which he belongs. Every undertaking which is more ambitious than this proves to be contradictory. The absolute is not attained, not, above all, created, through history. Politics is not religion, or, if it is, then it is nothing but the Inquisition. How would society define an absolute? Perhaps everyone is looking for this absolute on behalf of all. But society and politics only have the responsibility of arranging everyone's affairs so that each will have the leisure and the freedom to pursue this common search. History can then no longer be presented as an object of worship. It is only an opportunity which must be rendered fruitful by a vigilant rebellion.

'Obsession with the harvest and indifference to history', writes René Char admirably, 'are the two extremities of my bow.' If the duration of history is not synonymous with the duration of the harvest, then history, in effect, is no more than a fleeting and cruel shadow in which man has no more part. He who dedicates himself to this history dedicates himself to nothing and, in his turn, is nothing. But he who dedicates himself to the duration of his life, to the house he builds, to the dignity of mankind, dedicates himself to the earth and reaps from it the harvest which sows its seed and sustains the world again and again. Finally, it is those who know how to rebel, at the appropriate moment, against history who really advance its interests. To rebel against it supposes an interminable tension and the agonized serenity of which René Char also speaks. But the true life is present in the heart of this dichotomy. Life is this dichotomy itself, the mind soaring over volcanoes of light, the madness of justice, the extenuating intransigence of moderation. The words which reverberate for us at the confines of this long adventure of rebellion, are not formulae for optimism, for which we have no possible use in the extremities of our unhappiness, but words of courage and intelligence which, on the shores of the eternal seas, even have the qualities of virtue.

No possible form of wisdom today can claim to give more. Rebellion indefatigably confronts evil, from which it can only derive a new impetus. Man can master, in himself, everything that should be mastered. He should rectify in creation everything that can be rectified. And after he has done so, children will still die unjustly even in a perfect society. Even by his greatest effort, man can only propose to diminish, arithmetically, the sufferings of the world. But the injustice and the suffering of the world will remain and, no matter how limited they are, they will not cease to be an outrage. Dmitri Karamazov's cry of 'Why?' will continue to resound through history; art and rebellion will only die with the death of the last man on earth.

There is an evil, undoubtedly, which men accumulate in their passionate desire for unity. But yet another evil lies at the roots of this confused movement. Confronted with this evil, confronted with death, man from the very depths of his soul cries out for justice. Historic Christianity has only replied to this protest against evil by the Annunciation of the Kingdom and then of Eternal Life – accompanied by a demand for faith. But suffering exhausts hope and faith and then is left alone and unexplained. The toiling masses, worn out with suffering and death, are masses without God. Our place is henceforth at their side, far from teachers, old or new. Historic Christianity postpones, to a point beyond the span of history, the cure of evil and murder which are, nevertheless, experienced within the span of history. Contemporary materialism also believes that it can answer all questions. But, as a slave to history, it increases the domain of historic murder and at the same time leaves it without any justification, except in the future – which again demands faith. In both cases one must wait and, meanwhile, the innocent continue to die. For twenty centuries the sum-total of evil has not diminished in the world. No paradise, whether divine or revolutionary, has been realized. An injustice remains inextricably bound to all suffering, even the most deserved in the eyes of men. The long silence of Prometheus has seen, with the passage of time, men rail and turn against him. Crushed between human evil and destiny, between terror and the arbitrary, all that remains to him is his power to rebel in order to save from murder he who can still be a murderer, without surrendering to the arrogance of blasphemy.

Then we understand that rebellion cannot exist without a strange form of love. Those who find no rest in God or in history are condemned to live for those who, like themselves, cannot live: in fact, for the humiliated. The most pure form of the movement of rebellion is thus crowned with the heart-rending cry of Karamazov: if all are not saved, what good is the salvation of one only? Thus Catholic prisoners, in the prison cells of Spain, refuse communion today because the priests of the régime have made it obligatory in certain prisons. These lonely witnesses to the crucifixion of innocence refuse salvation, too, if it must be paid for by injustice and oppression. This insane generosity is the generosity of rebellion, which unhesitating gives the strength of its love and refuses injustice without a moment's delay. Its merit lies in making no calculations, distributing everything that it possesses to life and to living men. It is thus that it is prodigal in its gifts to men to come. Real generosity towards the future lies in giving all to the present.

Rebellion proves, in this way, that it is the very movement of life and that it cannot be denied without renouncing life. Its purest outburst, on each occasion, gives birth to existence. Thus, it is love and fecundity or it is nothing at all. Revolution without honour, calculated revolution which, in preferring an abstract concept of man to a man of flesh and blood, denies existence as many times as is necessary, puts resentment in the place of love. Immediately rebellion, forgetful of its generous origins, allows itself to be contaminated by resentment, it denies life, dashes towards destruction, and raises up the grimacing cohorts of petty rebels, embryo slaves all of them, who end by offering themselves for sale, in all the market-places of Europe, to no matter what form of servitude. It is no longer either revolution or rebellion but rancour, malice, and tyranny. Then, when revolution in the name of power and of history becomes that immoderate and mechanical murderer, a new rebellion is consecrated in the name of moderation and of life. We are at the extremity now. However, at the end of this tunnel of darkness, there is inevitably a light, which we already divine and for which we only have to fight to ensure its coming. All of us, among the ruins, are preparing a renaissance beyond the limits of nihilism. But few of us know it.

Already, in fact, rebellion without claiming to solve everything can at least pretend to do so. From this moment, high noon is borne away on the fast-moving stream of history. Around the devouring flames, shadows writhe in mortal combat for an instant of time and then as suddenly disappear and the blind, fingering their eyelids, cry out that this is history. The men of Europe, abandoned to the shadows, have turned their backs upon the fixed and radiant point of the present. They forget the present for the future, the fate of humanity for the delusion of power, the misery of the slums for the mirage of the Eternal City, ordinary justice for an empty promised land. They despair of personal freedom and dream of a strange freedom of the species; reject solitary death and give the name of immortality to a vast collective agony. They no longer believe in the things that exist in the world and in living man; the secret of Europe is that it no longer loves life. Its blind men entertain the puerile belief that to love one single day of life amounts to justifying whole centuries of oppression. That is why they wanted to efface joy from the world and to postpone it until a much later date. Impatience with limits, the rejection of their double life, despair at being a man have finally driven them to inhuman excesses. Denying the real grandeur of life, they have had to stake all on their own excellence. For want of something better to do, they deified themselves and their misfortune began; these gods have had their eyes put out. Kaliayev, and his brothers throughout the entire world, refuse, on the contrary, to be deified in that they reject the unlimited power to inflict death. They choose, and we offer as an example, the only original rule of life today: to learn to live and to die, and in order to be a man, to refuse to be a god.

In this noon of thought, the rebel thus disclaims divinity in order to share in the struggles and destiny of all men. We shall choose Ithaca, the faithful land, frugal and audacious thought, lucid action, the generosity of the man who understands. In the light, the earth remains our first and our last love. Our brothers are breathing under the same sky; justice is a living thing. Now is born that strange joy which helps one live and die, and which we shall never again renounce to a later time. On the sorrowing earth it is the unresting thorn, the bitter food, the harsh wind off the sea, the ancient dawn forever renewed. With this joy, through long struggle, we shall remake the soul of our time, and a Europe which will exclude nothing. Not even that phantom Nietzsche who, for twelve years after his downfall, was continually invoked by the West as the ruined image of its loftiest knowledge and its nihilism; nor the prophet of justice without mercy who rests, by mistake, in the unbelievers' plot at Highgate Cemetery; nor the deified mummy of the man of action in his glass coffin; nor any part of what the intelligence and energy of Europe have ceaselessly furnished to the pride of a contemptible period. All may indeed live again, side by side with the martyrs of 1905, but on condition that they shall understand how they correct one another, and that a limit, under the sun, shall curb them all. Each tells the other that he is not God; this is the end of romanticism. At this moment, when each of us must fit an arrow to his bow and enter the lists anew, to reconquer, within history and in spite of it, that which he owns already, the thin yield of his fields, the brief love of this earth, at this moment when at last a man is born, it is time to forsake our age and its adolescent rages. The bow bends; the wood complains. At the moment of supreme tension, there will leap into flight an unswerving arrow, a shaft that is inflexible and free.

MORE ABOUT PENGUINS, PELICANS
AND PUFFINS

For further information about books available from Penguins please write to Dept EP, Penguin Books Ltd, Harmondsworth, Middlesex UB7 0DA.

In the U.S.A.: For a complete list of books available from Penguins in the United States write to Dept DG, Penguin Books, 299 Murray Hill Parkway, East Rutherford, New Jersey 07073.

In Canada: For a complete list of books available from Penguins in Canada write to Penguin Books Canada Ltd, 2801 John Street, Markham, Ontario L3R 1B4.

In Australia: For a complete list of books available from Penguins in Australia write to the Marketing Department, Penguin Books Australia Ltd, P.O. Box 257, Ringwood, Victoria 3134.

In New Zealand: For a complete list of books available from Penguins in New Zealand write to the Marketing Department, Penguin Books (N.Z.) Ltd, P.O. Box 4019, Auckland 10.

In India: For a complete list of books available from Penguins in India write to Penguin Overseas Ltd, 706 Eros Apartments, 56 Nehru Place, New Delhi 110019.

Novels and Stories by Albert Camus

THE OUTSIDER

Meursault is a young man who lives in the usual manner of a French-Algerian, middle-class bachelor ... but he has a glaring fault in the eyes of society – he seems to lack the basic emotions and reactions (including hypocrisy) that are required of him. He observes the facts of life, death, and sex from the outside.
'Seldom have I read a work which says so much in so short a space' – John Betjeman.

THE PLAGUE

The Times described it as a 'carefully wrought metaphysical novel the machinery of which can be compared to a Sophoclean tragedy. The plague in question afflicted Oran in the 1940s; and on one plane the book is a straight-forward narrative. Into it, however, can be read all Camus's native anxieties, centred on the idea of plague as a symbol.' The symbol is that of the German occupation of France against which Camus fought so heroically during the war.

THE FALL

Jean-Baptiste Clamence appeared to himself and to others the epitome of good citizenship and decent behaviour. Suddenly he sees through the deep-seated hypocrisy of his existence to the condescension which motivates his every action. He turns to debauchery, and finally settles in Amsterdam where, a self-styled 'judge penitent', he describes his fall to a chance acquaintance.

EXILE AND THE KINGDOM

These six short stories show the same qualities that won a Nobel Prize for Literature for the late Albert Camus. Four of them are set in Algiers on the fringes of the desert – an environment which has often been associated with deep mystical and emotional experience.